THE PRINCIPLE OF NONVIOLENCE

A Philosophical Path

Jean-Marie Muller

Foreword by
Glenn D. Paige

 Center *for* Global **Nonkilling**

Honolulu
May 2014

© Jean-Marie Muller, 2014
© Center for Global Nonkilling, 2014 (this edition)

Translated by Rebecca James and Mike James, 2014.
Edited by Iolanda Mato Creo and Joám Evans Pim.

Cover design: In the circle of the universe, creative transformational initiatives (blue), drawing upon nonkilling human capabilities (white), work to end human killing (red).

First Edition: May 2014

ISBN-13   978-0-9839862-8-7

Cataloging in Publication Data (CIP)

The Principle of Nonviolence : A Philosophical Path / Jean-Marie Muller.
ISBN   978-0-9839862-8-7
1. Nonviolence 2. Philosophy. 3. Nonkilling.
I. Title. II. Muller, Jean-Marie.

CDU - 172.4: 327.36

A catalogue record is also available from the Library of Congress.

Also available for free download at: http://www.nonkilling.org

 Center *for* Global **Nonkilling**

3653 Tantalus Drive
Honolulu, Hawai'i 96822-5033
United States of America
Email: info@nonkilling.org
http://www.nonkilling.org

Ils ont bonne mine, les non-violents!
Nonviolent people certainly look well!
Jean-Paul Sartre

La non-violence est le point de départ comme le but final de la philosophie.
Nonviolence is philosophy's starting point, as well as its final goal.
Eric Weil

S'efforcer de devenir tel qu'on puisse être non-violent.
To strive to become such that we may be nonviolent.
Simone Weil

I believe that true democracy can only be an outcome of nonviolence.
Mahatma Gandhi

Le vrai problème pour nous autres Occidentaux, ne consiste plus tant à récuser la violence qu'à nous interroger sur une lutte contre la violence qui - sans s'étioler dans la non-résistance au Mal - puisse éviter l'institution de la violence à partir de cette lutte même. La guerre à la guerre ne perpétue-t-elle pas ce qu'elle est appelée à faire disparaître pour consacrer, dans la bonne conscience, la guerre et ses vertus viriles?

The true problem for us Westerners is not so much to refuse violence as to question ourselves about a struggle against violence which, without blanching in non-resistance to evil, could avoid the institution of violence out of this very struggle. Does not the war against war perpetuate that which it is called to make disappear, and consecrate war and its virile virtues in good conscience?
Emmanuel Levinas

Contents

Foreword	9
Preface	13
1. In a World of Conflict	19
2. A Reflection on Violence	31
3. Nonviolence as a Philosophical Imperative	51
4. The Nonviolent Man in the Face of Death	71
5. Principles of Nonviolent Action	81
6. Violence and Necessity	101
7. The State as Institutionalized Violence	115
8. Nonviolence as a Political Requirement	129
9. The Nonviolent Resolution of Conflicts	153
10. Nonviolent Alternatives to War	167
11. Violence and Nonviolence in History, According to Eric Weil	177
12. Dialogue with Eric Weil	191
13. Gandhi, the Requirement for Nonviolence	205
14. Gandhi, Architect of Nonviolence	221
15. The Chances of a Culture of Nonviolence	241
Conclusion	261
References	265
Index	271

Foreword

The Center for Global Nonkilling is pleased to present this English translation of Jean-Marie Muller's *Le principe de non-violence: Parcours philosophique* first published in 1995 by Desclée de Brouwer in Paris. It joins translations of Muller's works already available in other languages. Many more can be expected since the questions asked and answers sought respond to universal needs for new knowledge and practices to achieve and sustain nonviolent conditions of local and global life.

The first publisher's introduction succinctly summarizes the substance and significance of Muller's unique contribution: "The goal of this book is to found a philosophical concept of nonviolence... [It aims] to challenge once and for all the ideology that violence is necessary, legitimate, and honorable... Never, apparently has this been accomplished in such a masterly and complete manner."

As the reader will discover the publication of this book by the Center for Global Nonkilling is appropriate because the ethic of "nonkilling" underlies all discussions of nonviolence in the text. Frequently it becomes sharply explicit.

But while nonkilling is upheld as the ultimate truth to be pursued as the sustainer of human life—as in the biblical commandment "Thou shalt not kill"—Muller's philosophical inquiry does not pursue it as a matter of "absolutist abstraction." "Philosophical reflection does not allow us to assert that nonviolence is **the answer** that offers the technical means to face political realities under all circumstances, but it leads us to assert that it is **the question** which, in the face of political realities, allows us to look for the best answer under all circumstances."

Muller reminds us that philosophical inquiry itself is inherently nonviolent. By means of reason and words it seeks wisdom and virtue in pursuit of truth. He quotes Eric Weil, "Philosophy has no weapons" and "Nonviolence is the goal of philosophy from point of departure to final end." But nonviolent philosophy in action is not inherently passive. To end violence and injustices it is fearlessly active.

Jean-Marie Muller, born in France in 1939, identifies himself as a philosopher and writer. He is also an experienced nonviolent activist, consultant, workshop trainer, and institution-builder. By 1995 when *Le principe de nonviolence* was published—beginning in 1967 with conscientious objection to military killing—he had experienced periods of imprisonment; a hunger strike in solidarity with farmers to regain Larzac farmlands requisitioned for a military base; a hunger strike to protest sale of French Mirage fighters to Brazil's military regime; and had been arrested aboard the peace yacht FRI protesting French nuclear weapons tests in the South Pacific. He had journeyed for research, conferences, workshops, and trainings in 13 countries, including the United States and India, most frequently to Colombia and Chad. He had published 13 books, including on César Chávez and Gandhi on whom he is an acknowledged expert, plus many articles in the journal *Nonviolence Actualité* which he helped to found. He had participated in founding the Institute for Research on Nonviolent Conflict Resolution continuing to serve as research director.

Since 1995 Muller has engaged in solidarity work for peace and nonviolence in 14 countries, most recently in Syria, Lebanon, Jordan, and Cameroon. He has published 16 books to advance understanding of nonviolence culture and methods of action, including two on Gandhi. Most recently *Penser avec Camus: Meurtre est la question* (Thinking with Camus: Killing is the Question) (2014).

It is expected that *The Principle of Nonviolence* will be welcomed by scholars, activists, and the public as a uniquely significant companion to the English language literature on nonviolence. Among expected resonances are with the spiritually-rooted works of Tolstoy, Gandhi, King and others; the principled pragmatic power of Gene Sharp's *The Politics of Nonviolent Action*; the call for creativity to transcend deep cultural and structural violence of Johan Galtung's *Peace By Peaceful Means*; and the multi-faith, multi-disciplinary scientific approach proposed in *Nonkilling Global Political Science*. Synergy with the latter is forecast by Muller's foreword to its French translation *Non-meurtre: Vers une science politique mondiale* (2013).

We are grateful to the father-daughter translation team of Michael James and Rebecca James for making Jean-Marie Muller's pioneering philosophical exploration of *Le principe de non-violence* accessible to English readers throughout the world.

Glenn D. Paige
Founder and Chair
Center for Global Nonkilling
Author of *Nonkilling Global Political Science*

Preface

Violence is raw material for the news; it is the best ingredient for the sensational. Every day, we hear of violence which, here and there in the world, brutalizes and kills our fellow human beings. The information to which we are subjected turns us into voyeurs watching others suffer and die. We do not keep enough distance from the event happening before our eyes in real time anymore. Without this distance, there is no more space for thought. The mass media does not inform us of the reasons and stakes of violence, but of the violence itself. It does not arouse public opinion, but public emotion.

The violence we see on the news has circumstantial explanations concerning the economic and political situations in which it takes place, but all of them become rooted in what we can call a "culture of violence". In the confrontation of cultures happening all over the world and in each society, it is common to call for mutual tolerance. We put forward that if we make the effort to better know and understand other cultures, we will discover how much grandeur and nobility each holds. And we assert that, in order to live in peace with each other, we must accept our differences. All that is only partly true. For do not our resemblances trigger our quarrels, our conflicts and our battles? Does not the fact that we imitate each other cause us to be permanently at war against each other? Are not our cultures so similarly soaked in "the ideology of violence" that we are constantly about to hurt each other? In reality, the ideology of a necessary, legitimate and honourable violence tends to erase the differences between cultures and reveal horrific resemblances. Our cultures resemble each other because they are all cultures of violence. That is why, to live at peace with each other, we must not so much accept our difference as refuse our resemblances.

One of the main focuses of this book will be to analyse and undertake a radical critique of what we have just named the "culture of violence" and the "ideology of violence". We will then suggest the perspectives of a "philosophy of nonviolence" and endeavour to define its founding principles and elements.

When observing history, violence can seem to weigh on humanity as a fatality. Should man be an animal, he would be the cruelest of all. But man is a thinking being, and that's precisely why he's the cruelest of all living beings. Were not man a thinking being, he would not have been able—knowingly and scientifically—to plan the Auschwitz, Hiroshima and the Gulag Archipelago tragedies. Many other tragedies have occurred across the world before and after these and may equally symbolise the horror of the violence of mankind against mankind. However, how can human conscience not revolt when thinking back to all those whose faces, across the centuries, have been disfigured by fire and the sword? It is the scandal of such violence inflicted on men by other human beings which triggers the philosophical thought; it is the certitude that this evil should not be which creates the thought. We want to assert that the rebellion of thought when facing the violence which makes mankind suffer is the founding act of philosophy, and that the refusal to legitimate this violence is the basis of the *principle of nonviolence*.

Culture is, according to the definition of Marcel Mauss, "the acquired form of behaviour in human societies, as a whole"[1]. That is why we shall talk about a "culture of violence" to signify individuals, under the effect of social influence, directing their behaviour by focusing on violence as a normal way to defend their community from the threats made against it. Society cultivates violence (cultivate comes from the Latin word *colare* which means both cultivate and honour) by teaching individuals that it is the virtue of the strong man, of the brave man, of the honourable man who risks death to defend "values" which give meaning to his life. In peoples' imagination, the hero is the one who has taken up arms to defend the homeland. And society lionises and worships its heroes. Culture surrounds violence with prestige, but, precisely, to say that violence is prestigious is to admit (according to the etymological meaning of this word

---

[1] Quoted by the *Dictionnaire historique de la langue française* (Rey, Dir., 1993).

which comes from the Latin word *praestigiosus*, "which is deceptive") that it is deceptive, in other words that it deceives those who give in to its temptation. As soon as men start shedding blood for a cause, the latter, whatever it is, becomes sacred. They will always have to continue shedding their blood so that it cannot be said that the first victims shed theirs in vain. Violence, when all is said and done, sanctifies the cause, and not the other way round. Thus Zarathustra declares to his "brothers in war": "You say that a good cause will even sanctify war? I tell you: it is the good war that sanctifies every cause." (Nietzche, 1963: 59) If violence is sacred, nonviolence can only be sacrilege and whoever invokes it deserves anathema.

One of the most significant expressions of our culture of violence is the considerable extent of intellectual investment granted to the manufacture of weapons in our societies, in order to organize the mass killing of our fellow human beings. And we have reached such a degree of culture that this weapon production not only does not outrage us, but does not surprise us either. We even have at our disposal a great many arguments to justify this.

The culture of violence needs to refer to a rational construction which allows individuals to justify violence. That is where the "ideology of violence" steps in. Its function is to build a representation of violence that avoids seeing what it actually is—inhuman and scandalous. It aims to occult the irrational and the unacceptable in violence and to let an acceptable and rational representation prevail. It consists in hiding the scandalous reality of violence thanks to a representation that puts it in a positive light. The purpose—often attained—is to trivialize violence. *Instead of being banished*—declared unlawful—violence is trivialized, declared lawful. From then on, no other intellectual brake will oppose the use of violence.

"Morality", writes Emmanuel Levinas, "does not belong to culture: it makes it possible to judge it." (Levinas, 1994: 58) To be able to judge culture, it is necessary to suspend our support for the judgements that culture has taught us. A difficult task which requires us to distance ourselves from our culture, to unlearn what we have learnt, to renew our vision of man and the world, to reconsider our thoughts. It is about challenging our knowledge so as to put our ideas in order. It is about questioning our beliefs so as to become aware again. But in the name of what criteria, of what requirements? In the name of philosophy? But where should the source of philosophy be found, if not again within our culture? It would be an illusion to claim to be free of all influences, but perhaps is it possible to determine the cultural influences to which we have been subjected—they are numerous and contradictory—and to discern those that are openings towards more light, that are meaningful, and those, on the contrary, that shut us up and blind us? Perhaps is it possible to choose our influences. Man must challenge the idea that he is a predetermined being subjected to fatality. He isn't free, he isn't born free, but he can conquer his own freedom. Freedom is always a beginning, a new beginning. As a last resort, he has no other choice but to be his own judge of the truth that gives his life meaning. He could not submit to any external authority dictating him the truth, without giving up on his own responsibility. To become responsible and independent, he must absolutely trust his own reason, and not rely on others. A rational being, man has the ability to free himself from culture's conditioning and confinement little by little, in order to build little by little his own thoughts, his own morality, his own philosophy.

We have become used to blaming extremisms for the violence we condemn. *But the extremisms we refuse only exist through the orthodoxies we accept.* By definition, an extremist is the supporter of a doctrine driven to its extreme consequences, and this means that there is a link between this doctrine and the extremists' reason. The orthodoxy of the doctrine which extremists refer to is not innocent of the misdeeds and crimes that they commit. Extremists whose destructive impact we see everywhere can only exist because they borrow the arguments of their propaganda from orthodoxies. They certainly exaggerate, but precisely what they exaggerate, i.e. what they magnify, is orthodoxy. Orthodoxy offers raw material for the exaggerations of extremism; it provides it with pretexts for its excesses. Orthodoxies carry the seed for the growth of extremisms, and feed it themselves. In justifying "a reasonable use of violence", orthodoxies are already justifying the abuses of extremisms. For violence is not reasonable and it is an abuse. The violence that we imagine peacefully curled up within orthodoxy wakes up now and again, becoming angry and hideous. But orthodoxy is indeed the base camp where it leads its criminal operations. *To fight the violence of extremisms, it must be tracked down where it hides, within orthodoxies.*

Nationalist ideology that teaches contempt for foreigners leans on the cult of the homeland, which glorifies the peoples' national identity. The totalitarian State claims to base its legitimacy on the doctrine of democracy which attributes the monopoly of legitimate violence to the State. Total war bases its justification on the doctrine of a just war which legitimates and honours violence and killing whenever they serve a just cause. Religious fundamentalism takes its roots in the orthodoxy of religions that profess a doctrine of legitimate violence.

From then on, it is not possible to disavow, challenge and disarm extremisms without questioning the orthodoxies which provide them with justifications. To break the logic of violence of extremisms, we must begin by breaking with everything that legitimates and honours violence as well as the virtue of the powerful man, within our own culture. This change will be painful, for it will have to be deep. We will discover that to break with a culture of violence, it is actually necessary to break with our own culture. And it is inevitably difficult to challenge a tradition which was passed on to us as a sacred legacy. Even when we will have become convinced that this break is necessary to delegitimise violence permanently, it will still appear to us, somehow, as a sacrilegious abandonment, as an abjuration. It will especially be felt as sacrilegious by the others, by those who will want to defend tradition. This feeling of sacrilege will increase when, as is often the case, a conjunction of the ideology of violence and of a religious doctrine arises. Those wanting to defend the sound doctrine will denounce any rupture as a heresy and won't hesitate to curse infidels.

The traditions we have inherited, despite having given violence an important place, have barely left any space for nonviolence, even ignoring its name. There are however, in each of our traditions, solid foundations on which to build a wisdom of nonviolence. Each of us indeed bears "values" within him or herself, which confer dignity, grandeur and nobility upon each man, and ask for him to be respected and loved. These values in themselves contradict the claim of violence to rule over men and societies. And, in each of our cultures, at some point, women and men have found the strength to rebel against their contemporaries to assert the primacy of these values over the claims of violence. But most often, these values have been greatly buried under the waste of the ideology of violence, and thus denied and rejected. Loyalty to these values, as soon as they are purified from any confusion, will help convince each of us that demanding nonviolence is the basis of humanity. And we will learn that our loyalty will lead us beyond the break we have carried out, right into the heart of our culture.

That way, each of us, if willing to break away from the logic of violence and enter the dynamics of nonviolence, must face, within his or her own culture, both rupture and loyalty. It is by keeping the perspective which this double requirement has opened, and carrying out a double research process throughout some of the key texts that our culture is based on, that we have chosen to write this book.

1

In a World of Conflict

Nonviolence is still a new idea in Europe and throughout the world. The very word "nonviolence" gives rise to a great deal of ambiguity, misunderstanding and confusion. The first difficulty lies in the fact that it expresses a negation, an opposition, a refusal. It is thereby surrounded with ambiguity. But it does have the critical advantage of compelling us to face up to the many ambiguities of violence that we are usually tempted to conceal, for the sake of our own peace of mind. Nonviolence expresses not a lesser, but a greater degree of realism with respect to violence. Its full extent, depth and weight must be measured.

It will only be possible to define the meaning of nonviolence if we define the meaning of violence beforehand. Above all, it is necessary to define what exactly violence says no to, what it opposes, what it refuses. For all that, this will not be enough. For, knowing what nonviolence is not, we will still not know what it is. To know that, we will have to define what nonviolence seeks, what it wishes to state, what it offers, what its project is.

"Violence" unquestionably figures among the most widely used words in the written and spoken language of one and all. Looking at the meaning that we attach to the word, however, we see that it is used in many, very different ways. This linguistic confusion reflects confused thinking. And this dual confusion cannot help but give rise to mutual incomprehension in our discussions and attempts at dialogue. And the incomprehension is bound to be twice as great when we venture to talk about nonviolence. So, from the outset, a conceptual clarification that will enable us to agree on the meaning of the words we are using is of crucial importance. For that, we must define several concepts that we tend to confuse: conflict, aggressiveness, struggle, force, constraint and actual violence.

Conflict

"In the beginning there is conflict". Our relationships with others form our personalities. An individual's existence as a human being has less to do with *being in the world* than with *being with others*. Man is essentially born for contact. I only exist in relation to others. Yet my experience of encounters with others tends to be marked by adversity and confrontation. It disturbs me when others come to my home ground. They are invading my area of tranquility; they are tearing me away from my peace of mind. Others, by their very existence, are forcing their way into the space I have secured for myself, as if they were threatening my own existence. Others are those whose desires go against my desires, whose interests clash with my interests, whose ambitions oppose my ambitions, whose plans thwart my plans, whose freedom threatens my freedom, whose rights encroach upon my rights.

The appearance of others by my side is dangerous, or at least it could be. I have no idea whether it is or not; that's why I feel it to be dangerous. Others do not necessarily wish me harm; they may even wish me well, but I do not know. That is why others, strangers, cloud my future. Other people worry me, they even scare me. Even if they do mean me no harm, they trouble me. They will inevitably get in the way. I have no choice but to make room for them, to give way to them, maybe give up my own place. At first I feel other people's proximity as a promiscuity. They may not want to threaten me, perhaps they just want to ask for my help? But even then it still means trouble. My fear of others is twice as great when they do not look like me, when they do not speak the same language, when they do not have the same skin colour, when they do not believe in the same God. This man, above all others, disturbs me. Why did he not stay at home where he belonged?

René Girard has developed a theory which sheds light on the way in which human beings come to compete with each other. As a premise to his thinking, René Girard states that "Everything, or almost everything, in human behaviour is learned, and that learning always boils down to imitation." (Girard, 1978: 15) He then seeks to develop a science of humanity by "specifying the properly human modalities of mimetic behaviour" (Id.). Contrary to those who see imitation as a process geared to social harmony, René Girard strives to show that it essentially is a matter of opposition and antagonism, of rivalry and conflict. For what is at stake in the mimetic behaviour of human beings is the appropriation of an object that gives rise to rivalry because several members of a group want it at the same time. "If an individual sees one of his or her peers reaching out for an object, he or she is immediately tempted to imitate that gesture". (Girard, 1978: 16) According to René Girard, conflict between individuals originally stems from such mimetic rivalry over the appropriation of a single object. And conflict is the confrontation between my will and another's, both of us struggling to make each other yield.

Individuals are jealous when another person possesses an object that they themselves do not possess. Jealousy, wanting the object possessed by another, is thus one of the most powerful sources of conflict between individuals.

Power over objects begets power over others. The desire for possession is profoundly interlinked with the desire for power. While competing for the possession of objects, individuals are also struggling to assert their power over one another. So there is an organic link between property and power. Power is often what is at stake in clashes between human beings. Naturally, everyone has to have enough to meet his or her basic needs—food, shelter, clothing—as well as enough power to ensure that his or her rights are respected. Desiring property and power is legitimate insofar as it enables an individual to achieve independence from others. Adversaries in a conflict, however, each have a natural tendency always to demand more. Nothing is enough for them, and they are never satisfied. "They do not know when to stop"; they know no limits. *Desire demands more, much more, than need.* "There is always a sense of limitlessness in desire", writes Simone Weil (1951: 140). To begin with, individuals seek power so as not to be dominated by others. But if they are not careful, they can soon find themselves overstepping the limit beyond which they are actually seeking to dominate others. And so, rivalry between human beings can only be overcome when each individual puts a limit on his or her own desires. "Limited desires", notes Simone Weil, "are in harmony with the world; desires that contain the infinite are not." (1951: 80)

An individual cannot run away from a conflict situation without giving up on his or her own rights. He or she has to accept confrontation, for it is through conflict that a person is able to gain recognition on the part of others. Conflict can be destructive, but it can also be constructive. Conflict is a means of reaching an agreement, a pact that satisfies the respective rights of each adversary and, as such, of managing to build equitable and just relationships between individuals within a single community and between different communities. Conflict is therefore a structural component of every relationship with others and, hence, of social life as a whole.

Any political situation is conflictual, at least potentially so. The coexistence of people and peoples must become peaceful, but will always remain conflictual. Peace is not, cannot, and never will be conflict-free but it does depend on the control, management and resolution of conflicts through means other than those of destructive and lethal violence. Political action must therefore seek nonviolent conflict resolution (from the Latin *resolutio*, the act of undoing).

In actual fact it is only possible to speak of nonviolence in conflict situations. Pacifist discourse, be it legally or spiritually-based, is wrongheaded and wanders off into idealism when it stigmatizes conflict and argues exclusively in favour of rights, trust, fraternity, reconciliation, forgiveness and love. This amounts to a Utopian flight of fantasy, away from the realm of history.

Nonviolence does not imply a world without conflict. Its political aim is not to build a society where human relations would solely be based on trust. The latter can only be established through relations of proximity, among fellow human beings. In society, any relations with distant "others that I do not know" are, as a rule, a challenge, and should be approached with caution. Hence, life in society is not organized on the basis of trust, but on that of justice. Political action must be geared to organizing justice between all "distant others". It involves creating institutions and drafting laws that provide practical modes of social regulation for dealing with conflicts which can break out between individuals at any time.

In the final analysis, however, conflict must not be regarded as the norm in one's relations with others. Man may be a wolf to his fellow man, but he then lives as a wolf, and not as a man. Human beings fulfil their humanity not outside, but beyond conflict. Conflict may be part of human nature, but only when it has yet to be transformed by the stamp of human beings. Conflict may come first, but it must not have the last word. It is not the primordial, but the most primal means of relating to others. It must be overcome, surpassed. Human beings must ensure that their relations with others are peaceful, devoid of all threat and fear. Human beings must not fall into a relationship of *hostility* with those with whom they come into contact, where each is the enemy of the other; they must seek to establish a relationship of hospitality, where each is the other's host. Significantly, the words hostility and hospitality belong to the same etymological family: originally, both Latin words *hostes* and *hospes* refer to the stranger, who can either be excluded as an enemy, or greeted as a host.

Hospitality calls for more than justice. Justice alone, that is to say merely respecting each other's rights, is not enough to establish relationships between human beings. It still keeps fellow human beings apart from each other. Demanding respect still means making oneself feared. Respect, by its very nature, involves a degree of distance. "*Se tenir en respect*"—as the French expression has it—involves keeping a distance from each other. In order to form a human community, human beings must maintain a two-way relationship based on giving and sharing. Let us anticipate in saying that it is in goodness that hospitality resides.

Aggressiveness

Violence is so central to human history that we are sometimes tempted to think that it is inherent to human nature. Violence would therefore be "natural" for human beings. Believing in nonviolence would then be in vain, for it would be fighting nature itself. Yet in fact it is not violence that is written in human nature, but aggressiveness. Violence is not aggressiveness itself, but an expression of it, and it is not a necessity of nature that aggressiveness should be expressed by violence.

Humans can become rational beings, but first of all they are instinctual and impulsive ones. Instincts are a bundle of energies: when the bundle is properly tied, it gives structure and unity to the individual's personality, while if it becomes undone then the entire individual loses structure and unity. Aggressiveness is one of these energies; like fire, it can do good or harm, destroy or create.

Aggressiveness is a power of combativeness and self-assertion which helps build my own personality. It allows me to face others without flinching. To be aggressive is to assert oneself in the face of something other by walking towards it. The word "aggression" come from the Latin *aggredi*, whose roots, *ad-gradi*, mean "walking towards", "moving towards". Only in a derivative sense does aggression mean "moving against": it comes from the fact that in a war, marching towards the enemy is marching against it, that is to say, attacking it. In its origins, then, the word "a-ggression" does not imply more violence than the word "pro-gression" that means moving forward. Showing aggressiveness is accepting conflict with another without submitting to its domination. Without aggressiveness, I would constantly be running away from the threats that others pressure me with. Without aggressiveness, I would be incapable of overcoming the fear that paralyses me and holds me back from fighting my adversaries and struggling to have my rights recognised and respected. To move towards others, one must show boldness and courage, for it is to face the unknown, and to embark on an adventure.

Fear lies within each individual, and the point is not to drive it away by refusing to acknowledge it. On the contrary, one must become aware of it, try hard to accept it, to tame and overcome it, all the while knowing that this effort will have to be renewed again and again, endlessly. This fear may cause human beings, sometimes unwittingly, to feel anxiety, anguish and suffering, which can become rooted as an attitude of intolerance and hostility towards others. An irrational factor then affects the development of interpersonal relations and may even become predominant. Fear is not shameful, however, merely human.

What can be shameful is to give in to one's fear. For fear can give us bad advice, both when counselling submission and when inciting to violence. To tame one's fear, to master the feelings and passions it provokes, this is what makes it possible to express one's aggressiveness through other means than destructive violence. Once that is achieved, aggressiveness becomes a fundamental constituent of one's relationships to others, in which mutual respect can replace domination and submission.

In actual fact, in the face of injustice, passivity is a more widespread attitude than violence. People's capacity for resignation is considerably greater than their capacity for revolt. One of the first tasks of nonviolent action is therefore that of "mobilizing", that is to say to stir the victims of injustice into action, rousing their aggressiveness so that they are ready to struggle: provoking conflict. While slaves submit to their master, there is no conflict. On the contrary, it is at such times that "order" is restored, and "social peace" reigns, uncontested by anything or anyone. Conflict only arises from the moment when slaves show sufficient aggressiveness to "move towards" (*ad-gradi*) their masters, dare to face them and claim their rights. Nonviolence presupposes a capacity for aggressiveness before all else. In that sense, we should say that nonviolence is the opposite of passivity and resignation, rather than of violence. But collective nonviolent action must allow the channeling of individual's natural aggressiveness in such a way that it expresses itself not through destructive violence, which could lead to further violence and more injustice, but through fair and peaceful measures suitable for building a fair and peaceful society. In the end, violence is nothing other than a perversion of aggressiveness.

The anger that can take hold of a person and cause the loss of all self-control, is an overflowing of aggressiveness. But we know that anger is a sign of weakness and not strength of character. "*Ira brevis furor est*": "anger", writes Horace, "is a momentary madness". The Latin poet specifies that: "He who cannot learn to dominate his anger will later regret having done what resentment and passion advised him to, looking to violence for a ready satisfaction for his unappeased hatred. …. Govern your passions, for they will rule where they are not ruled; they must be held back, they must be tied down." (*Epistles*, I, II, 59-64)

Jesus of Nazareth is not content with condemning he who kills his own brother, he also accuses he who "loses his temper with his own brother" and heaps insults on him. (Mt 5, 21-22) John of Bethsaida clearly voices Jesus' thoughts when he claims: "Whoever hates his own brother is a homicide." (1Jn 3, 15) Hatred is, indeed, deadly enough.

Struggle

Simply existing is, indeed, a struggle for life. To fend for my own rights, but also to fend for the rights of those I wish to support, I must struggle against those who threaten or harm them. "It is sheer madness", stated Charles Peguy in contradiction with pacifist dogma, "to want to link the Declaration of Human Rights to a Declaration of Peace. As if a Declaration of Justice was not a declaration of war in itself. …. As if one single point of law, one single claim, could appear in the world without immediately becoming a cause for trouble and cause to start a war." (Péguy, 1961: 1250-1) If we take the word war in its broadest sense (meaning a struggle, a confrontation, a battle), from the point of view of formal principles, Peguy is right to contradict the pacifists: they remain prisoners of their own refusal of war and do not suggest any other means by which to fight injustice and defend human rights.

Nonviolent action certainly intends to use up all the possibilities of dialogue with the adversary by appealing to his reason in an attempt to convince him; by appealing to his conscience in an attempt to convert him. If he agrees to a discussion, it is then possible to undertake a negotiation process in an attempt to come to an agreement that does everybody justice. Sadly, appeals to reason are rarely enough to resolve a conflict. What generally characterizes a situation of injustice, is precisely the impossibility of dialogue between adversaries. And it is because dialogue is impossible that struggle is necessary. Whenever it is not possible to resolve a conflict through dialogue, struggle is the only way to make dialogue possible. Struggle serves to create the conditions for dialogue by establishing a new balance of power, thus forcing others to see me as a necessary interlocutor.

From then on, it becomes possible to start negotiating the terms of agreement that will end the conflict.

Force

There is yet another distinction to be established, between the use of violence and the exercise of force. Any struggle is a trial of strength. In a given economic, social and political context, all relations with others can be viewed as a balance of forces. The quest for justice is a quest to find balance between antagonistic forces, so that the rights of each and every one should be respected. Struggle seeks to create a new balance of forces in order to establish that equilibrium. "Social order", writes Simone Weil, "can only be a balance of forces." (Weil, 1956: 111) Social justice is the balance of forces pulling in opposite directions. That is why "the scales, representing an equal balance of power, has always been, throughout antiquity and especially in Egypt, the symbol for justice." (Weil, 1963: 129) Injustice is therefore the result of an imbalance of forces in which the weaker are dominated and oppressed by the stronger. From then on, acting for justice is to establish a balance of forces, and that can only happen by exercising a force which limits the force responsible for the imbalance. Hence, for Simone Weil, the "beautiful action", is "an action which concludes, suspends the indefinite dialogue between the unbalanced elements that respond to each other, and establishes the unique balance corresponding to the given situation." (Weil, 1951: 52) Nonviolent action wants to be that "beautiful action", aiming to establish the balance of forces which ensures justice and peace.

This balance of forces allows human beings to live in symbiosis (from the Greek *sun*, with, and *bios*, life) with each other. Symbiosis is a "life in common" based on reciprocally beneficial relations for all partners involved; it is an association between several living beings which enables them to satisfy their respective needs without doing others any harm. It is therefore in all their best interests to respect the terms of this association, despite the constraints it imposes on them. It is thus enduring because all may benefit from it.

Michel Serres praised the "contract of symbiosis" which allows adversaries to become partners by deciding to live together in mutual respect of their rights and interests. "What is an enemy", he asks, "who is he for us, and how should he be treated? In other words and for example: what is cancer? A growing set of malignant cells that we must at all costs expel, sever, reject? Or something like a parasite with which we must negotiate a contract of symbiosis?"As for Michel Serres, he "inclines towards the second solution, as life itself does." (Serres, 1992: 281) That is why "it is better to find a symbiotic balance, even a poorly adapted one, than to revive a perpetually lost war." (Ibid., 282)

It is pointless to claim that rights must take precedence over force, when wanting to discredit force in the name of rights. As a matter of fact, rights can indeed have no other guarantee than force. In a just and free society, political life is governed by law, but the respect for the law is guaranteed by strength. Alain voices legal pacifism's fundamental error as he writes: "Not the solution to a problem of law through forceful means, but quite the opposite, the solution to a problem of force through legal means." (Alain, 1939: 214) These "legal means" in themselves actually remain powerless to solve a "legal problem." Idealism by its very nature credits "rights" with a specific force which would act throughout history and would truly lay the foundations for progress. Everything points to the opposite: such a force cannot exist. Max Scheler clearly pointed out the illusion of "the strength of rights": "such a spontaneous force", he writes, "inherent to the very idea of rights, has never existed. Any "positive" right is, when it emerges, but a legal formulation of a given balance of forces, of a given set of interests." (Scheler, 1953: 110)

Only the force of an organized action can actually be effective in fighting against injustice and restoring what is right. It is therefore mere self-deception to aim to disparage "force" in contrast with "right", since, when it comes to deeds, rights can have no other guarantee than force. But force is not violence and it is not possible to discredit violence until force has been rehabilitated, given its rightful place and has had its legitimacy recognized. We must also at one and the same time reject the so-called realism which justifies violence as being the very foundation of all political action, and the so-called spiritualism which refuses to recognize force as an inherent element in political action. And since force exists only in action, it is not possible to denounce and fight against violence except by offering another method of action which, although it owes nothing to lethal violence, is nevertheless capable of establishing a balance of power that guarantees rights.

The strategic discourse on which the concept of a nonviolent struggle is based rejects the idealist view which would like to establish peace on the "force of justice", "the force of reason", "the force of truth", "the force of love". Such expressions are certainly not without meaning. Hence there is a sense in which we can speak of the "force of truth", and "telling the truth" is never in vain. But in that case it is a persuasive force that comes from outside, and must be welcomed. The truth can only be acknowledged by those who decide to support it of their own accord; it could not force itself onto those who refuse to submit to it. Lies easily triumph over truth. Triumph bears the mark of violence; it already has its appearance. He who announces triumph loud and clear is a dangerous man; he is already preparing for war.

Of course, in a conflict, it is theoretically possible for those who bear responsibility for injustice, because they are also human and have a sense of justice, to freely admit their wrongs and to do their adversaries justice. But this is not very likely in practice. And if they do not willingly do so, they will simply have to be forced into it.

Most often, as Pascal noted in his twelfth *Provinciale*: "Violence and truth cannot impose on each other." For if it is true that "all of violence's efforts cannot weaken the truth, and only serve to make it stronger", it is nonetheless true that "all of truth's illuminations cannot do anything to stop violence, and can only irritate it even further." (Pascal, 1963: 429)

Justice and truth by themselves are thus generally incapable of forcing the master to acknowledge the slave's rights. Strength, as a matter of fact, only exists in action and unity is the strength in the action. That is why those who suffer from injustice must unite and act together in order to get justice. "The people, united", states a Spanish proverb, "shall never be defeated."

Constraint

To prove my adversaries wrong, I must therefore pressure them with a real force of constraint that forces them to do me justice.

If nonviolent action's long-term aim is to get my adversaries to become reasonable, its short-term objective is to constrain them, without waiting for them to be convinced.

To constrain people is to force them to act against their will: they did not want to agree before, but now they do. They finally accept what they first refused. They accept because they cannot do otherwise or, more exactly, because more disadvantages than advantages would result from them doing otherwise. They accept because, all things considered, in doing otherwise, they would have more to lose than to gain. They accept because, in the end, it is in their best interest to do so. They find themselves compelled to change their selection and decision criteria. So they make concessions, they give up. They comply, that is to say, when facing constraint, they temper their desires, restrain their ambitions, become less demanding while taking other people's requirements into account. As the French expression has it, they "add water to their wine", learn to compromise (to comply is *obtempérer* in French, from the Latin *temperare*, meaning mixing, blending, diluting).

Nonviolent struggle cannot simply amount to a debate, it really is a battle in which several forces oppose each other. Within economic, social and political conflicts, adversaries are not people, nor even groups of people, but indeed groups of interests. And it is generally not possible for a rational dialogue to settle between them, one in which truth could triumph over error in a demonstration which no objection could contradict. The relationships between these groups are that of power and, when power is at stake and calls antagonistic interests into question, human beings are generally not reasonable. That is why, when it comes to struggling against the structural injustice of an "established disorder", constraint, exerted by collective action, determines the success of a nonviolent resistance.

Naturally, within a given group, some individuals may be aware of the justice of the cause defended by the opposition. They could then, so to speak, advocate that same cause within their own group. But, in all likelihood, they will be but a small minority and risk being rejected as traitors. Their role could be important, however, once the struggle has changed its balance of forces, and the time has come to negotiate a solution to the conflict.

2

A Reflection on Violence

The exercise of aggressiveness, force and constraint within a struggle makes it possible to move beyond conflict by looking for rules whereby all adversaries are done justice. Violence, on the other hand, immediately seems like an instant de-regulation of conflict with the result that it can no longer fulfil its function of establishing justice between adversaries.

Let us return now to René Girard's thesis on mimetic rivalry. Two individuals are contending for the possession of the same object, which is more desirable to each for the other's desiring it. Very soon, the two individuals, now adversaries, will turn their attention from the object itself and focus entirely on their rival. And they will fight, not to have the object which from this moment tends to be left out and forgotten, but to eliminate this rival. They may even prefer destroying the object of their desire rather than letting it become the other's property. Their contention "becomes pure rivalry" (Girard, 1978: 35), and from this moment on, the mimetic relationship between the two rivals will be dominated by the logic of violence. "Violence", writes René Girard, "is a perfect mimetic relationship, and therefore perfectly reciprocal. Each imitates the other's violence, repaying it, 'with interest'." (Ibid., 324)

Violence, as we have noted, occurs when human beings have boundless desires, and when these desires become thwarted by others. "I have the right, observes Simone Weil, to make anything my own, but others get in the way of that. I have to take up arms to get these obstacles out of the way." (Weil,

1956: 47) Violence stems from a boundless desire colliding with bounds set by others' desires.

Violence appears in a conflict when one of its protagonists does everything he or she can to threaten the other with death. "For make no mistake", would have us observe Paul Ricoeur, "the aim of violence, the end it has in view, implicitly or explicitly, directly or indirectly, is the other's death—at the very least; or maybe something even worse." (Ricoeur, 1955: 227) Hence every manifestation of violence is a murderous process, a death sentence. The process might not reach its final deed, but the desire to eliminate one's adversaries, to get them out of the way, exclude them, silence them, suppress them, becomes stronger than the will to come to an agreement with them. From insults to humiliation, from torture to murder, the forms of violence are many, and so are the forms of death. To compromise a person's dignity is itself to compromise that person's life. Silencing them is already an act of violence; for to deny the right to speak is to deny the right to life.

It is wrong to speak of "violence" as if it existed on its own among people, in a sense "outside" them; or acted as an independent agent, where in fact violence exists and operates only through people; it is always some person who is responsible for violence.

If, when defining violence, we put ourselves on the side of the person exercising it, we run a serious risk of mistaking its true nature by embarking instantly on those processes of legitimation which justify means by the end. We must therefore in defining violence place ourselves first on the side of the victim. Here, the perception is immediate and it involves a mindset which considers the means used, and not, as before, the end sought. According to Simone Weil, violence, "is that which turns any person subjected to it into a thing". "When it goes all the way", she explains further, "it turns a person into a thing in the most literal sense: a corpse". But violence that kills is a crude, summary form of violence. There is another violence, far more varied in its procedures, and surprising in its effects, and this is "the one that does not kill; or rather, that has not killed yet". "It will most certainly kill in the end, or perhaps it will kill;

or again is it just hanging over the person, ready to kill at any minute; in any case, it turns a person to stone. Out of the power to turn a person into a thing by killing arises another power, far more remarkable: the power to make a thing of a still-living person." (Weil, 1953: 12-13)

However, what distinguishes a still-living person affected by violence from a thing, is that the person suffers. Making people suffer is an act of violence, for suffering can be far more dreadful than death. "The supreme test of the will", writes Emmanuel Levinas, "is not death, but suffering." (Levinas, 1992: 267) That is why, he goes on to explain, "hatred does not always wish for the other's death, or, at least, it only wishes for the other's death by inflicting it as a supreme suffering. .... In suffering, the subject must be aware of its own objectification, but for that the subject must precisely remain subject." (Ibid., 266-267)

It seems to us that a definition of violence could be formulated using Kant's second imperative in the *Foundations of the metaphysics of morals*: "Act in such a way that you treat humanity, in your own person as well as any other, always as an end too, and never simply as a means." (Kant, 1952: 150-151) According to Kant, the basis for that principle is that, unlike *things* that are only means, *people* exist as end in themselves. "Humans, and in general all rational beings, exist as ends in themselves, and not only as means which this person or that can make use of as they will; in all the actions of a rational being, whether self or other-regarding, any other rational being must be considered also as an end." (Ibid., 149) The person, accordingly, who uses other humans simply as mere instruments (means), violates their humanity, and does violence to them. We can therefore define violence in this way, by taking Kant's suggestion literally: to be violent is "to use another person simply as a means, disregarding that other people, as rational beings, must always be considered as ends as well." (Ibid., 152)

Violence, we are told, is the abuse of force. But there is more to it than that: violence is in itself an abuse; the very use of violence constitutes abuse. To abuse someone, is to violate them. All violence against a human being is a violation: a violation of its body, its identity, its personality, its humanity. All violence is brutal, offensive, destructive, cruel. Violence always affects the face, deforming it through the effect of suffering; all violence is disfiguring. *Violence wounds and bruises the humanity of its victim.*

But people do not only feel the violence they suffer; they also find out from experience that they themselves are capable of violence against others. Human beings, through re-flection, or turning their gaze upon themselves, discover that they are violent. *And violence wounds and bruises also the humanity of the perpetrator.* "Striking or being struck", says Simone Weil (1960: 80), "the befoulment is one and the same. Cold steel is fatal at the handle and at the blade alike." So whether we practice violence or undergo it, "its touch is petrifying in every way, and turns a person into a thing" (1985: 54).

"Structural violence"

Violence is not only the *direct violence* of *violent actions*; the *indirect violence* of *violent situations* also exists. In the sixties, the Norwegian researcher Johan Galtung invented the expression "structural violence", referring to violence caused by political, economic and social structures which create situations of oppression, exploitation or alienation. There was much debate to know whether or not it was right to resort to the same concept, that of "violence", to designate both violent actions and situations of injustice (See Mellon, 1980). Naturally, the destructive intention in violent action is immediately perceptible, whereas it is more difficult to detect that same intention in situations of injustice. However, there is no doubt that victims of these situations undergo a form of violence that infringes upon their dignity and freedom, and which can genuinely threaten them with death. A situation of injustice matches the definition we have given of violence: it violates the humanity of those who suffer from it. And if we refer to Kant's second maxim on which we based our definition of violence, in a situation of oppression, of exploitation or of alienation, a person is indeed treated as a means and not considered to be an end in itself. Besides, it does not seem to us that the *intentionality* criterion should be the one to be remembered here, more so the *responsibility* criterion. Yet, human responsibility is directly engaged in these situations of injustice, clearly not due to imponderable factors. Not only "are we all responsible", but there is no oppression without oppressors, no exploitation without exploiters, no dictatorships without dictators.

We therefore think that it is in no way a metaphor to qualify as "violence" the situations of injustice which hurt human beings and can kill them. On the other hand, it is only a metaphor to speak of the "violence" of nature. Nature can certainly kill, but it *is not* "violent". Not only does it not intend to kill, but it bears no responsibility whatsoever over the deaths it causes. Hence is no responsibility engaged in the case of a volcano eruption, an earthquake or a hurricane. *What we have qualified as violence can only be the result of human action.*

Understanding the violence of revolt

Armed violence is often caused by the violence of unjust situations. And it is necessary to understand violence that is born from the revolt of the oppressed, as they try to break free from the yoke that weighs heavily on them. If nonviolence initially condemns and fights the violence of oppression, it inevitably leads to an active solidarity with its victims. When these very victims resort to violence, most often out of sheer desperation, we must not turn our back on them in the name of an abstract nonviolent ideal. We must not tar with the same brush those who are responsible for the injustice, and those who are its victims. It is important to remember that those who are truly to blame are those who take advantage of the existing disorder, defending nothing but their own privileges. But to liberate the oppressed, is also to attempt to allow them to free themselves from their own violence. It is also a duty generated by the solidarity we owe them.

The violence of the oppressed and excluded is often a means of expression rather than a means of action. It is not so much seeking effectiveness as claiming an identity; it is a way to gain recognition for those whose very existence remains not just unknown, but ignored. Violence then becomes a way to revolt against this ignorance. It is the ultimate means of expression for those that society has deprived of all other means. Because they have not had the possibility to express themselves and communicate through speech, they attempt to do so through violence, which thus replaces the right to speak that they have been refused. Violence seeks to be a language and first and foremost expresses suffering; it is a "distress signal" which must be read as such by other members of society. Violence is a desperate attempt for the excluded to reclaim lost power over their own lives, and then becomes a way to prove their existence: "I am violent, therefore, I am." And violence makes recognition all the more possible for its being forbidden by society. It symbolizes the transgression of a social order that does not deserve to be respected. This transgression is precisely what the people involved in violence are after. For those that law deprives of all recognition, the violation of that same law seems like the best way to be acknowledged. This can be true for individuals as well as groups: a group can also seek to prove that it exists as such by asserting itself through the use of violence. That way, it forces others to acknowledge its existence, if only in fighting it through violence, on the territory where it has chosen to express itself. Furthermore, the violence of transgression brings real and malicious pleasure, in destroying the symbols of an unjust society, and throwing the attributes of an unfair order to the floor. Violence is thereby fascinating for those who feel the frustration and humiliation caused by being excluded.

But understanding violence does not mean it can be *justified*. For if violence is just, as soon as it serves a just cause, will it not become every person's, group's, people's and nation's right and duty? Have we never indeed, over the centuries and across the world, met or seen a person, a group, a people, a nation claiming loud and clear that its cause is just? And if today we rally behind speeches that approve of violence to defend a good cause, how will we oppose those that approve of violence for the wrong cause tomorrow? Will it be enough simply to discuss the cause, and not the violence? *Probably not*. As soon as violence is legitimized as a human right, every one will eagerly take advantage of this right whenever they consider that their interests require such defence. In actual fact, *the ideology of violence allows everyone to justify their own violence*. History is then sucked into an endless spiral of violence. There follows a chain reaction of violent acts, each as legitimate as the others, that no one can interrupt. Violence thus becomes a fatality, which nonviolence intends to break.

According to the ideologies which dominate our societies, it is necessary to oppose the original violence of oppression or aggression by a *counter-violence* that can contain it, and eventually overcome it. The same ideologies legitimise and justify this second violence, asserting that its purpose lies in establishing justice or defending freedom. The argument that is constantly put forward to justify violence—and that is claimed to be above suspicion—is that it is inevitable in order to fight against violence. This argument implies a corollary: turning one's back on violence, would be giving way to violence. But whatever the reasons that are put forward, this argument remains filled with an implacable contradiction, both in theory and practice: using violence to fight against violence does not make it possible to eliminate violence. The ideologies of violence seek to cover up this contradiction, whereas the philosophy of nonviolence and the political strategy that it inspires as we shall see—devotes all its attention to it, in an attempt to overcome it. For an essential and decisive question arises here: does using violence with the intention of serving a just cause change the nature of violence, or not? In other words, is it possible to describe violence differently depending on the purpose it is claimed to be serving? The ideologies of violence seek a positive response to this dual question, insinuating that the use of violence for a just cause is nothing but the use of force. The philosophy of nonviolence radically criticizes this response, and absolutely refutes it. Violence, after all, is violence, and remains unjust and therefore unjustifiable because it remains inhuman whatever the purpose it may be serving.

The violent man in the face of death

A person's attitude towards violence is greatly determined by his or her attitude towards death. Deep within themselves, human beings know fear: fear of others, fear of the future, fear of the unknown, that they picture filled with threat and danger. But people's fear is always rooted in their fear of dying. According to Aristotle—and with him, all the western philosophical tradition—the virtue of the strong man who is able to overcome his fear and face up to danger, is courage. In the *Nicomachean Ethics,* he writes that "naturally, we dread danger and, generally speaking, what we fear are evils." (Book III, Ch. VI) But humans must show courage and control their fear: "The characteristic of courage is indeed to consistently endure what is or seems frightening to humans, for the simple reason that it is good to confront danger and shameful to avoid it." (Book III, Ch. IX) Yet the most frightening of evils "is death, which is the final conclusion beyond which there is, it seems, neither good, nor evil" (Book III, Ch. IX). Aristotle then asks in what circumstances human beings show courage, and war is the example he singles out above all others. Hence does the strong man mainly manifest himself « in the death one finds in war, among the greatest and most glorious perils" (Book III, Ch. VI). For Aristotle the sole evidence lies in the honours conferred upon many for military courage. He concludes: "Hence can one legitimately pronounce a person brave when he or she remains fearless in the face of a beautiful death and in front of sudden dangers, likely to cause death; those are especially to be found in war." (Book III, Ch. VI) And when he states that "law orders all people to act like brave men" he is yet again referring to war as an example: the law thus requires soldiers "not to leave battle, not to flee, not to lay down their arms". (Book V, Ch. I). As for those who "feel excessive fear" in the face of danger, they are "cowards" (Book III, Ch. VIII).

Plato already considered courage to be an essentially warlike virtue. In *The Republic*, Socrates addresses Adeimantus in these terms: "Who would describe a city as cowardly or courageous by looking at anything other than that part which defends it and wages war on its behalf?" And Adeimantus replies: "No one would look at anything else." (Book IV, 429a) Many centuries later, speaking through Zarathustra, Nietzsche equally maintains the predominance of warlike courage over all other virtues: "War and courage have achieved more great things than loving your neighbour." (1963: 59) Hegel, we shall see, will not state otherwise. We have therefore always been used to the thought that the courageous man is he who overcomes fear and risks dying by resorting to violence to defend a just cause. A person who shows courage in the face of danger is said to *get tougher**, which means precisely that he becomes capable of confronting the risks of war in overcoming his fear.

But is not the challenge of the person who decides to use violence really to kill before he or she is killed? People who choose violence risk being killed, but do not wish to acknowledge it; in fact, they know it, but do not wish to believe it, for they are entirely preoccupied with the determination to kill and want to convince themselves that they will defeat their adversaries in this fight to the death. In an imaginary dialogue with a general, Alain, the philosopher, declares to the military man: "Since (the) destiny (of citizens) is after all, to risk everything, including their own lives, will they not choose peace over all risks? For any war plan contains risk of death. What worse risk could there be in a real and honest peace plan?" But the general replies: "The first article of our doctrine is to believe that we shall overcome." (Alain, 1939: 284) For those who choose violence, the risk of being killed is therefore covered up by their absolute belief in victory. This risk certainly really exists, since an adversary must be confronted, one who is as determined to kill so as not to die and as certain of triumphing, but each feigns to ignore it and prefers not to think about it.

Since they are all mortal, should human beings not show compassion for each other? It is in fact precisely because they are mortal that human beings are cruel to each other. Humans kill, not only because they do not want to get killed, but because they do not want to die: they kill to defeat death. We kill, says Simone Weil (1953: 116), "because we feel as if we are escaping the death that we are inflicting"; we kill to "revenge our mortality" (Id.). In conclusion, what justifies violence for human beings, is that it appears to them as the only way to protect themselves from death.

In his great book *Crowds and Power*, Elias Canetti thoroughly analyses "the desire to survive" (1966: 244) which lies deep within human beings. "The lowest form of survival", he writes, "is killing. .... One wants to kill anyone who stands in one's way, thwarts one's plans, sets himself up against one as an

---

* Translator's note. In French, *s'aguerrir*, from the word *guerre*, meaning war.

enemy. One wants to strike him down so that one feels that one still stands while the other lies prostrate. .... This moment of confronting the man one has killed fills the survivor with a special, incomparable kind of force. There is no moment which more demands repetition." (Ibid., 241-242) That way, by outliving those they kill in battle, humans have the great satisfaction of feeling invulnerable, and somehow immortal. "The survivor looks upon all these corpses surrounding him and feels happy, privileged even", writes Elias Canetti. "The dead lie powerless, and he stands among them, as if the battle had been fought for his survival only. He has diverted death from himself onto others." (Ibid., 242) What gives the warrior prestige and the status of a hero, the reason why others admire and envy him, is that he has outlived all those he has killed, as well as all those who died by his side: he has outlived his enemies as well as his friends.

Should we not be surprised that human beings across the years and centuries have not realized the full extent of all the suffering, destruction and death caused by war, that they have not revolted against the inevitability of violence which has weighed on history by their own hand and which they have not yet decided to break with? How is it that they have learnt nothing from the past and that they have always been eager for history to repeat itself? Is it not precisely because they only know about war through the memory of its survivors who, all things considered, can no longer complain about it? Naturally, the survivors are always the ones to make speeches during war memorial ceremonies. For one minute of silence in memory of the dead, how many hours of noise in memory of survivors? Remembering the dead does nothing but fill the memory of survivors, who have every reason to think that fate has treated them generously. In actual fact, the survivors more or less consciously honour themselves in honouring the dead; they honour themselves for having survived and get great satisfaction from it. The survivors' narcissism thus erases the misery of war victims. The memory of survivors, and not the thought of the dead, is what lives on through the centuries and form peoples' collective memory. That is why all things considered, these do not hold painful memories of the horrors of war and do not feel the need to reject violence.

History is nothing else but the history of survivors. "Written by the victors, their meditation based on the victories", Emmanuel Levinas notes, "our western history and philosophy of history announce the achievement of a humanist ideal while ignoring the defeated, the victims and the persecuted as if they had no significance whatsoever. .... Humanism of the great! The denunciation of violence might turn into the installation of a form of violence and a certain haughtiness or superiority: alienation and Stalinism. War against war perpetuates war by ridding it of its guilty conscience." But Levinas concludes strangely, showing an optimism we have difficulty sharing: "Our times certainly do not need to be convinced of the importance of nonviolence anymore." (1990: 239) It seems to us that he still has everything to learn about nonviolence.

Violent people refer to the judgment of history to justify their deeds. But the judgment of history does not exist; the survivors are the ones judging history. History cannot be the judge, it can only be judged, and is judged so by the victors. History seems to prove violent people right, but that is only the history of violent people. As for the history of violence, it still remains to be written, which will involve taking the victims' opinions into account.

The illusion of killing to defeat death

In his book *Psychoanalysis of the Atomic War*, the Italian psychiatrist and philosopher Franco Fornari considers that we come to terms with life and death in "a sort of bad faith" (1969: 12). We refuse to acknowledge "the imminence of death within ourselves" and "we picture death as if it were detached" (Ibid., 12-13): "We cheat, at this game where life and death fight over our existence, by hiding the death cards." (Ibid., 13).

The fear of death is therefore the cause for our fear of others—unknown, strangers, undesirables, intruders. We consequently consider others to be enemies intending to kill us, even if they show no hostility towards us. Fear creates danger more than danger creates fear. People often regress to the situation they were in when, as children, the inoffensive sounds of nighttime made them fear the worst. "By keeping death at bay", writes

Franco Fornari, "humans kill insofar as, having placed death outside themselves, they see it as the attack of an enemy seeking to kill them. That is why every crime is prompted by the illusion that death can be defeated by killing the enemy." (Ibid., 23)

Franco Fornari then refers to Freud's words from a text written at the beginning of the First World War, *Thoughts for the times on war and death*: "Once a decision", writes the Austrian psychiatrist, "will have put an end to the brutal confrontation of this war, every victorious combatant will happily go home to his wife and children, with no preoccupation or thought for the enemies he will have killed with his bare hands or with a long-range weapon." (Freud, 1981: 34) The civilized man therefore does not feel any guilt when it comes to murder. Freud points out that it was a different matter altogether for the primitive man. "The savage", he notes, "is by no means an unrepentant murderer. When he comes back from war a victor, he cannot enter his village nor touch his wife until he has expiated his war crimes in an often long and painful penance." (Id.) Freud concludes by emphasizing that in doing so the primitive man showed "a moral consideration that has been lost among us civilised men" (Ibid., 35).

The Chinese philosopher Laozi, in chapter 31 of *Tao Te Ching*, expresses the same obligation to go into mourning for those who, out of necessity, have had to resort to violence against their adversary:

> As shiny as they look, weapons are nothing but instruments of misfortune
> Those who live rightly loathe them.
> That is why the Tao man never interferes with them....
> For the noble man, there are no fortunate weapons:
> The instrument of misfortune cannot be his own.
> He turns to it against his will, if necessary,
> Above all loving peace and quiet;
> Even in victory he does not rejoice;
> For to rejoice, one must love killing,
> And he who takes pleasure in the massacre of men,
> What can he accomplish in the world of men? ....
> Mourning and lament for the massacre of men,
> A funeral rite to give the victor his rank.

Laozi and Freud's thoughts on the obligation of mourning for the man who murdered his adversary must not be looked upon with amused indifference, as is often the case for edifying anecdotes on the habits and customs of a bygone age. They should not only be taken seriously, but also literally. The truly "civilized" man, if he is trapped by necessity and forced to kill his opponent, does not feel like celebrating any victory, does not seek to exonerate himself with any justification, but wants to go into mourning for those who died because of him. Laozi and Freud's assertions are irrefutable: after the killing of an enemy, "civilization" demands mourning, whereas "savagery" encourages the celebration of victory. For, to celebrate, "one must enjoy killing".

The women behind war

War is Man's domain. Not that it is of no concern to women, quite the opposite: it concerns them directly, but they have stood behind war or, more exactly, they have been kept behind war, most often invisible, in the same way that they have been kept behind men. Women have probably suffered from war more than men, but their suffering and tears were resigned and silent, as their lives were. Even as they cursed war, they did not protest against it. Until now women have suffered from the violence of men without daring to revolt against it. They have been oppressed and dominated by men, and have most often been submissive. They have generally accepted men's laws; in doing so, they have accepted the rules of war.

Hence the warlike virtues that heroes are made of, belong to men. Women seem to be lacking them, as if they did not have the necessary skills to carry a sword and defy death on battlefields, as if they were not worthy of sharing the glory of warriors and had to be kept for their amusement and consolation. But in refusing to submit to men's power, will women refuse to imitate their violence? Nothing would be worse than women, in the name of equality, claiming their place in war. Could women be "naturally" loath to "taking lives", because they give birth to human beings? Could they have a "natural" tendency to refuse violence and to prefer nonviolence because of their biological status? Could violence be essentially masculine and nonviolence essentially feminine? It is probably better to say that violence is essentially masculine and that nonviolence is essentially masculine *and* feminine. It is thus certainly not fruitless to hope that by freeing themselves from men's yoke, women will make a decisive contribution to the culture of nonviolence. But this also means that men must liberate the feminine element which makes up part of their being.

Guilt and responsibility

Man kills to escape the fear of death but, in killing, is confronted with the fear of murder. That is why as he kills his enemy, man simultaneously needs to justify his murder and deny the feeling of guilt that seizes him. This justification process causes man to commit violence without considering it as such. He can kill without feeling violent.

Man's imperative need to justify his own violence actually indicates that he is aware that it is not fair. Because he feels guilty, he needs to exonerate himself and protest his innocence by justifying himself. He therefore resorts to prevarication which causes a distortion and hardening of his moral conscience, and in that way he can continue to act without feeling guilty. All the justification mechanisms for violence are nothing but defence mechanisms for man, who wants to protect himself against the guilt he feels over his own violence.

To say that violence wounds the humanity of the person committing it, is not simply to state an abstract metaphysical principle, it expresses a psychological reality that leaves its marks on the violent man's life experience. Violence literally traumatizes (to traumatize, etymologically, means to wound, to hurt) whoever takes to it. Man hurts himself by his own violence, he hurts himself deep within and must shelter behind a protective shell in order to avoid suffering. The more or less repressed and more or less admitted guilt of a man who commits violence against his fellow men, gives rise to anxiety. The justifications of violence that are offered by the prevailing ideology aim to allow him to find reassurance and peace. If he internalizes these justifications, he is in a position to convince himself that he has done nothing but his duty and not only can he have a clear conscience, but he can feel proud of what he has just done. On the other hand, if despite everything he is aware that these justifications are nothing but propaganda, and if he cannot be satisfied with them, he finds himself alone with his infamy, racked with overwhelming pain. This suffering, caused by the psychic trauma he has suffered, can become fatal, in so far as it can make him go insane. Some war injuries cannot simply be slung over one's shoulder. Hence do the agents and victims of violence find themselves locked together in the same process of degradation and destruction.

Because he feels guilty towards the victims of his own violence, man needs to shift the blame onto them. To clear himself, he projects his feeling of guilt onto his enemy. He is responsible, he is guilty: "It is his fault!". First, "He started it!". It is always the others who started things. Violence is always committed in response to the violence of *others-who-started-things*. From then on, "He got just what he deserved"; "He should not have started it"; "It serves him right". Well no, it precisely does not serve anybody right: to commit violence is never to "serve right". For others to have started something is not a reason to continue. Because if others were wrong to start, I am certainly not right in continuing. If I continue, they will necessarily start again with renewed violence. And we will all be caught up in an endless spiral of violence.

The justification of the murder that a person is about to commit is necessarily followed by the criminalisation of whoever he is about to kill: this is the foundation of the theory of self-defence. A person always becomes a murderer in defence against those who want to kill him. He must kill so as not to be killed and to be able to continue defending the "sacred" values of his cause. Killing is consequently not felt to be a fault, but an act of bravery that deserves to be honoured as such. That change, that inversion of the meaning of the murderous act characterizes the moral perversion of a man alienated by what we have named "the ideology of violence".

The feeling of guilt must not plunge the individual into a morbid bad conscience, it must make him realize his fault and invent a new behaviour, respecting the dynamics of his inner life. The feeling of guilt towards violence is the source of the feeling of personal responsibility of the individual; it must generate a need for reparation, and not for justification.

The individual generally does not resort to violence in isolation, but does so within the social group that he belongs to. The justification of violence is immediately brought to him by this community, which not only justifies it, but honours, glorifies and regards it as sacred it by putting forward the defence of its values, rights and interests. Most often, the individual alienates his personal responsibility within the community. As soon as the latter justifies killing by presenting it as the ultimate mean of defence of the civilized man against barbarians, the individual stops feeling responsible for his own violence. Not only does he feel no guilt whatsoever, but it makes him feel proud.

These justification processes of violence have another consequence: because he does not experience violence as such, man loses the possibility of controlling his own violence. Once violence is justified, there are no more limits to its development. Furthermore, the justification of violence causes a chain reaction by which all violence is legitimized. So, ultimately, man does not judge violence according to what it really is, but from the mental representation he has of it. As soon as this representation shows violence as a just and legitimate way to fight injustice, he will lose any reluctance to kill. Every last one of these justifications of violence are "derivations" (in Vilfredo Pareto's sense of the word), that is to say superficial and logical constructions which hide the feelings, desires and passions that are the true motives behind the acts of individuals and social groups; their aim is to give a logical appearance to non-logical acts. To justify his own violence, man makes and produces forgeries; the violent man is a forger.

Violence relies on propaganda to maintain its hold on people's minds. Violence must be dressed in prestige and, as Simone Weil pointed out, "nothing is more essential to a policy of prestige than propaganda" (1962: 33-34). No good reasons can be put forward to justify violence, but Simone Weil adds that "pretexts that are marred by contradiction and lies are nonetheless quite plausible when they are those of the strong. .... They alone provide excuses for the adulation of cowards, for the silence and submission of the unfortunate, and allow the winner to forget that he is committing crimes" (1957: 40) These bad pretexts are very useful to violence for they repress the thoughts that seek to formulate a conscientious objection: "The art of keeping up appearances stops or slows down the impulse that indignation would give, and prevents one from being weakened by hesitation." (1963: 143) Propaganda's function is therefore to prove those who use violence right, for "one must be really convinced that one is always right, that one has not just the right of the strongest, but also the right, purely and simply, even when it is far from being the case" (1962: 33). The essence of propaganda is the lie that imputes all the faults, all the misdeeds, all the crimes to the enemy.

At the same time, propaganda aims to convince the members of a group that they have qualities which others lack. "In fact", writes Raymond Rehnicer, "intra-specific struggle only becomes possible when each belligerent group finds its survival force in the firm and unwavering conviction of its own superiority over other groups." (1993: 42) Propaganda thus creates and maintains an "esprit de corps" that ensures group cohesion. Driven by this so-called superiority, members of the group will be all the more convinced that it is legitimate, necessary even, to fight other groups to death in order to guarantee the security and prosperity of their own group.

Submission to authority

The person who commits violence is generally not just a part of, but is also surrounded by relations of domination and submission, of command and obedience. It is most often in following the orders of the supposedly legitimate authority of the community to which he belongs that the individual commits acts of violence. Man becomes a torturer out of discipline, he becomes a killer by command. For the obedient subject, the universal commandment of moral conscience "Thou shalt not kill" is rubbed out by the commandment of that authority: "Thou shalt kill".

Numerous experiments have shown man to be capable of inflicting violence of a particularly cruel nature on other defenceless men, with no other motivation but submission to authority. This is a discovery of which we are far from having drawn all the consequences, especially regarding the ethics of the exertion of power.

Among these experiments, those carried out by the American psycho-sociologist Stanley Milgram, and described in his book *Obedience to Authority*, could be the most significant. A psychology laboratory was supposed to be conducting a study on memory, and specifically on the effects of punishment on the learning process. To this end, it published advertisements in the local press, asking for volunteers willing to take part in this research. The experimenter asked each of these people to inflict harsher and harsher punishment on a "student", in the form of electric shocks of increasing intensity, each time he made a mistake. In actual fact, the student was an actor who did not receive any electric shock, but had to express more and more vehement suffering and protest. At seventy-five volts, he moaned, at a hundred and fifty volts, he begged for the experiment to stop, at two hundred and eighty-five volts, his only reaction was a scream of pain. Milgram explains that "for the subject, the situation is not a game, but very real and intense conflict. On the one hand, the manifest suffering of the student encourages him to stop; on the other, the experimenter, a legitimate authority to whom he feels committed, orders him to continue. Each time he hesitates before administering a shock, he receives the order to carry on. To get himself out of an unbearable situation, he must break with authority." (1974: 20) Yet, while no one refused to take part in the experiment, close to two thirds of the participants agreed to keep going until the stimulator's highest level of electric shock. Milgram summarized the essential outcome of his study in those words: "Ordinary people, simply doing their jobs, and without any particular hostility on their part, can become agents in a terrible destructive process. Moreover, even when the destructive effects of their work become patently clear, and they are asked to carry out actions incompatible with fundamental standards of morality, relatively few people have the resources needed to resist authority." (Ibid., 22)

Obedience to the injunctions and orders of authority is one of the main factors of human behaviour. "We can observe", Hannah Arendt writes, "that the instinct of submission, an ardent desire to obey and be ruled by some strong man, is at least as prominent in human psychology as the will-to-power, and politically perhaps more relevant." (1972: 148) Among all the social rules an individual has interiorized from a very young age, respect for authority holds a central and preponderant place. Everything in a child's education seeks to convince him that obedience is a duty and a virtue, and that consequently, disobedience is a wrong action and a fault. However, this conditioning is never total and as he becomes an adult, man gains a relative personal autonomy by giving himself certain rules of conduct, according to moral criteria he has personally selected. But as soon as he finds himself incorporated within an organized hierarchy, his behaviour pattern changes deeply. He then risks losing the best part of his personal knowledge; his intellectual, moral and spiritual life could suffer a major regression. The individual finds himself in a situation of dependence in relation to the other members of the community, and even more so in relation to the leader. According to Freud, "rather than a "gregarious animal", man is a horde animal, an individual creature in a horde led by a chief." (1981: 148) He adds that "the individual gives up on his *ego ideal* in favour of the group ideal embodied by the leader." (Ibid., 158) The submission of an individual to authority is simultaneously part constraint, resulting from a lot of pressure, and part consent—and it is very difficult to measure the exact importance of each of these. The tendency of an individual towards submission is strongly heightened by the rewards for obedience and the punishments for disobedience.

The man who commits violence out of obedience to authority is generally merely "doing his duty". He only wants to take the indisputable moral value of this rule of conduct in consideration, by trying hard to conceal the immorality of what he is doing. The moral value of obedience prevails over the immorality of the order. The subject can then convince himself that to obey is the right thing to do, even if what he is doing is wrong. And while he obeys, he worries above all about complying with the instructions he has received, so as to satisfy the authority that trusts him. Technical occupation tends to outshine any ethical preoccupation for the obedient subject.

Obedience manipulates whoever submits himself to the orders of authority. The obedient subject relies on authority to decide on his or her conduct and its legitimacy. For the submissive individual, the legitimacy of the given order is based on the legitimacy of the authority, and the legitimacy of the ordered act is based on the legitimacy of the order. He who obeys does not feel responsible for the consequences of his own actions, because he acts under the cloak of authority. He attributes all responsibility to authority itself. Man can therefore omit to assess his own conduct on the pretext of obeying the orders of his superiors. "People", writes Stanley Milgram, "are inclined to accept the definition of the action supplied by the legitimate authority. In other words, although the subject accomplishes the action, he allows the authority to decide its significance. It is this ideological abdication which constitutes the essential cognitive basis of obedience." (1974: 181)

People find a certain security in submission, and would have to leave it, should they go down the steep road of open disobedience. First of all, obedience guarantees that the individual remains integrated within the group, the community, and society. To break with authority is to exclude oneself from the community in which one finds the means to live in relative comfort; to refuse to obey is surely to expose oneself to all the inconvenience of excommunication and exclusion. Secondly, and above all, in submitting to authority, the individual feels that he has its protection. More than that, he somehow has the feeling that he is part of the power he submits to. "My obedience", writes Erich Fromm, "makes me part of the power I worship, and hence I feel strong." (1983: 17) From then on, to break with power, is to find oneself powerless, alone, abandoned, weak, at least until power has been defeated, which could take a long time. And no one is guaranteed to survive the power one is contesting, and which is about to break one. However, in the eyes of moral requirement, there can be no doubt: when there is a conflict between the requirements of conscience and the obligation of command, the individual must break with authority and refuse to obey. Conscientious objection is then the only way for an individual to retain his autonomy, his responsibility and his freedom.

3

Nonviolence as a Philosophical Imperative

When man becomes aware of violence as a radical perversion of his relation to humanity—to his own humanity and the humanity of others—he realizes that he must categorically object to it. This refusal to acknowledge the legitimacy of violence is the basis for the concept of nonviolence.

When man experiences violence, within himself and others, he finds out that he is the bearer of an appeal for nonviolence. This appeal of reason, this requirement of conscience, this claim of the spirit certainly exist in man before he experiences violence, but he only becomes aware of his own inhumanity, folly and senselessness after he has experienced violence. *We consider man's necessity for nonviolence to be prior and superior to his desire for violence.* But it is only in a painful confrontation with the reality of violence, that the idea of nonviolence occurs to man. He then understands that he can only build his humanity and claim his identity, conquer truth and gain authenticity by resolutely adopting the dynamics of nonviolence. Nonviolence is not the conclusion to a reasoning, nor is it a deduction, but one of reason's options. Man understands that he can only give meaning to his life by refusing to give in to the call of violence. To say no to violence, by asserting that the requirement for nonviolence is the basis and structure of man's humanity, is to refuse the allegiance that violence requires and to wilfully remain the master of one's destiny. And it is not enough simply to refuse to legitimize violence, it must be de-legitimized.

Nonviolence, a principle of philosophy

It is not possible to consider man in his relation to violence—violence that fits into the relation to other men—without seeing and asserting the requirement for nonviolence. The possibility of nonviolence appears as the primordial inaugural event of philosophical knowledge. The architecture that structures philosophy—at once ontology, knowledge of the nature of being, ethics, knowledge of what is good, and metaphysics, knowledge of the Absolute—rests on the requirement for nonviolence. That same requirement gives meaning and transcendence to man's life. The first founding principle of ethics is the obligation, according to Simone Weil's formula, to "endeavour to become a nonviolent being" (1951: 154).

Nonviolence is not a possible philosophy, it is not one of philosophy's possibilities, it is the structure of philosophy itself. No philosophy is possible, that would not state that the requirement for nonviolence is indisputable, that it is the irrefutable expression of man's humanity, that is essential to man's humanity. To ignore this requirement or, worse still, to reject it, is to deny the human possibility to break the law of necessity, it is to deprive man of the freedom to cut himself loose from fatality, and become a reasonable being.

Nonviolence then becomes the founding principle of philosophy, its first and guiding proposition, its first and guiding proposition from beginning to end. In other words, philosophical research, which aspires to get closer to the wisdom that gives human life meaning, is based on *the principle of nonviolence*. This principle is not laid down a priori, but upon reflection, and upon reflection, it is universal.

Any philosophy that neither de-legitimizes violence nor opts for nonviolence fails to meet its goal. For violence, entirely man-made, which throughout history has accumulated destruction, suffering, cruelty and death, is the true scandal of this world, and any philosophy that does not radically contest it, basically allows violence to soar. If only by default, it colludes with the ideologies that call for crime in the defence of just causes, which in turn become detestable; it also gives credence to the propaganda that justifies killing by developing a rhetoric which distorts truth by all possible means, and provides pretexts for the worst doings; it justifies the countless massacres that regularly cover the planet in blood.

Paradoxically, people who have opted for nonviolence tend to be criticized for being intolerant towards those who have not made that choice. Should tolerance not be one of nonviolence's dimensions? If tolerance is respect for others, nonviolence naturally implies the greatest respect for one's interlocutor. But this respect not only does not exclude the confrontation of ideas, on the contrary, it requires it. It is not true that all ideas are respectable. If violence is detestable, the ideas that support and justify it are themselves detestable. The conviction of people who have opted for nonviolence is rooted in the awareness that violence is intolerable. They can only deeply disagree with those who tolerate it and cannot keep this disagreement to themselves: any tolerance towards violence, but also towards the ideas and ideologies on which this tolerance is based, already seem like an objective collusion with the violence that mutilates and wounds people's humanity. It is in the very nature of a disagreement to be conflictual. Admittedly, it is a conflict of ideas and not of people, but it would be vain to ignore that ideas also involve people. Those who have opted for nonviolence cannot avoid this conflict. Not only must they accept and take responsibility for it, but they often cannot do anything other than provoke it. Hence the requirement for nonviolence calls for the virtue of intransigence; and that is why the nonviolent option demands great intellectual rigour, refusing the easy solution of complacency, and implying a certain harshness.

Man generally uses necessity as an argument for his having to resort to violence. But to justify violence by necessity is the proof that violence has no human justification; for man only fulfils his humanity and conquers his freedom beyond necessity. It is precisely because violence bears the permanent mark of necessity that it is inhuman. In agreeing to serve violence, man chains himself up to necessity and therefore loses his freedom. Necessity is what man must learn to free himself from in order to conquer his dignity, as a free being. Necessity does not match up to legitimacy. In Plato's *Republic*, Socrates denounces the sophist who deceives the people by asserting that "the necessary is just and noble, never having himself seen, and not having the power to explain to others how much the nature of the necessary differs from that of the good." (1966: 251). Simone Weil often highlighted the distinction between the necessary and the good established by Plato: in *Pre-Christian Intuitions*, she writes that "There is an infinite distance between the essence of the necessary and that of the good." (1985: 83-84) Even when violence appears necessary, the requirement for nonviolence remains; *the necessity of violence does not do away with the obligation of nonviolence.*

Ahimsa

The term nonviolence is a literal translation of the Sanscrit word *ahimsa* that frequently appears in Buddhist and Hindu literature. It is composed of the negative prefix *a-* and the noun *himsa* which means the desire to harm or to do violence to another living being. *Ahimsa* is therefore the absence of all desire for violence, that is to say the respect of all living beings, in thoughts, words and deeds. If we were to follow the etymology faithfully, one translation of *a-himsa* might be in-nocence, for the two words have in fact analogous etymologies: in-nocent is from the Latin in-*nocens*, and the verb *nocere* (to hurt or harm) itself comes from *nex, necis* meaning violent death, murder. So innocence would quite literally be the term for someone who is free of all murderous or violent intent towards others. The word innocence nowadays, however, evokes rather the somewhat doubtful purity of someone who is harmless much more from ignorance or inability than by virtue. Nonviolence must not be confused with that form of innocence—yet this distortion of the word's connotation is significant: as if not doing harm somehow revealed a sort of impotence... Nonviolence is in fact innocence rehabilitated as the virtue of the strong and the wisdom of the just.

The first of the five precepts taught by Buddha concerns *ahimsa*: "to abstain from taking the life of another living being" (1991: 69). In another text, Buddha teaches that among the "eightfold paths" making it possible for man to free himself of evil desires and therefore to reach wisdom, the "right intention" carries "the intention not to harm", "the right speech" involves "abstaining from abusive speech", and the "right action" consists in "abstaining from killing". (Ibid., 159)

According to Patanjali, the founder of the *yoga* philosophy, *ahimsa* is the first ethical requirement to which those wishing to reach perfection must submit; in other words, "refrainment" from violence is the first task for whoever wants to enter the road to purification. Pantajali's teachings are found in the *Yoga-Sutra*, a short text composed of 195 aphorisms divided into 4 chapters. We know nothing of Patanjali's life. We do not even know if he lived in the second century B.C. or in the fourth century A.D. What is certain is that the teachings of the *Yoga-Sutra* refer to very ancient wisdom. In book II, Patanjali exposes "the rules to live by in relation to others": they are "nonviolence, truth, selflessness, moderation and the refusal of useless possessions" (1991: 30). These rules are universal, for they "neither depend on ways of living, nor on places, times, nor circumstances" (Ibid., 31). When people break these rules, their attitude is troubled by their own thoughts and "these thoughts—such as violence, whether it is endured, caused or approved of—are the results of impatience, anger and error". (Ibid., 34) If, by their inner attitude, humans live in a state of nonviolence, they can succeed in disarming the violence of others: "Around one who is solidly established in *nonviolence, hostility disappears*." (Ibid., 35)

The word *ahimsa* has a negative form, but its meaning is positive, since it expresses a liberation from the desire for violence which is, in itself, entirely negative. The meaning of *ahimsa* is as positive as that of the Sanscrit word *arogya* which refers to health, but whose literal meaning is the "absence of illness". *Ahimsa* is much more than an interdiction, it is a requirement. It is a principle.

The word nonviolence seems ambiguous because, as we have previously pointed out, it is covered in all of the word violence's ambiguities. But its crucial advantage lies precisely in the fact that it forces us to face up to these ambiguities, while we usually try to occult and work around them. Nonviolence does not express a lesser realism, but on the contrary, a greater realism towards violence. Nonviolence demands that the full extent of the depth and weight of violence, should be gauged.

Violence, when all is said and done, is an error of thought. The just thought is represented by accurate scales; and these scales also symbolize justice. A fair judgment is a well-balanced judgment; and the basis of justice is a just thought. Only a just thought can challenge violence, de-legitimize it, and deprive it of the privileged place it has been unduly given by the dominant ideologies. Only a just thought can be the basis for the requirement for nonviolence. Etymologically, the French verb *"penser"* (to think) comes from the Latin word *pensare*, whose first meaning is "to weigh": the just thought ("la pensée juste") is the search for a well-balanced judgment. Any imbalance in a judgment is an error in weighing, an error of thought. And the unbalanced judgment introduces an imbalance in behaviour, in action, which shows itself as violence. Violence is, in essence, an imbalance. Nonviolence aims to seek balance through conflict itself.

If we initially have a negative way of looking at nonviolence, it is because we have a positive outlook on violence. Precisely because of its negative form, it has often been said that the word nonviolence was badly chosen and that it would be preferable to imagine another, which would express the respect for humanity in a positive way. A large number of these words actually exist, the first of which being the word love. It is indeed possible to assert that genuine love implies the requirement for nonviolence. But the word love has numerous meanings: in semanticists' language, it is polysemous (from the Greek *poly*, numerous, and *sêmainen*, to mean). Linguists have us observe that the more frequent a word is, the more polysemous it is. In fact, the word love has been used so much that it is damaged. The teachings of love across different spiritual traditions, have most often been made prisoner by a rhetoric which has not prevented men from submitting to the law of violence. On the contrary, how many times have love and violence been combined into one and only exaltation of a inevitably sacred cause? How many times has violence been advocated in the name of love? "Love", writes Simone Weil, "makes war as well as it does peace. Love goes to war more naturally than it does to peace, with the fanaticism that is the foundation of tyranny. .... Peace will not be created by love, but by thought." (1988: 48)

Therefore, spiritualities—whether of religious inspiration or not—have most often sought to preach love while accepting violence. Yet, as Henri-Bernard Vergote observes, one can only speak of spirituality in relation to nonviolence. However, he points out, "not having been able to recognise clearly in violence the other absolute of the spirit, and therefore of any life invoking the spirit's name, in its religious or secular form, a certain "spirituality" has almost always become its unconscious accomplice, giving it an un-hoped for alibi in the form of a justification that makes it seem less brutal, because apparently less questionable. One could even envisage a history of violence which would be nothing other than the history of this incomprehension." (Vergote, 1987: 363)

In praise of goodness

Love, because of the too close relationship it claims to have with the Absolute, too often finds itself in the shadow of violence. That is why we prefer to speak in praise of goodness when defining the requirement for nonviolence. In doing so, we have no intention of opposing goodness to love but, on the contrary, wish to claim that genuine love is expressed in the goodness that excludes all forms of violence. The philosophy of nonviolence does not assert man's natural, intrinsic, goodness. Man is not good, but he can be good. It is not in his essence to be good, but to be able to be good; this implies that it is also in his essence to be able to be evil: it is part of man's nature to be able to be good and/or evil. This ambivalence characterizes his essence.

Man does not experience goodness when he himself is good—for that matter, how could he be certain when that it is the case?—but when he encounters another man who shows goodness towards him. I experience the goodness of others through the good that it does me, through the well-being that it brings me. Thanks to the goodness of others, I feel good, in my body, in my life. Thanks to the goodness of others, I experience the gentle pleasures of life. Because, by showing me goodness, others respect me, I can respect myself; they literally offer me all their respect.

The philosopher will therefore prefer to write a hymn to goodness, in the same way that Saint Paul of Tarsus once wrote a hymn to charity, in which he saw the realisation of love. Goodness refuses all forms of discrimination against people; it takes care of each and everyone. Goodness does everybody justice, but it does more than what justice requires. Goodness welcomes the other, the stranger, the unknown, with solicitude. Goodness is benevolent; it tries hard to be beneficent. Goodness is magnanimous. Goodness does not lose its patience; it does not become angry. Goodness does not pick quarrels with anyone; it does not provoke. Goodness is strong enough not to render evil for evil; it does not seek revenge. Goodness does not use violence, for violence is not good; goodness is essentially nonviolent. Goodness is indulgent. Goodness rejoices over others' happiness; it suffers from their unhappiness. Goodness is sympathy, it is com-passion. Goodness worries for others; it generates solicitude (from the Latin *sollicitudo*, worry, concern). Goodness is faithful; it does not change over time. Goodness is a gift, it does not require anything in return. Goodness is selfless; it does not seek compensation, reward or remuneration. Goodness does not draw attention to itself; it avoids ostentation. Goodness acts straightaway; it does not postpone for the future what the present now demands. Goodness defends the weak and the destitute; it stands up to the conceit of the powerful and the overconfidence of the rich. But even in conflict, which it does not avoid, goodness only seeks goodness. Thus speaks the wise man, in Laozi's chapter 49 of the Tao Te Ching: "I treat those who are good with goodness; I treat those who are not good with goodness. Thus I attain goodness."

Because it is negative word-form, the word nonviolence only expresses a necessary condition for the respect of humanity in Man. This condition is not enough, but it is absolutely necessary. It is a *sine qua non* without which it is impossible to define an attitude that is respectful of human life. The question that violence asks of man is prior to any other. Man needs to give it a final answer in the form of a rejection. The slightest hesitation or procrastination already shows complicity, and is a sign of weakness. That is why the word nonviolence is the most appropriate, rigorous and rational term to express what it implies. It is decisive because it expresses a principle. The requirement for nonviolence is an absolute necessity: first, all personal complicity with violence must be refused—and the worst complicity is that of intelligence—to attempt to clear the paths leading to the full and complete recognition of the humanity in people. "To be ready to hope for what is not misleading", writes Bernanos, "one must first despair at what is misleading." (1953: 249) So to put our hope in means which are not misleading, we must first despair at violence as a means to build a human world. The first requirement of justice towards others is never to do them any wrong, never to harm them.

According to Arthur Schopenhauer, the founding principle of man's moral attitude towards other men is "compassion": it is the absolute opposite of a feeling of condescension and contempt, and has its root in the com-passion towards others that is so essential to human conscience. Schopenhauer highlights the negative nature of the requirement contained in compassion: "Thus the first degree of the effectiveness of this genuine and natural moral incentive is called negative. Originally, we are all inclined to injustice and violence, because our needs, desires, anger, and hatred immediately enter consciousness .... on the other hand, the sufferings of others that are caused by our injustice and violence, enter consciousness merely on the secondary path of the representation. .... Therefore the first degree of the effect of compassion is that it opposes and impedes those sufferings that I intend to cause to others by my inherent antimoral forces. It calls out to me: "Stop !"; it stands before the other man like a bulwark, protecting him from the injury that my egoism or malice would otherwise urge me to do." (Schopenhauer, 1991: 162) So justice, which is rooted in compassion, demands nothing but negative: it requires that I never cause suffering to others, nor do them any harm. At a higher degree, compassion has a positive effect and encourages me to help my fellow men. Similarly goodness, which in the eyes of Schopenhauer is the highest expression of compassion, first holds me back from harming anyone in any way, and then asks me to come to the assistance of any suffering person.

The *dictates* of moral conscience are more imperative and more categorical when advising man not to commit evil, rather than inviting him to do good. It is always the case: we are more certain of evil than we are of good, and only in becoming aware of evil, do we reach an understanding of good. "We do not feel uncertain about evil", writes Hans Jonas. "We generally only become certain of good by making a detour through evil." (1993: 49) If the necessity for nonviolence is not a certainty for man, he is very likely to lead a life based on uncertainty. The obligation not to wish the death of others is therefore the first "commandment" of ethics. "If the commandment", writes Paul Ricoeur, "cannot avoid taking the form of an interdict, it is precisely because of evil: all the faces of evil are met with the "no" of morality. This is probably the ultimate reason for which the negative form of interdiction is inexpugnable." (1990: 258) But Ricoeur immediately notes that interdiction is nothing but the expression of an affirmation which, in fact, precedes it: "On the ethical level solicitude, as the mutual exchange of self-esteem, is affirmative throughout. This affirmation, which can well be said to be *inherent* (it is our decision to highlight this) and is the hidden soul of prohibition. It is what, ultimately, arms our indignation, that is our rejection of indignities inflicted on others." (Id.)

"Thou shalt not kill"

Nonviolence is the realization, in human history, of the deepest requirement of man's rational and therefore universal conscience, which is expressed in the imperative, itself formally negative: "Thou shalt not kill", opposing all reasons ordering man: "Thou shalt kill". (It is of no importance here that this requirement may have taken on a religious form. It would however prove necessary to understand why religions have supported so many bloodbaths throughout history.) This prohibition of killing is necessary because the desire to kill exists in man. Killing is forbidden because it is possible, and because this possibility for man is inhuman. *Prohibition is essential because temptation is pressing; and the former is all the more essential given that the latter is more pressing.* However, the imperative "Thou shalt not kill" is not a commandment that comes from the outside or from above, and is imposed on consciences by an external constraint; it is a commandment given to man by an internal requirement of his own conscience. It is the autonomous man—that is to say the free man—who asserts the ethical affirmation not to kill.

The requirement "Thou shalt not kill" cannot allow any exceptions. Wanting to seek pretexts—if they are sought, they will necessarily be found—to justify an exception, is to deny the requirement. Even when violence seems necessary to man, the prohibition of killing remains essential and the requirement of nonviolence lives on. Necessity can constrain man, but it gives him no rights. The necessity of killing is a dis-order, and not a counter-order; it does not clear the murderer. *The necessity to kill does not do away with the commandment not to kill.* Only if men firmly stand their ground will the commandment not to kill free them from the necessity to kill. If the necessity to kill does away with the commandment not to kill, anyone is at liberty to plead necessity whenever they find themselves in a legitimate self-defence situation, in order to kill and justify killing. There is nothing new about this: it is precisely the history of humanity to this day...

Karol Wojtyla (1995) empties the commandment: "Thou shalt not kill" of all substance when he writes, in his book *The Gospel of Life*, that it "has absolute value when it refers to the *innocent person*"; by these very words, he circumvents and renders ineffective the ethical imperative of nonviolence. For in our eyes, the other man who is our enemy and against whom we claim to defend our rights, is never innocent; on the contrary, we always put multiple reasons forward to declare him guilty, precisely in order to clear ourselves from the obligation to kill him. He is the only one to bear responsibility for this murder. "It is his fault". This is exactly the conclusion reached by Karol Wojtyla. After he has acknowledged the right to legitimate self-defence—that is, in actual fact, the right to legitimate violence—he concludes: "In such a case, the fatal outcome must be attributed to the attacker, since he exposed himself to it through his own action." (Id.) Following the same logic, he recognizes the legitimacy of the death penalty. Of course, he only admits it "in cases of absolute necessity" and thinks that today "thanks to an increasingly efficient organization of penal institutions, these cases are now relatively rare, if not almost non-existent." (Id.) But this reservation regarding the application of the death penalty is of little importance here. The commandment "Thou shalt not kill" loses its meaning as soon as it is considered that it does not imply the absolute refusal of the death penalty. It is an absolute question of principle.

In his *Analects*, Confucius mentions the Golden Rule—which those wishing to achieve the virtue of humanity must conform to—on several occasions. These are his words: "What you do not wish for yourself, do not do to others". (Book X, Art. 2) Here again, this Golden Rule is formulated in a negative way. Jesus of Nazareth actually formulates the Golden Rule—which all wise men must conform to—in a positive form: "What you wish for yourself, do it to others." (Mt 7, 12) And hence does he teach the necessity of love for one's fellow men. But as Leo Tolstoy writes, "if we cannot do to others what we wish for ourselves, let us at least not do to them what we do not wish for ourselves" (1906: 315). For, he adds, "before good can be achieved, it is necessary to step outside evil, into conditions that allow one to do good." (1891: 212) Before we are held responsible for all the good we do not do, we are entirely responsible for all the evil we do.

The reciprocity of positive attitudes and behaviour in the relationships between individuals and communities is one of the founding principles of justice and concord between men. Reciprocity—or more exactly, the possibility of reciprocity—therefore is a decisive criterion in the conduct of the moral man. This principle of reciprocity comes to establish the law of universality, which must control the actions of the rational man. Yet violence precisely cannot be universalized without life simply becoming impossible. The Golden Rule can then be thus formulated: "Act towards others in such a way that others can act likewise towards anyone"; which first and foremost entails the following categorical imperative: "Do not act towards others in such a way that, if others acted likewise, life would be impossible." And this requires of each and every person to renounce the use of violence towards others. Hence can nonviolence alone establish the universality of the moral law, to which rational beings must conform.

Even the violence of others does not justify my own violence, my counter-violence. Others being violent towards myself, does not give me the right to resort to violence against them. I could perhaps invoke necessity, but not rights. The requirement "love your enemy" formulated by Jesus of Nazareth (Mt 5, 44) clearly expresses that the requirement of nonviolence remains for violent, aggressive, and murderous people.

When Michel Serres attempts to define wisdom for contemporary man, he bases it on the refusal of violence. He states that "Before we organise the good of others, which often amounts to doing them violence—that is to say evil—the minimum obligation demands that we carefully avoid doing evil." (1992: 294) He admits that "the maximum obligation" would consist in loving not only unknown or fellow men, but also mankind as a whole, all living beings and the entire planet; but in order to aspire to this, it is necessary to fight against the violence which plunges men into sorrow. "The meaning comes from evil and the problem it crushes us with. .... Universal morality ...., because it deals with the problem of evil, objective, and because it is summed up in the question of violence, is in turn summed up in the old commandment: 'Thou shalt not kill', which we naturally keep, and within it: 'Thou shalt not use violence'." (Ibid., 293)

According to the *Ancient Egyptian book of the dead*, in order to be saved, those who have just died must make a "negative confession" in which they attest that they have committed no violence against their fellow men:

> I now bring Truth and Justice into my heart,
> For I have ripped all Evil out of it.
> I have not caused suffering to men.
> I have not used violence against my family.
> I have not substituted Injustice for Justice.
> I have not associated with the wicked.
> I have not committed any crimes.
> I have not made others work for me to excess.
> I have not intrigued out of ambition.
> I have not mistreated my servants.
> I have not deprived the indigent of subsistence.
> I have not allowed a servant to be mistreated by his master.
> I have not made anyone suffer.
> I have not caused famine.
> I have not made my fellow men cry.

> I have not killed nor ordered killing.
> I have not caused illness among men.
> I have not tried to increase my estate
> By unlawful means
> Nor to usurp others' fields.
> I have not altered the scale's weights, nor its beam.
> I have not taken the milk away from the child's mouth.
> I have not seized hold of the cattle in the meadows.
> I have not obstructed the waters when they had to flow
> I have not cut off the dams built across running waters.
> I have not put out the flame in a fire
> When it had to burn. (1985: 213-214)

Those who choose nonviolence take the risk of suffering the violence of others. One of the founding principles of nonviolence is that *it is a greater misfortune for man to commit violence than to suffer it*. The ultimate consequence of this principle is that in the eyes of ethics, it is better to be murdered than to be a murderer, to be a victim than a executioner, to be killed than to kill, and that murder must be feared more than death. Even in the face of death, Socrates intends to remain faithful to the principle according to which "it is never good to do injustice, neither is it to do injustice in response to injustice, nor—when we are hurt—to seek revenge in the same way" (Plato, 1965: 73-74). And in the *Gorgias*, Socrates thus answers Polus, who asks him if he would rather suffer than commit injustice: "I for one would wish neither; but if it were absolutely necessary to do or to suffer injustice, I would choose rather to suffer than to do injustice." (Plato, 1967: 201) Aristotle reaffirms the same principle in the *Nicomachean Ethics*: "All things considered", he writes, "it is worse to do than to suffer injustice; for unjust actions are blameable and imply vice. .... On the contrary, to have injustice done to you is no token of a vicious or unjust character." (Book V, Ch. XI) For all that, at no point does Aristotle deduce the requirement of nonviolence from this principle.

Emmanuel Levinas: The Humanism of the Other

Emmanuel Levinas questions the primacy given to ontology in the Western philosophical tradition. Ontology sees existence as persistence in the being: "Being is the endeavour to be, to persevere in being." (Levinas, 1992: 96) The being then contents itself with a re-flection on existence which turns into introversion, egoism. It is only concerned with meeting its own needs, and seeks to assert itself in possession and domination. "In all my effort", states Emmanuel Levinas, "there is a kind of devaluation of the notion of being which, in its obstinacy to be, contains violence and evil, ego and egoism." (Ibid., 90)

The freedom of men who only care about themselves loses itself in arbitrariness: they are allowed everything, including killing. Such a way of looking at existence maintains beings in a state of self-satisfaction, and ignorance of others. In this sense, ontology is a philosophy of power, domination, conquest, violence and war. Even if man's only source of worry is to persevere in his being, he is inevitably faced with others, who suddenly stand before him like adversaries. According to Emmanuel Levinas, "to be or not to be, that is probably not the right question" (Ibid., 140); for "being is never—contrary to what so many reassuring traditions claim—its own reason for being" (1992: 121).

The encounter with the other interrupts the solitude and egoism of man; the acknowledgement of the other is the decisive event that marks the beginning of man's human existence. In coming closer, the other asks for my assistance (from the Latin *ad-sistere*: stand near to) and makes a request; in doing so, he disturbs my peace and quiet, reassesses my freedom and affects my clear conscience.

The encounter with the other man reveals his face to me, for "the face is a being's very identity" (Levinas, 1991: 46). Through the face of the other man appear both the vulnerability of the being, and its transcendence. His vulnerability, for "the face, in its nudity, shows me the destitution of the poor and the stranger" (1992: 234); his transcendence, for "the infinite comes to my mind in the significance of the face" (1992: 101) and "the idea of the Infinite refers to nobility, transcendence" (1992: 31).

The discovery of the Other's face—in its vulnerability and transcendence—makes me realize both the possibility and the impossibility of killing; this realization is the affirmation of my moral conscience. "The relation to the face", claims Emmanuel

Levinas, "is immediately ethical. The *face* is what one *cannot* kill, or at least it is that whose meaning consists in saying: "thou shalt not kill." Killing, it is true, is a commonplace act: one can kill others; ethical requirements are not an ontological necessity. The prohibition against killing does not render murder impossible, even if the authority of the prohibition is maintained in the clear conscience of the evil committed—malignity of evil." (Levinas, 1992: 81) At the same time when others "at sword or gun point", they meet the force that threatens to hit them, "not with a greater force .... but with the very transcendence of their own being. .... This Infinite, more powerful than killing, already resists us in their faces, it is indeed their face, it is the original expression, it is the first word: "Thou shalt not commit murder"." (1992: 217) The look of others, by the resistance to killing that it expresses, paralyses my power and disarms my will. That way, "the idea of the Infinite, far from violating the spirit, determines nonviolence itself, that is, it establishes ethics" (Ibid., 223). According to Emmanuel Levinas, philosophy does not begin with ontology, but with ethics. Ethics are not a branch of philosophy, but "the first philosophy" (1992: 71).

The essential affirmation of ethics is the requirement for nonviolence, which must prevail in the relationship between man and the other man. "To the idea of the "Thou shalt not kill", writes Emmanuel Levinas, "I give a meaning which is not that of a simple characteristic killing prohibition; it becomes a fundamental definition or description of the human event of being, which is a constant caution as regards violent and murderous acts towards others." (1992: 100) "Thou shalt not kill", he adds, "is not a simple rule of conduct. It appears to be the principle of discourse itself, and of spiritual life." (1990: 21)

I cannot meet others without somehow striking up a conversation with them. Meeting others, is to speak with them: "Speaking is to make oneself known to others while one gets to know them. .... This *trade* implied by speech is precisely action without violence." (Levinas, 1990: 20) Language is the action of rational men who put violence aside in order to make contact with others. "Reason and language lie outside violence. They are the spiritual order! And if morality must truly exclude violence, a profound link must join reason, language and morality." (Ibid., 19)

In approaching me, and coming towards me, the other man calls out and appeals to me, to my responsibility. To answer him, is to answer for him. As I discover the face of the Other, I become responsible for him. I could of course turn away from him, but humanly, I cannot: "The face imposes itself upon me, and I can neither turn a deaf ear to its call, nor forget it, I cannot cease to be responsible for its misery." (Levinas, 1994: 52-53) In meeting the other man, I become his ob-ligor (from the Latin *ob-ligare*, to be linked); I have an obligation not to leave him alone. In becoming responsible for the Other, I am granted the dignity of a unique and irreplaceable being: my responsibility is an election. "From then on, being myself means I cannot escape responsibility. .... But the responsibility that empties the Self of its independence and egoism .... confirms the uniqueness of the Self. It is the reason why nobody can answer instead of me." (Levinas, 1994: 53-54) Man thus becomes himself, not by re-flecting upon himself, but by becoming responsible for others: "The point is to show the very identity of the human self starting with responsibility." (1992: 97) What is the basis and structure of the humanity of man, is the responsibility for other men. This responsibility gives meaning, dignity and greatness to human existence. Emmanuel Levinas never ceases to plead in favour of the reversal, the turnaround which substitutes the Self-orientation of ontology for the Other-orientation of ethics.

This presence of the other man by my side disturbs and bothers me; it tears me away from comfort and forces me to leave shelter. In meeting the Other, I expose myself to him, I run risks, I become vulnerable. As I stand opposite the Other, I expose myself to wounds and outrages: "One is exposed to the Other as a skin is exposed to what wounds it, as a cheek is offered to a smiter." (Levinas, 1990: 83) But man must have the courage to face these dangers: "Communication with others can only be transcendent in the form of a dangerous life, of a beautiful risk to be run" (Ibid., 190).

My responsibility towards the Other imposes itself upon me, regardless of his attitude towards me. The relationship to the Other is "non-symmetrical", for "I am responsible for the Other but do not expect reciprocity, should it cost me my life. Reciprocity is his [the Other's] business." (Levinas, 1992: 94-95) I am never even with the Other, and I always arrive late for the appointment I have with him. My responsibility towards others consists in "moving in the direction of the Other without worrying about his moving towards me, or more exactly, in approaching in such a way that—beyond all the reciprocal relationships that will not fail to happen between myself and my fellow men—I can always be a step ahead of him." (1990: 134) Emmanuel Levinas never tires of quoting words uttered by one of the characters from *The Brothers Karamazov* by Dostoyevsky, Starets Zosima's brother, Markel: "Each of us is guilty before all for everyone and everything, and I most of all." (Dostoyevsky, 1948: 264)

The responsibility towards the other man is essentially expressed through goodness towards him. It is through goodness that man becomes a peacemaker: "Peace can therefore not be identified with the end of battles that cease for want of soldiers, with the defeat of some and the victory of others, that is with cemeteries or future universal empires. Peace must be my own peace, in a relationship that starts with the Self and moves towards the Other, in desire and goodness where the Self both survives and exists without egoism." (Levinas, 1992: 342)

Emmanuel Levinas thus defines a new ontology which is not based on self-knowledge, but on goodness towards others: being, is being-for-others, that is being good. While western philosophical tradition establishes the rights of the Self when facing the Other, Levinas' philosophy establishes the privileges of the Other as regards the Self. Human rights are above all the rights of the other man: charity begins at the home of others. It is in goodness towards others that the Self asserts itself and develops into a human being. Goodness is the true response to the solicitation written in the face of others. It is goodness that introduces man to the Infinite expressed in the face of others: "An absolute adventure within an essential imprudence, goodness is transcendence itself." (Levinas, 1992: 341) In the movement of goodness, the I unselfishly changes the centre of interest towards the Other. Goodness is unselfishness: Goodness consists of posing yourself in your being in such a way as the Other has more importance than yourself." (Ibid., 277) In this perspective, Levinas no longer defines philosophy as the love of wisdom, but as "wisdom at the service of love" (1990: 253).

In becoming responsible for the Other, I become responsible for his death: "Fear of the Other's death is certainly the basis of responsibility for others." (Levinas, 1992: 117-118) In discovering the Other's face, in its nudity and vulnerability, I become aware that he is faced with death and I worry about him. This non-indifference to the death of the Other is one of the expressions of my goodness towards him. And "this concern over the Other's death comes before concerns over myself" (1991: 228). Man thus carries within himself "a vocation to exist for others that is stronger than the threat of death" (Ibid., 10). It is this vocation which Levinas calls the vocation "for holiness". As soon as man fears the death of others more than his own, he would rather die than kill. Hence does man fulfil his humanity by deciding to "exist for others, that is to question himself and to dread killing more than death" (1992: 275). In taking the risk of dying so as not to kill, man gives his life a meaning that life itself cannot take away. The responsibility for others, expressed through goodness, gives life meaning, which in turn gives meaning to death itself, a "meaning that cannot be measured by the Being or not-Being, on the contrary, the Being developing from meaning." (1990: 205)

It seems to us that Levinas' reflections on man's responsibility towards other men, and on the essential nature of the commandment "Thou shalt not kill", form an extremely precious contribution to the foundation of a philosophy of nonviolence. Several of Levinas' assertions would certainly be worth discussing. It is thus difficult to share all of his ideas when he restricts the relationship between oneself and others to an entirely dissymmetrical and totally non-reciprocal situation. On this point, Paul Ricoeur is right to ask Levinas this question: "Should not the Other's voice telling me "Thou shalt not kill", be made my own, to the point of becoming my conviction?" (Ricoeur, 1990: 391) And if indeed, I welcome, acknowledge and internalize the Other's voice, speaking to me through his face, then can communication, dialogue, and therefore reciprocity be established with him? From then on, the Self is not kept in an attitude of pure "passivity", as Levinas claims. But even if it may be necessary to keep one's distance from some of his formulations, it would not—at least as we see it—call the truth of his intuitions into question. These intuitions, should we wish to follow them, lead us to the heart of true philosophy, that is to genuine "wisdom of love", a genuine wisdom of goodness. (We will have the opportunity, later on, to meet up with Levinas once again, and to question him about nonviolent *action*, without him—according to us—succeeding in giving us a satisfactory answer.)

4

The Nonviolent Man in the Face of Death

According to Thomas Aquinas, "the role of the virtue of fortitude is to maintain human will in line with moral good, despite fears of a physical evil. .... Yet the most terrible of physical evils, is death, which takes away all good and all material wealth." (*Summa Theologica* II, II, Q. 123, Art. 4). Thus according to him, "the role of fortitude is to reinforce the soul against the dangers of death" (Ibid., Art. 5). He then claims that the principal act of the virtue of fortitude is not to attack, but to endure: "It is more difficult to endure than to attack." (Ibid., Art. 6) For he who endures the attack of adversaries without fighting back faces the fear of death, whereas he who attacks adversaries does nothing but push them aside. "For he who attacks", writes Thomas Aquinas, "danger stays away, whereas it is present for he who endures the attack. .... He who endures fears not, though he is confronted with the cause of fear, whereas this cause is not present with the aggressor." (Id.) Commenting on these words by Thomas Aquinas, Jacques Maritain writes: "Force that strikes, aims to destroy evil through another evil (physical) inflicted upon bodies. From then on evil, however reduced it may be, will continue to go from one to the other, with no end. .... Force that endures aims to annihilate evil, by welcoming and exhausting it through love, by absorbing it into the soul as a consented pain; there it stops, and cannot go any further." (1933: 207)

Quite the opposite, the man who chooses nonviolence is aware that in refusing to kill, he takes the risk of being killed. Not that this risk is necessarily greater for the nonviolent man than for the violent man; it may be, it is even probable that the risk is lesser for the latter, than for the former. But however that may be, the real difference does not lie here. What really changes, is that the nonviolent man directly faces the risk of dying without having the chance to prevaricate. He too knows the fear of death—how could it be otherwise?—but in choosing nonviolence, he has chosen to face it, and try to overcome it without cheating. That is why, in the final analysis, only he who accepts death can take the risk of being killed without threatening to kill. "If one knows with all one's soul that one is mortal", writes Simone Weil, "and one accepts it with all one's soul, one cannot kill." (1951: 147) True Wisdom, true freedom, is to be able to face death without fear, to be able to say, like Socrates as he is sentenced to death: "I do not care about death in any way at all, but my whole care is to commit no unjust or impious deed." (Plato, 1965: 45) In becoming free in the face of death, man becomes free in the face of violence; in controlling his fear of dying, he gains the freedom of nonviolence. But to accept to die rather than having to kill is not necessarily to accept death. Quite the opposite, in order truly to protest against death, one must first refuse to kill.

Great spiritual thinkers have often used the language of philosophy to say that love for others involves overcoming the fear of dying. Guy Riobe, who was an authentic mystical Christian, thus writes: "True love of men requires one to become the fellowman of others, seen as others, as different from oneself, as foreign to oneself, in their impenetrable mystery. The fraternal encounter between two beings always surrounds a deadly challenge; there is always a boundary wall to climb; and the encounter only reaches true perfection in a victorious answer to this challenge. It is clear that the challenge reaches extreme proportions when a man has to meet his enemy fraternally, or, more generally, when men have to overcome the boundary walls they have erected between their people, or between the cultural universes to which they belong." (1988: 69)

In the logic of violence, accepting to die for a good cause is above all wanting to kill for it. The logic of nonviolence also involves accepting to die for a good cause, but only in order to avoid killing, because the will not to kill precedes the will not to die, because the fear of killing is stronger than the fear of dying. The fear of death then becomes the fear of the Other's death. *The transcendence of man is this possibility to choose to die in order to avoid killing, because the dignity of his own life is worth much more to him than life itself.* Because it gives meaning to man's life, the risk of nonviolence really is worthwhile: suffering is worthwhile, and, if need be, dying is worthwhile.

When he becomes the victim of a plot by the ruling powers, forming a coalition against him, Jesus of Nazareth faces death with an attitude of absolute nonviolence. While he knows that he will be arrested and handed in to his pursuers, he feels "sadness and anguish" (Mt 26, 37), but he knows that he will be able to overcome both. As one of his companions seeks to resort to violence to defend him, he asks him to sheathe his sword (Mt 26, 51-52). Later, it is with the greatest determination that he faces up to his accusers who are about to sentence him to death. Jesus dies in perfect accordance with the advice that he has given his friends: "Do not fear those who kill the body, and after that can do no more." (Lk 12, 4)

If Jesus of Nazareth acts in such a way in the face of death, it is that for him, as René Girard pointed out, "the choice of nonviolence cannot constitute a revocable commitment, a kind of contract whose clauses could only be respected insofar as other contracting parties equally respect them." (1978: 230) It is therefore to remain faithful to the requirement of nonviolence that Jesus accepts to die rather than having to use violence: "It is about dying because to continue to live would mean submitting to violence." (Ibid., 237) René Girard thus formulates what lies at the very centre of Jesus' wisdom: "One must not hesitate to give one's own life to avoid killing, and to escape, in doing so, the circle of killing and death." (Ibid., 238) The precept according to which "he who wants to save his life will lose it" (Mt 16, 25) must be taken at face value, for "he will indeed have to kill his brother, and that is to die in fatal ignorance of others and of oneself" (Girard, 1978: 238). As for he who accepts to lose his life, "he is the only one who does not kill, the only one to know the fullness of love" (Id.).

To take the risk of nonviolence, is to want to risk life completely. The beauty and nobility of life, is to take the risk of dying and to overcome it at each moment. If death is by our side at the beginning of our lives, should we not realize, not that we are coming closer to it all the time, but on the contrary, that we are constantly moving away from it? Every moment in life is a victory over death. The very meaning of life is to constantly defeat death. Death, in reality, is not present, but always future; every day, it is postponed. We therefore still have time to live. It is in choosing nonviolence, in preferring the risk of dying to the risk of killing, that man maintains the transcendence of life. Violence then seems like the negation of the transcendence of life.

Violence and nonviolence are seen and judged through the distorted prism of the ideology of violence: we always put down to bravery, honour and heroism the death of whoever was killed in a violent battle, while we put down to failure and inefficiency the death of whoever was killed in a nonviolent combat. We consider on the one hand, that the failure of violence is not an argument which proves its inefficiency, but which proves that victory requires more than violence, and on the other hand, that the failure of nonviolence is an argument which proves its inefficiency, and which shows that only violence can make it possible to achieve victory.

The tragic extreme of the nonviolent option is not to die in order to avoid killing, it is to avoid killing when violence could perhaps prevent the death of my nearest fellow man. In this case, man reaches the ultimate limit of the requirement of nonviolence. However, it is advisable to remember that he who has opted for violence can equally experience such a tragic situation, for his action is likely to cause an even greater violence which may kill his closest fellow man. But, then again, even if he is aware of that risk, the violent man thinks he will avoid it, while the nonviolent-man must face it knowingly.

Nonviolence is a physical attitude

The body, and not only the reason, must also opt for nonviolence. A person who is afraid of violence, that is to say of death, is an incarnate, carnal, and physical being. Fear is physical, and to overcome it, the person must control his own body. The techniques which allow individuals to reach self-knowledge and to control their body, are most useful here, in order to move forward on the path to nonviolence. In nonviolent action, the body ventures and remains on the front line, exposes itself to blows, defies violence and confronts death. If the body is far too recalcitrant, if it is petrified and rears up, it will be difficult for reason to persuade it. The body must prepare, educate and train itself in order to control its own emotions and fears.

Hence is nonviolence simultaneously both a physical, and a rational attitude. Any thought is inseparable from its physical expression. The thought of the incarnate being takes root within its body, and it is in nonviolent action that the being experiences nonviolence physically. It is in nonviolent action that the carnal man can think nonviolence, and it is not possible for him to have a clear and precise idea of nonviolence if it is not rooted in a physical experience of nonviolent action.

Philosophy is always a re-flection, that is to say it involves looking back on oneself, on one's own experience, on one's own action. And if the philosopher has no physical experience of nonviolent action, how could he develop a rational nonviolent thought? It is necessary to have physically felt that nonviolent action is possible—which does not mean that it is always victorious—in order to reach a clear conception of the philosophy of nonviolence. It is not enough to experience violence so as to understand nonviolence, nonviolence itself—that is, nonviolent action—must yet be experienced. Nonviolence clearly can not be thought if it is not experienced first. Hence the philosophy of nonviolence is only intelligible through the experience of nonviolent action. If the philosopher stays outside nonviolent action, he will only see its limits—in the same way that anybody who remains outside a house can only see its walls—he will only observe its weaknesses and will be unable to understand the internal dynamics which give it strength.

From then on, can the philosopher reflect on nonviolence if he himself is not a militant? But the rational man is suspicious of the militant. Does the latter not have the bad reputation of being an activist? Because he takes sides, is he not accused of being intolerant? Is he not suspected of having ideas too set to be able to think? Of course, no one doubts that the militant is a man of conviction, but that is precisely why his being a man of reflection is questioned. As if acting with conviction did not allow him the necessary hindsight for reflection, as if it were preferable not to act in order to think more clearly... Should not the image of the philosopher thinking, while he stands outside the city conflicts, be questioned? As if not committing, not taking sides helped to improve thinking... Should it not be stated, on the contrary, that if philosophy is a re-flection upon action, the philosopher cannot not act, and in that sense, he cannot not be a militant? Indeed, we think that it is necessary to proceed to a philosophical rehabilitation of militancy. It is not without significance that the word *militant* has the same etymological root as the word military (from the Latin *miles*: soldier): just as soldiers practice the art of armed combat, nonviolent militants practice the art of nonviolent struggle.

The four cardinal virtues

The true fortitude of the strong man—and courage, as its etymological sense suggests, is unique to man: the Latin word *virtus*, of which it is the translation, indeed comes from the root *vir*, which means "man"—is to be ready to take the risk of nonviolence rather than that of violence. Fortitude is one of the four cardinal virtues on which must rest, as if on "hinges"—"cardinal" comes from the Latin word *cardo* which refers to the hinge of a door—the life of the moral man who intends to conform his thoughts and actions to the requirements of good. And indeed, the man who becomes violent.* More so than anger, violence is madness. The other three cardinal virtues are Prudence, Temperance and Justice, and they are also foundations of the nonviolent attitude of

---

* Translator's note. In French *sort de ses gonds*, which means "flies off the handle" or becomes unhinged.

the moral man. According to Aristotle, "Prudence is a true habit, in conjunction with reason, practical on the subjects of human good and evil" (*Nicomachean Ethics*, Book VI, Ch. V). "Prudent people", he adds, "are characterized by their ability to decide wisely, wise deliberation being the rectitude of judgment in accordance with usefulness, and referring to a goal of which prudence has allowed just appreciation" (Ibid., Book VI, Ch. X) Violence is indeed always an im-prudence, and there is an organic link between the virtue of prudence and the requirement of nonviolence. On temperance, Aristotle says that "on the subject of pleasures, it is a median" (Ibid., Book III, Ch. V). "Our ability to desire", he writes, "must conform to the prescriptions of reason. Thus in the temperate man, there must be an agreement between this ability and reason. Indeed, both offer the same goal, which is goodness." (Ibid., Book III, Ch. XII) As for justice, Aristotle defines it as "the habit from which men are disposed to do just actions, and from which they act justly, and desire just things" (Ibid., Book V, Ch. 1).

But, because of a tragic misunderstanding between history and geography, the cardinal virtues were born in exile in a land of violence. For centuries, armed people have forced them to speak their language, to share their beliefs, to abide by their ideologies, to adopt their habits and customs, to support their causes. But today, they call louder and louder for their true identity to be acknowledged, and ask to be let to live in a land of nonviolence. It has become urgent to organize their repatriation.

Forgiveness

It must be said that forgiveness does not have a good reputation. It too often has a religious connotation, which clouds its meaning by associating it to the obscure notion of sin. Historical religions—and above all Christianity—thus developed an elaborate rhetoric on the forgiveness of sins which, in the end, hardly concerned the history of humanity. It is therefore a difficult—but all the same necessary, legitimate and rich—initiative, to repatriate forgiveness to its rightful order, that of philosophy.

The decisive importance of the ethical requirement of forgiveness within human relations is highlighted by what its negation inevitably implies: the relentless chain of vengeance and revenge. Vengeance is strictly reciprocity, it is a pure imitation of the violence of adversaries. First of all, forgiveness breaks with this reciprocity and imitation. While resentment, rancour and hate imprison individuals with the chains of the past, forgiveness frees them from it, and allow them to enter the future. "Forgiveness", writes Vladimir Jankelevitch, "thus undoes the last shackles that tie us down to the past, draw us backward, and hold us down. By allowing the coming times to come to pass, and, in doing so, accelerating this coming, forgiveness indeed confirms the general direction and the sense of a becoming that puts the tonic accent on the future." (1967: 24) Vengeance prolongs and passes on into the future the destructive consequences of an evil act committed in circumstances that already no longer exist. Vengeance is inopportune, untimely, anachronistic; it is always ill-timed.

He who forgives does not ignore the desire for vengeance, but decides to overcome and surpass it. The decision not to take vengeance cannot be made, precisely because the desire to take vengeance lies here within ourselves, and that it wants to carry the day. That is why forgiveness requires great courage. It is because vengeance is desirable that forgiveness is a difficult duty. Forgiveness is not the result of an inclination, it is not rooted in a feeling, but in a wilful decision; it is an act, an action, it is, says Jankelevitch, "an event" (Jankelevitch, 1967: 12) which happens in history, in order to change its course. "Forgiveness", writes Hannah Arendt, "is the only reaction which does not merely re-act, but acts anew and unexpectedly, unconditioned by the act which provoked it and therefore freeing from its consequences both the one who forgives and the one who is forgiven." (1988: 307)

Forgiveness certainly does not lose the memory of the past—forgetting is not a virtue, but only a distraction—but it resolutely looks towards the future. There is an "obligation to remember" the past which is a duty to remain vigilant about the future, but it is also important to ensure that the memory of evil does not clutter the future. "Forgetting", writes Emmanuel Levinas, "nullifies relations with the past, whereas forgiveness conserves the past pardoned in the purified present. The pardoned being is not the innocent being." (1992: 316) Hence forgiveness does not destroy memory, but it is a bet on the future. This bet can be lost, but it does not necessarily lose its meaning. Forgiveness is unconditional, it therefore offers no guarantee. Forgiveness is a gift, so it can neither be earned, nor taken back. To become effective in the evolution of history, the decision to forgive must develop over time. When one of his companions asks him whether he should forgive up to seven times the offences that his brother will cause him, Jesus replies: "I do not tell you to forgive up to seven times, but up to seventy times seven." (Mt 18, 21-22) While vengeance is a form of despair, forgiveness is entirely driven by the hope of a new beginning. To refuse vengeance and to offer forgiveness to one's adversary, is not to give up on justice. This presupposes that to take vengeance is not to do justice, which we indeed admit. Quite the opposite, to forgive is to open the path to justice.

The duty of forgiveness lies at the very heart of the requirement of nonviolence. To forgive, in the end, is always to forgive an act of violence. To forgive, is to decide unilaterally to break the never-ending chain of violent acts that justify each other, it is to refuse to continue war indefinitely, it is to wish to make peace with others as well as with oneself. For he who is preoccupied with the desire for vengeance does not find peace. To forgive is to pacify one's own future by refusing to remain the prisoner of a perpetual circle of violence. Vengeance truly renders life impossible, and death quite probable.

But the refusal of vengeance does not cover all of forgiveness' task: it has yet to rebuild a new relationship between offended and offender. It is important to distinguish between personal forgiveness, when the offence itself lies directly within a person to person relationship, and impersonal forgiveness, when the offence takes place within the relationship between one community and another, that is within a social or political relationship. In a personal relationship, one must forgive those who are close; in a political relationship, one must forgive those who are distant. In both cases, forgiveness makes reconciliation possible, or if not, at least conciliation, that is to say it makes it possible to reestablish or to establish just relationships. But for these to become effective, the evildoer must recognize his responsibilities, enter the history of forgiveness himself, and take part in its dynamics.

In reality, the great massacres of history have not been caused by personal resentment, but by collective hatred. It is the latter then that must therefore especially be extinguished, and only forgiveness can succeed in doing so. Forgiveness then appears to be a decisive moment, within political action, whose purpose is to free history from the blind mechanism of violence.

5

Principles of Nonviolent Action

Violence is also a method of action that seems necessary for men of good will, to defend the established order when it guarantees freedom, and to fight the established disorder when it maintains oppression. But if action is truly necessary, is it also the case for violence? However hateful violence may be, it is important for its refusal not to lead to inaction, and leave the field open for the violence of evil doers. That is why *violence not only deserves a condemnation, it demands an alternative.* It is therefore essential to look for a "functional equivalent" of violence, that is a method of nonviolent action which makes it possible to face oppression and aggression. As long as the "feasibility" of such a method has not been established, the philosophical requirement of nonviolence will be ruled out by the technical necessity of violence. But also, as long as the philosophical requirement of nonviolence has not clearly been asserted, violence will continue to be tolerated, and no other method of action will be searched for, which constitutes a good enough condition for none to be found. The requirements of philosophy therefore meet political realism in searching for means to a strategy of nonviolent action. These means, while exerting a force of real constraint on adversaries, make it possible to solve inevitable human conflicts humanely, without resorting to murderous violence.

Nonviolence upsets the balance of weapons

The extreme difficulty that we have in perceiving the pertinence of the concept of nonviolent action is mainly due to the fact that we are used to seeing the confrontation between two individuals or groups as being "on equal footing"*: the two adversaries have the same or, at least, equivalent means at their disposal. Yet precisely, as soon as one of the adversaries renounces the use of violent means employed by the other, the struggle seems totally unequal and the imbalance of forces that seems to result from this points to the immediate and definitive victory of the one who is armed over the one who is not. In other words, we cannot imagine a struggle otherwise than through the implementation of symmetrical means by the two adversaries. Any asymmetry, any dissymmetry of arms is immediately seen as an insurmountable disadvantage, as the absolute inferiority of the one who is less armed in comparison to the one who is better armed.

Yet, the concept of nonviolent action by itself implies an inequality and dissymmetry between the means of the aggressor and those of the victim. This consideration alone upsets our usual references and disorientates us. Whoever chooses nonviolence seems completely ill-equipped to deal with he who does not hesitate to choose violence. It seems to us that he is very likely to be defeated. He will undoubtedly be put to death, just like the lamb facing the wolf. It is true that if one only considers the technical tools that the armed man has and that the nonviolent man has not, the latter is not in a position to resist the former. From a purely theoretical point of view, violence can be exerted without limits by the armed man over the nonviolent man. This possibility cannot be excluded simply because it is technically possible. It remains abstract, however, and might not necessarily come true. Experience shows us that it may not be the most likely. In order to appreciate the probabilities of the armed man passing into action, not only must the technical factors be taken into account, but also the human, psychological, ethical, social and political factors. In reality, these factors are likely to set the armed

---

* Translator's note. In French "à armes égales", meaning "with the same weapons"

man limits which he cannot overstep without experiencing major inconvenience. Violence without limits would be blind, in every sense of the expression. It would imply rushing ahead, with no rational purpose. That is why, despite being technically possible, it is not necessarily the most likely eventuality.

Each side arms itself against others, but each also considers the others' arms as a threat. Hence the armament of one calls for and justifies the armament of all. However, if everyone only arms himself for his own defence, where can the offence come from? In reality, our armament, which we see as a protection against adversaries, is very likely to be seen by them as a provocation. Furthermore, the constant search for the equality of arms and the balance of forces causes an endless arms race. The outcome is that balance is sought at an even higher level, thereby becoming more and more unstable and likely to break under the sole effect of the laws of gravity. The pursuit for equality of arms by itself favours the triggering of violence. The strategy of nonviolent action seeks to implement conflict regulation mechanisms in order to defuse conflicts, and have them evolve towards a peaceful solution.

He who renounces the possession of arms poses no threat towards potential adversaries. The latter now have no reason to fear an aggression. They find themselves lacking the self-defence argument, which always serves to justify the use of arms. The spring arming the will of those who are ready to make war in response to provocation, is slack. From then on, the risk that they should be the first to resort to arms to prevent an aggression, on the pretext that attacking is the best defence, is considerably lowered, if not reduced to nothing. In the case of a conflict, it is then possible to take the time to engage in negotiations, allowing to appreciate the stakes of the disagreement, and to consider the possible terms of agreement between the two parties. It is then important for he who has renounced the arms of violence to show his determination to resist by all the means of nonviolent action. This should allow him to face the armed blackmail of adversaries, and to dissuade them from acting out. The probability of an aggression is certainly not nonexistent—one cannot simply state that adversaries "will not dare"—but it may not be the strongest.

"Whoever wants the end, wants the means"

"The end justifies the means", says the proverb, and this means that the end justifies all means. Of course, the means are only just if, first of all, the end is just. But it is not enough for the end to be just in order for the means equally to be. It is also important that the means should be in harmony with the end, coherent with it. Violent means, should they be employed to reach a just end, themselves hold a great deal of injustice, which is always visible in the end. If the choice of means comes second to the chosen end, it is not secondary; on the contrary, it is essential in order to reach the pursued end. In the end, one only reaps what one has sowed, and whoever sows violence, reaps violence.

Not only do the means of violence pervert its end, but they are substituted for it. The man who chooses violence neglects the end that he had first invoked as a reason to do battle and does not worry about it anymore, for the means keep him entirely busy. The means become his first cause for concern, and the end his second, therefore the least of his worries. He will of course continue to mention it in his propaganda, but it will only serve to justify the means. That way, the means do not serve the end, on the contrary: the end serves the means. "It is this reversal of the relationship between means and end", writes Simone Weil, "it is this fundamental folly that accounts for all that is senseless and bloody right through history." (1955: 95)

To use the end to justify the means, is to consider violence as a mere technical means, a tool, an instrument which must be judged solely on its effectiveness. Violence would neither be good nor bad, but only more or less effective. It thus leaves the field of ethics to enter that of pragmatics. Violence is then ethically neutral and only the probability of its success and failure makes it possible to appreciate its usefulness. The decision ordering the action is not a choice anymore, but only a calculation.

"Whoever wants the end, wants the means" says another proverb, expressing the true wisdom of nations better than the previous one, as long as it is interpreted as it should be. Indeed, whoever wants justice, wants just means; whoever wants peace, wants peaceful means. It is the action that counts, and not the intention of the protagonist. Yet precisely, the end is linked to intention, and only the means are linked to action. Nothing is more perverse than a morality of intention judging action solely on the quality of its intention.

In the end, it is wrong to consider the action of man as a mere means to an external end. *Human action always finds meaning within itself, and not only within its result.* The latter cannot be sought "at all costs", that is to say, at any cost. The end cannot be sought "at any cost", "at any price". In other words, the first result of the action, is the action itself, and it must therefore be seen as an end in itself. Political action does not use instruments to create objects, it acts in order to build the present of men; that is why its meaning lies first in action itself, that is in its means, and not its end. To do good is good in itself, independently of the action's success or failure. It is not that the success or failure of the action is a matter of indifference—but efficiency cannot be the decisive criterion for the decision.

During the action, we are only in control of the means and not of the end or, more specifically, we are only in control of the end through the means. The end relates to the future, only the means are concerned with the present. It is therefore important for the means to be the beginning of the end... But we are always tempted to give up on the present and lose ourselves in the future. "We never keep to the present, Pascal noted. We anticipate the future as if we found it too slow in coming and were trying to hurry it up. .... We wander about in times that do not belong to us, and do not think of the only one that does. .... We try to give it (the present) the support of the future, and think how we are going to arrange things over which we have no control for a time we can never be sure of reaching. .... Thus we do not actually live, but hope to live." (Thought 172) Hence the violent man loses himself into the future. He promises justice, he promises peace, but always for tomorrow. Each day, he renews the same promise, putting off justice and peace till tomorrow. And so forth until the end of history. And each today is filled with violence and suffering, destruction and death. The present of man cannot merely be considered to be a means to reach a future which will be its end; it is its own end in itself.

The violent man therefore sacrifices the present to an uncertain future by hiding behind an ideology which encourages him to prefer tomorrow's abstraction over today's reality. In doing so, he wilfully resorts to means that radically contradict the end he claims to be pursuing, but whose realisation is endlessly postponed until a hypothetical future. The nonviolent man has realized that he is essentially responsible for the present, and thus focuses entirely on the present. That is why he seeks means which already hold within themselves the effective realization of the sought-after end. "Real generosity towards the future", wrote Albert Camus, "lies in giving everything to the present." (1951: 365)

In 1978, when Vaclav Havel wants to express the political philosophy behind the resistance of dissidents against the Soviet Empire's totalitarian order, he asserts that it intends to refuse any use of violence to change society. According to him, the main reason for this choice is precisely because the dissidents want to conquer their dignity as free men today, by living according to values that give their existence meaning now, and that they do not intend to do battle to make a hypothetical future happen, a future which might allow them, but much later, to live according to these values. "This attitude", writes Havel, "that turns away from abstract political visions of the future towards concrete human beings and the way to defend them effectively in the here and now is quite naturally accompanied by an intensified antipathy to all forms of violence carried out in the name of "a better future"." (1989: 127)

However, for the means to be employed to make it possible to reach the pursued end, they cannot simply be nonviolent, they must also be efficient. But what is efficiency? And what is the efficiency of efficiency? What criteria allow to appreciate and judge the efficiency of an action? The notion of efficiency conveyed by the prevailing ideology is directly linked to the idea of violence. The paradigm of efficiency, is the efficiency of violence. Such that we cannot imagine a form of efficiency that would not be violent; through the distorting prism of the ideology of violence, we simultaneously perceive the efficiency of violence and the violence of efficiency. And yet violence, by itself, is a nonsense, and is a factor of inefficiency. If man's purpose is to give his existence and history meaning, the action that allows him to do so is efficient. The efficiency of nonviolence is first and finally to give meaning to human action. But the strategy of nonviolent action must still find the appropriate tactical means that really allow to reduce and, as much as possible, to eliminate the violence of oppression and aggression. *Nonviolent action must seek victory, even if failure, always a possibility, does not take away its meaning.*

The principle of non-cooperation

Most often, during social and political conflicts, the side which is in power, and which therefore is in a position of force, does not accept the intervention of any given mediator. It claims the legitimacy of its power—it is in the very nature of power, even in its most hateful form, to claim its legitimacy—and is determined to maintain its attributes and prerogatives. In these conditions, the opposing side, which is the victim of the injustice of power, has no other option but to act directly in order to change the existing balance of forces and enforce its rights.

The essential principle of the strategy of nonviolent action is that of non-cooperation. It rests on the following analysis: in a society, complicity—that is to say the voluntary or passive cooperation of the majority of citizens with the ideologies, institutions, structures, systems, regimes and laws that generate and maintain injustice—is the strength of the injustice of the established disorder. Nonviolent resistance aims to break with this complicity through the organization of collective actions of non-cooperation.

Étienne de la Boétie (1530-1563) was one of the first to clearly express the potential efficiency of a policy of non-cooperation in his *Discourse on voluntary servitude*. Noting that the power of a tyrant entirely rests on the voluntary complicity of the people, he asks to understand "how it is possible that so many men, so many cities, so many nations sometimes suffer under a single tyrant who has no other power than the power they give him; who is able to harm them only to the extent to which they have the willingness to bear with him; who could do them absolutely no injury unless they preferred to put up with him rather than contradict him" (1978: 174-175). In reality, the people themselves give the tyrant the necessary means to oppress them. La Boétie thus addresses those who endure tyranny: "The tyrant, indeed, has nothing more than the power that you confer upon him to destroy you. .... How can he have so many arms to beat you with, if he does not borrow them from you? .... How does he have any power over you except through you? .... What could he do to you if you yourself did not connive with the thief who plunders you, if you were not accomplices of the murderer who kills you, if you were not traitors to yourselves?" (Ibid., 181-182) From then on, the tyrant's subjects need only cease to lend him their support for the tyranny to collapse. "You can deliver yourselves if you try", La Boétie asserted, "not by taking action, but merely by willing to be free. Resolve to serve no more, and you are at once freed. I do not ask that you place hands upon the tyrant to topple him over, but simply that you support him no longer; then you will behold him, like a great Colossus whose pedestal has been pulled away, fall of his own weight and break in pieces." (Ibid., 183) Tyrants are capable of great cruelty as long as they can count on the cooperation of their subjects, "but if not one thing is yielded to them, if, without any violence they are simply not obeyed, they become naked and undone and as nothing, just as, when the root receives no nourishment, the branch withers and dies." (Ibid., 180)

The American Henry-David Thoreau (1817-1862) expounds the same principle of non-cooperation in a short essay titled *On the duty of civil disobedience*. He asserts that, in order to fulfil his duty as a citizen, the individual should not adjust his behaviour according to the obligations of law, but according to the requirements of his conscience. "I think, he states, that we should be men first, and subjects afterwards. It is not advisable to cultivate a respect for the law, as much as for what is right." (1967: 57) From then on, the duty of a citizen does not amount to voting for what he considers just: "Even voting for the right is doing nothing for it. It is only expressing to men feebly your desire that it should prevail. A wise man will not leave the right to the mercy of chance, nor wish it to prevail through the power of the majority. There is but little virtue in the action of the masses of men." (Ibid., 67) The honest man cannot wait for the majority itself to rally behind justice in order to act according to his own requirements: "Any man more right than his neighbours constitutes a majority of one already." (Ibid., 76) Of course, to fight an injustice of the established disorder, one must first implement all the means provided for by law. But when these prove to be ineffective, it then becomes necessary to disregard the obligations and restrictions of law.

The citizen who intends to act responsibly, must not hesitate to disobey the State when it orders him to cooperate with injustice. "Unjust laws exist; shall we be content to obey them", asks Thoreau, "or shall we endeavour to amend them, and obey them until we have succeeded, or shall we transgress them at once?" (Ibid., 72) This is his reply: "If the machine of government is of such nature that it requires you to be the agent of injustice to another, then, I say, break the law. Let your life be a counterfriction to stop the machine. What I have to do is to see, at any rate, that I do not lend myself to the wrong which I condemn." (Ibid., 74) A minority of just men, as soon as it has the courage to confront the State directly, and to defy it by disobeying its unjust laws, can force it to give in. "A minority is powerless while it conforms to the majority; it is not even a minority; but it is irresistible when it clogs by its whole weight. If the alternative is to keep all just men in prison, or give up war and slavery, the State will not hesitate which to choose." (Ibid., 80)

In his *Socialist History*, Jean Jaurès quotes this declaration which Mirabeau made to the Assembly of the States of Provence, addressing "all the gentlemen and minor gentry who wished to hold sway over the productive class": "Take care, do not oppress this people that produces everything, and that, to make itself formidable, has only to become motionless." And Jean Jaurès notes that Mirabeau, on that occasion, gave "the most powerful and the most dazzling description of what we now call the general strike" (Jaurès, 1969: 136). Thus defined, the general strike of an entire people, determined to break the yoke of oppression that weighs upon its shoulders, and to become master of its own destiny, is the perfect illustration of the principle of non-cooperation.

In his book *Reflections on Violence*, Georges Sorel seeks to justify "revolutionary violence", and many philosophical texts refer to Sorel's way of thinking in order to gain a better understanding of the phenomenon of violence. But that is actually a tremendous misunderstanding, for, in highlighting the necessity of violence for the liberation of the proletariat, Sorel has no intention whatsoever of encouraging workers to throw themselves into a murderous confrontation with the armies of the bourgeoisie. On the contrary, he deeply regrets that this image is generally what the word revolution conveys, and refuses this perspective, which, he claims, belongs in the past. "For a very long time", he writes, "the Revolution appeared essentially to be a succession of glorious wars, which a people famished for liberty and carried away by the noblest passions, had maintained against a coalition of all the powers of oppression and error." (Sorel, 1972: 112) But, notably leaning on the tragic events of the Commune which happened in 1871, he shows that the proletariat has had to turn its imagination and reason away from any warlike epic. He strongly refutes "the barbaric acts which the superstition of the State suggested to the revolutionaries of 93" and wants to "hope that a socialist revolution carried out by pure trades unionists would not be defiled by the abominations which sullied the bourgeois revolutions" (Ibid., 138-139).

Moreover, Georges Sorel strongly protests against "Socialist Parliamentarians" who would like to convince workers that it is henceforth possible for their rights to be acknowledged merely through the game of formal democracy. He asserts that from then on the proletarian must put all his ideals and hopes in the general strike only. In saying that, he does not consider the practical organization of this gigantic action: he is only concerned with showing that the idea of the general strike corresponds to the deep aspirations of the working soul, and that it is capable of mobilizing the proletariat in the struggle against the middle-class. For him the general strike is a *myth* and must be considered as such, but he thinks precisely that only the power of that myth can create the necessary dynamics to the revolutionary movement. "The general strike", he writes, "is the *myth* in which socialism is wholly comprised, a body of images capable of evoking instinctively all the sentiments which correspond to the different manifestations of the war undertaken by Socialism against modern society. Strikes have engendered in the proletariat the noblest, deepest, and most moving sentiments that they possess; the general strike groups them all in a co-ordinated picture, and, by bringing them together, gives to each of them its maximum of intensity. .... We thus obtain that intuition of Socialism which language cannot give us with perfect clearness—and we obtain it as a whole, perceived instantaneously? (Sorel, 1972: 153-154)

Civil disobedience

It would be in vain, in the name of an abstract ideal of absolute nonviolence, to build a society where justice and order could be ensured by individuals acting of their own free will, without the need to resort to obligations imposed by law. The latter has an undeniable social function: that of forcing citizens to act reasonably, so that neither arbitrariness nor violence can be allowed free rein. It would therefore not be just to consider the restraints exerted by law as mere obstacles to freedom; they also guarantee it.

The social pact through which citizens unite to create a society, is the *constitution*. In theory, it is based on the consent of all citizens. The law is the application of the constitution. For this purpose, it instructs the appropriate behaviour for the common good, and gives the government the means to act against the activities of those who do not respect the clauses of the social pact. As far as the law fulfils its function and serves justice, it deserves the obedience of citizens. But when it covers up, supports or generates injustice itself, it deserves their disobedience. Obedience to the law does not free citizens from their responsibility: those who submit themselves to an unjust law are responsible for this injustice. For what makes injustice is not the unjust law, but the obedience to the unjust law. According to the official doctrine of States which claim to be democratic, each citizen, because he has the possibility to vote freely, must abide by universal suffrage. But it is not for the law to dictate what is just, what is just must dictate the law. And so, when there is a conflict between the law and justice, one must choose justice and disobey the law.

Democracy requires responsible citizens, and not disciplined citizens. George Bernanos claims that "a free people is a people undisciplined" (1949: 77) History teaches us that democracy is more often threatened by the blind obedience of citizens than by their disobedience. If the obedience of citizens is the strength of totalitarian regimes, their disobedience should become the foundation for the resistance to these same regimes. Vladimir Bukovsky, who was a prisoner in Soviet camps for a long time, writes that "We had grasped the great truth that it was not rifles, not tanks, and not atom bombs that created power, nor upon them that power rested. Power depended upon public obedience, upon a willingness to submit. .... We knew of the implacable force of one man's refusal to submit. The authorities knew it too." (Bukovsky, 1978: 35)

As a political action, civil disobedience is a collective initiative. It is not only about defining the right to conscientious objection, based on the obligation of the individual conscience to refuse to obey unjust laws; it goes beyond this recognition, and tries to define the rights of citizens to disobey the law in order to assert their power and see their claims come to something. In that case, civil disobedience does not express the moral protest of the individual faced with an unjust law, but the political will of a community of citizens seeking to exert their power.

Speak out and tell the truth

Because the first act of complicity with lies and injustice is to remain silent, the first act of non-cooperation will be to break that silence and speak out in public, in order to bring out the requirements of truth and the demands of justice. This action of speaking out is already a seizure of power. Thanks to this action the monopoly of speech claimed by the established powers is broken. From the moment that the individual speaks out to contest the established order and protest against its injustice, he can give in to the temptation of violence. Precisely because violent speech deliberately transgresses the norms of the conformist speech that claims to justify injustice, it can seem like a radical questioning of the established order in the eyes of the revolted man. From then on, so as to express his refusal clearly, he will seek to express himself in another language than that of the order he is contesting. To respect the standards of language set by society, would yet again be to accept to submit to its laws. The cry of the outraged man will then be a blasphemy, it will seek to be sacrilegious. In expressing his anger, his contempt and hate for society loudly, he will feel that he is freeing himself from the restraints which sought to silence him.

But in reality, there is a radical contradiction between speech and violence; one begins where the other ends. Speech which becomes violence denies itself as speech. It is therefore a decisive error to disregard the requirements of reason in order to denounce the wrong reasons which the powerful use in an attempt to hide the injustice of the established order. Only rational speech is capable of revealing the sophisms, contradictions and lies within official speeches by which citizens are summoned to approve silently.

The pacification of speech is one of the requirements of nonviolence. Furthermore, the teachings of nonviolent speech are much more efficient than those of the violent cry. The authority of speech comes from its justness, and not from its violence. Hence public opinion is much more receptive to pacific speech than to violent speech that comes to aggress it. Reasonable speech and nonviolent action reinforce each other, speech highlighting the significance of the action, and vice versa. So that when the struggle is at its most intense, speech becomes action and action becomes speech.

The challenge of the dissidents

On February the 12th 1974, a few hours before KGB agents came to knock on his door and arrest him, Aleksandr Solzhenitsyn (1974) signed the last text he would write on Russian land before his expulsion. In that text, the author of *The Gulag Archipelago* directly addresses his fellow citizens, asking them to resist the oppression that weighs upon them. More precisely, he asks them to refuse any cooperation with the lies on which the totalitarian order of Soviet society rests. Such is his analysis: the strength of the totalitarian State comes from the fact that it benefits from the collaboration of most citizens, who resign themselves and give in because they are afraid of losing the few advantages which have been promised to those who remain silent. "Violence", he writes, "can conceal itself with nothing except lies, and the lies can be maintained only by violence. And violence lays its ponderous paw not every day and not on every shoulder. It demands from us only obedience to lies and daily participation in lies—all loyalty lies in that. The simplest and most accessible key to our liberation, neglected until now, lies right here: in personal non-participation in lies." For Solzhenitsyn, this path to resistance is the only one that is accessible to all. It certainly is not easy and is littered with obstacles, but "it will be easier and shorter for all of us if we take it by mutual efforts and in closed ranks. If there are thousands of us, they will not be able to do anything with us." Solzhenitsyn warns his fellow citizens that if they do not have the civic courage to run the risk of that resistance, they will themselves become complicit in their own oppression: "If we are too frightened", he writes, "we should stop complaining that someone is suffocating us. We ourselves are doing it."

But in the end, Solzhenitsyn remains convinced that the human mind is capable of holding back the wild rush of violence. In another text, he states that "the idea that the lethal course of history is irreversible, and that the confident Spirit cannot act upon the most powerful force in the world, is unacceptable …. Only the inflexibility of the human spirit, standing firmly erect on the moving line of violence which is looming, and saying, ready for sacrifice and death, "do not come any closer!", only this inflexibility of the mind can be the true defence of private and universal peace and that of all of humanity." (Solzhenitsyn, 1974: 110) Already in freeing himself from the hold of lies, and openly daring to speak the truth, did Solzhenitsyn make a dent in the totalitarian wall surrounding his people. By condemning him to exile, the leaders of the Soviet union admitted their own weakness: "Why was Solzhenitsyn expelled from his homeland," asked Vaclav Havel in 1978? "Surely not", he answered, "as the holder of an effective power by which any representative of the regime could have felt threatened to lose his place. His expulsion meant something else: the desperate attempt to hide that terrible source of truth, of which nobody could tell what changes or political upheavals it would lead to within the conscience of society." (Havel, 1989: 91)

Vaclav Havel himself became a dissident by refusing to co-operate with the lies. According to him, the fundamental task of all those who intend to face up to rigid ideologies and anonymous bureaucracies consists in letting their own reason guide them, and "in serving the truth under all circumstances as our own existential experience" (Havel, 1989: 243). The totalitarian State wants to force individuals to submit to a social ritual, which in turn forces them to live a lie. Naturally, they do not have to believe in all the mystification justifying this ritual, but they must act as if they believed in it. "For this reason, however", notes Havel, "they must live within a lie. It is enough for them to have accepted to live with it, and in it. For by this very fact, individuals confirm the system, fulfil the system, make the system, are the system." (Ibid., 77)

There is no possible coexistence between "living a lie", and "living in truth". Each expression of the former constitutes a threat for the latter, for it strips it of its deceptive appearance, which alone allows it to subsist. That is why living in truth not only has an "existential dimension" allowing individuals to recover their own identity and come to terms with their own humanity, "it also has a political dimension" (Havel, 1989: 88) allowing citizens to fight efficiently against the totalitarian system. Living in truth consists in a real power of protest, a genuine power of opposition, an authentic counter-power that confronts the established power. The latter will certainly not allow itself to be openly challenged, and will try to silence the rebels by all possible means, but it cannot recapture words that have been released from its grip. As soon as they have been pronounced by a free man, they have been said once and for all, and remain active. The persecutions that may rain on their author do nothing but increase his strength. They will not cease to resonate in the conscience of all those who are living a lie. Whatever compromises these have stooped to, it is not possible for the word of truth not to find somewhere deep within them their repressed desires for a life of dignity. That is why "they may be struck at any moment—in theory, at least—by the force of truth" (Havel, 1989: 90). Although no one can foresee it, it is legitimate to think that this force of opposition may increase to the point that it can express itself through a political movement, directly competing with the effective power. That is how Vaclav Havel, after many years of roaming and wandering in dissidence, became President of the Czechoslovak Republic.

The force of humour

Among the reasons for which central European dissidents were able to face so many painful events with dignity, Vaclav Havel highlighted the importance of their sense of humour. He then says that "we might not be in a position to take on our historical tasks, were it not for that gap between reality and ourselves." (1989: 101) And he speaks of the surprise of foreigners who find it difficult to understand how they can both endure such ordeals and not cease to laugh about them. For him, that sense of humour was precisely what made it possible for them to face the gravity of the situation with serenity: "If we must not lose ourselves in our own seriousness to the point of becoming comical, we must however have a sense of humour and irony. When we lose them, our activity also paradoxically loses its seriousness." (Ibid., 102)

Vaclav Havel's words are far from fortuitous, and it is important to reflect upon the meaning of humour by asking whether it might not be linked to nonviolence. The word "humour" in English is borrowed from the old French word *humeur* which in turn comes from the Latin *humor*, meaning a liquid. *Humeur* first referred to an organic liquid present in the human body, and then to character, for in the past, the latter was said to depend on the composition of the "humours" of the human body (the four main 'humours' being blood, black bile, yellow bile and phlegm). *Humeur* then had two antinomic uses, sometimes meaning a "disposition to be merry" (good mood/humour), sometimes meaning a "disposition to be irritated" (bad mood/humour). The English word "humour" took the first of these meanings from the French (and it reintegrated the French language as such).

This backward look to retrace the formation of the word humour allows us to have a better understanding of its meaning. He who adopts a humorous attitude towards events, is the one who finds himself in a situation where everything should contribute to his feeling disposed to irritation, and who, against all odds, changes the normal course of things and himself decides to be inclined towards joking. He is the one who, given the circumstances, should be in a bad mood ("bad humour"), and who decides to be in a good mood ("good humour"). To summarize the relation of the humorous man to the four humours, he is the one who, faced with the difficulties of his life, is determined not to be in a foul mood (black humour), not to worry himself sick (bile) nor to fret, to refuse to become cantankerous (sang froid), but, on the contrary, to stay calm, not to lose his composure and to make the best of a bad job (phlegm).

According to Freud, who offered many penetrating reflections on the subject, the pleasure of humour comes from "an economy in expenditure of feeling" (1993: 411), "an economy of affection" (1993: 321). He specifies that, as a general rule, we display humour "at the cost of irritation—instead of getting angry" (1993: 404). The "humorist" finds himself in a situation such as he would normally be expected to show signs of some affection, "he will get angry, will express grief, fright, horror, perhaps even despair" and yet, "he fails to show affection, and instead makes a joke" (1993: 322).

Freud sets out to consider humour "in the light of a defence mechanism" which aims to "avoid the constraint of suffering" (Ibid., 324), to "prevent the appearance of displeasure" (1993: 407) and sees it as "the highest of defence mechanisms" (Id.). What he who resorts to humour seeks to express in order to face up to a situation that holds real danger, could be conveyed in those words: "I am too big (and too great) for such occasions to distress me" (Ibid., 408). The ego therefore intends to assert its invincibility, its invulnerability to external dangers, through humour: "The ego refuses to be distressed by the provocations of reality, to let itself be compelled to suffer; it insists that it cannot be affected by the traumas of the external world; it shows, in fact, that such traumas are no more than occasions for it to gain pleasure." (1993: 323). Hence humour is a method of resistance against adversity: "humour is not resigned, it is rebellious" (Ibid., 324).

By allowing individuals to defend themselves against irritation, fear and suffering, humour offers them the possibility to protect themselves against hate and violence. Furthermore, humour is tremendously contagious, hugely convincing. The spectator-listener who watches and listens to the humorist find himself inclined to follow him down the road he has chosen, and willingly accepts the invitation he receives to come and share his humorous pleasure.

"Combine justice and force"

Blaise Pascal's incisive phrases on justice and force are well-known: "It is necessary to combine justice and force; and, for this end, make what is just, strong, and what is strong, just." (Thought 298)[1] These statements define the ambition of nonviolence perfectly: it is indeed to "combine justice and force". And since violent action contains an irreducible part of injustice, only the force of nonviolent action can be just. But it is clear that Pascal was not thinking of nonviolence at all while he wrote his *Pensées* (literally, Thoughts).

What are his thoughts exactly? First he notes that "justice without force is powerless", that "justice without force meets with opposition, for there will be always the wicked" (298). He thus challenges idealism, which claims that there is a "force of justice", with reason. Pascal makes a second observation: "Force without justice is tyrannical", "force without justice is arraigned" (298). Here, when he uses the word "force", he actually means "violence": violence is indeed here accused of being tyrannical when it is exerted at the cost of justice. As for nonviolent force, it does not have the means for tyranny. But if it is really about violence, how can what is violent be made to be truly just? More exactly, is it possible for what is violent to be truly just? Pascal is well aware of the difficulty. For all that, he does not think we have solved it, but that we have only circumvented it: "We cannot give force to justice, because it is opposed to justice, calling it injustice, averring its own justice; and so, not being able to make that what is just strong they have made that which was strong just." (298) Pascal thus acknowledges that violence can-

---

[1] We will indicate the numbers of Pascal's Thoughts in brackets, according to the order in which they appear in Brunschvigg's edition.

not give force to justice because violence is opposed to justice. It is therefore not possible to combine justice and violence, unless one claims, but against the truth, that violence is just. That is precisely what has been done: violence has been justified. And that is how "force", that is to say violence, is "Queen of the world" (303) or, more precisely, how it is "its tyrant" (311).

But Pascal is not misled: justice imposed by violence is not true justice. The justice that prevails in society, is only the one that is defined by "custom", by "fashion": "A fashion makes what is agreeable, so it makes what is justice." (309) "Customs" therefore decide on the criteria and norms of justice for men and that is why the latter is so unpredictable, depending on the time and place. In reality, we do not know true justice, for if we knew it, "we would not have established the maxim most generally accepted among men, that each must follow the custom of his country." (297). Hence the established order serves as justice: "Justice is that which is established; and thus all established laws will necessarily be held as just without further examination because they are established." (312) If men obey laws, it is because they are compelled to, by the violence of the princes who rule them. The right that prevails in society is therefore "the right of the sword", "for the sword gives a true right" (878). Pascal acknowledges the need to base justice on the violence of the sword, so that men can thus see that justice and violence are indeed together, and that by submitting to violence they believe they are submitting to justice. "Otherwise", he points out, "we should see violence on one side and justice on the other." (878) Pascal considers that men must submit to the right of the sword, because should they not, there would be a civil war, which is "the greatest of evils" (320) and that peace, which is "the sovereign good" (219), must be maintained. But he knows very well that the established order does not meet the requirements of true justice. For he is not unaware that in "true justice", there is "no violence" (878).

We certainly would not wish to support Pascal's political choices concerning the organization of society. In the end, on the pretext that he prefers unjust order to disorder, he resigns himself to injustice, and putting the corruption of human nature forward, he preaches for the obedience of the people to a power whose violence and lies are its main foundations. What interests us here, is the analysis of the facts presented by Pascal, for it seems to show great lucidity. Indeed, things often happen as he says they do, even if they do not go well: violence is the basis of the established order, and indeed, making the people believe that this order meets the requirements of justice, is to deceive them.

Pascal's reflections thus help us to understand that the method of nonviolent action makes it possible to combine justice and force without opposing justice, that only nonviolence can give force to justice. *Opting for nonviolence, is refusing to make what is violent just, and to make what is just strong.*

6

Violence and Necessity

On the rare occasions when some interest towards nonviolence is shown, it is generally to assert that it can be the choice of individuals in the way they lead their personal life, but it cannot be the rule in political life, which calls for violence. Hence violence would be inherent in political action.

Machiavelli and well-used cruelty

Niccolo Machiavelli is at the top of the list of those who have proclaimed the necessity of resorting to violence in governing the city of men. Among the advice that he gives the Prince in order to remain in power, he insists on many occasions that he should not have scruples about showing cruelty whenever necessary. "The prince", he writes, "ought not to worry about having a reputation for cruelty in order to keep his subjects unified and loyal." (Machiavelli, 1962: 117) Evil does not lie within cruelty, but in cruelty "ill-used"; consequently, well-used cruelty can be said to be "good", "if one can speak well of evil" (Ibid., 66). For Machiavelli is careful not to praise violence, he only asserts its implacable necessity. He does not dispute the fact that cruelty is "inhuman" (Ibid., 120), he only claims that it is necessary in so far as it alone can be efficient.

One of the major characteristics of Machiavelli's undertaking is to define the efficiency criteria of the action as seen from the point of view of political artifice, beyond all consideration for the categories of good and evil. "It is necessary", he claims, "for a prince to have the ability to change his mind according to the way the winds of fortune and conditions require; if possible, he ought not turn away from what is good, but he should be able to do evil if necessary." (Machiavelli, 1962: 126) But according to him, a prince is more often faced with the necessity to show cruelty, than with the possibility to show goodness: "a prince cannot observe all those things for which men are considered good in order to maintain the state." (Machiavelli, 1962: 137)

He suggests that, in the end, cruelty is less cruel than goodness, which gives free rein to evildoers. Hence does he condemn the attitude of "those who, because of too much leniency, allow disorder to erupt, whence arise murders and lootings." (Machiavelli, 1962: 117) Thus wanting to contain the cruelty of men, he gives free rein to the cruelty of princes by giving it no other limits than the inconvenience which might ensue for them.

A prince whose code of conduct involved behaving as a good man under all circumstances would be responsible for his own defeat. He must above all comply with the constraints of necessity, even if it meant that he should trample on the requirements of humanity. "There is such a difference between how we live and how we ought to live that he who turns away from what actually does occur for the sake of what ought to occur, does something that will ruin him rather than save him. For he who wants to be a good man all the time will be ruined among so many who are not good. It is therefore necessary for a prince who wants to survive to learn how not to be good and to use goodness, or not use it, according to what needs to be done." (Machiavelli, 1962: 109-110)

According to Machiavelli, political power essentially rests on the power of arms. "All armed prophets have conquered, he observes, and the unarmed ones have been destroyed.". (1962: 46) Only the power of arms make it possible for a prince to rule and to be obeyed, "for there is nothing proportionate between the armed and the unarmed; and it is not reasonable that he who is armed should yield obedience willingly to him who is unarmed." (Machiavelli, 1962: 104) A prince should worry more about having "good arms" than "good laws", since laws have no other force than that of arms (Ibid., 85). Of course, Machiavelli willingly admits that it is in the nature of men to be governed by laws, and that is in the nature of animals to be gov-

governed by force, but he asserts that men, generally, must be ruled like animals. A prince must therefore be "half-animal and half-man" (Machiavelli, 1962: 124). He must be both as cunning as the fox, in order to avoid traps, and as cruel as the lion, in order to defend himself against the attack of wolves (Id.).

According to Machiavelli, the prince should stop at nothing to maintain order among his subjects: "In the actions of individuals, especially princes, when there is no judge to appeal to, people look at the results. A prince only has to conquer and maintain the state. His means will always be considered honourable, and everyone will praise them." (Machiavelli, 1962: 126) The main question asked by Machiavelli, the only one in the end, is to know how a prince can obtain the submission of his subjects. He answers this question without hesitation: he should stop at nothing as long as it allows him effectively to reach that end.

The reason why a prince must rule his subjects with an iron fist, without ever softening his threats, is that "men are always evil in the end, if they are not constrained to be good out of necessity" (Machiavelli, 1962: 165-166); "For it can be said of men in general that they are ungrateful, talkative, tricky and deceitful, eager to avoid dangers, anxious for gain" (Ibid., 118). Between a prince and his subjects, there must therefore be complete distrust. Machiavelli concludes that "since men love as they please but fear as the prince wills, a wise prince ought to rely on what is his power and not in the power of others, only being careful to avoid being hated" (Ibid., 121).

In the final analysis, Machiavelli is really developing the political doctrine of despotism, if despotism is the form of government in which all powers are conferred on one single man, without citizens being able to enjoy any kind of power. It was said that the Florentine was "the founder of political science"—the formula comes from Raymond Aron (Machiavelli 1962: 7)—, but, in reality, he only founded the political science of despotism.

Machiavelli's entire undertaking lies outside the political project that we call democracy, and which is characterized by the participation of citizens in political power. One could argue that democracy was not on the agenda at the time or place where

Machiavelli lived. One could add that the Florentine understood the full extent of the political problems happening within the Italian peninsula, confronted with the warlike rivalries between France, Spain, Germany and the Vatican. One could also highlight the fact that as an informed and sorry spectator of an Italy "without a ruler, without order, beaten, looted, dismembered, chased by foreigners", he could only be right in saying that "it is waiting for whoever will be able to heal its wounds and end the lootings of Lombardia, the ransoming of Naples and Tuscany, and heal its wounds, which have long festered", and that "it prays that God may send someone who can save it from cruelty and barbaric tyranny" (Machiavelli 1962: 178). But in reality, are not the misfortunes of Italy which Machiavelli deplores largely due to the actions of princes who put his own advice into practice? If all men are as evil as the Florentine says, princes are as evil as their subjects. It is therefore a mistake to expect them to use the position that they are awarded solely in order to ensure public order and peace, for the benefit of public order.

The principles that Machiavelli formulated might make it possible to establish a police state, but they are of no use in the construction of a democratic order, one in which citizens could live with the dignity of free men. Yet Machiavelli's reflections on the necessity of violence are often regarded with benevolence by the very people who profess democracy. It is as if the Florentine's commentators feared—in stepping back from his "realism"—that they may deserve his criticism of those who think it possible to act in politics while seeking to respect moral principles.

Machiavelli's analysis, reasoning and advice undoubtedly show rigorous logic. This logic is all the stronger—and so all the more attractive—given that he asserts his raw thoughts with imperturbable coldness and refuses anything that might soften its brutality. With his confession, he disarms all the accusations. He does not prevaricate and never equivocates. He is cynical, but he acclaims it loud and clear. The question is not whether to accept or refuse his logic, but whether to accept or refuse the premises on which he has based it. As for us, it is precisely these premises that we refuse.

Hegel and the apology of war

Hegel's political philosophy illustrates in a particularly significant manner the prevailing theory according to which violence is the driving force behind history. Hegel starts with this observation: when left to themselves, individuals behave according to their own interests and desires and they can therefore only come into conflict with each other. The "state of nature" in which men find themselves within civil society, is "the state of violence" (Hegel, 1989: 138). It is a state of savagery "linked to the passions of brutality and to acts of violence" (Hegel, 1988: 141). The individual deludes himself in believing that he is free in the state of nature. Man only becomes free if—going beyond his own interests—he acts for the general interest which, in every society, is embodied by the State. "Freedom", writes Hegel, "is confused with instincts, desires, passions, whims and the arbitrary of individuals, and their limitations are considered to be the limitation of freedom. On the contrary, this limitation is the very condition of freedom. The State and society are precisely the conditions in which freedom is attained." (Hegel, 1988: 143)

Hence man is incapable of achieving his own freedom. Hegel seeks to criticize radically the moral individualism in which man claims to seek refuge in order to cultivate his own virtue, hidden away from the fury of history. He stigmatizes the individual who "holds himself for a fine creature": "a swollen enlargement which gives itself and others a mighty size of the head, but blistered with emptiness". To this deceiving moral individualism, Hegel opposes the ideal of the antique citizen, who linked his own destiny to that of the city: "Virtue in the olden time had its secure and determinate significance, for it found the fullness of its content and its solid basis in the substantial life of the nation, and had for its purpose and end a concrete good that existed and lay at hand." (Hegel, 1992: 319) The individual therefore reaches his true destination by integrating the life of the people: "Thus, in a free people, reason has already been made real; this reason is the presence of the living spirit." (Ibid., 292)

The people builds its unity in the organization of the State. "The spiritual individual", writes Hegel, "the nation—in so far as it is internally differentiated so as to form an organic whole—is what we call the State." (1988: 139) Without the organization of the State, the people is nothing but a crowd in the grip of its own passions: "The many, as single individuals—and this is a favourite interpretation of the term people—do indeed live together, but only as a crowd—a formless mass whose movement and activity can consequently only be elemental, irrational, barbarous, and terrifying." (Hegel, 1989: 310)

The State is the objective incarnation in history, both of the rational requirement, the universal requirement and the ethical requirement that lies within each individual. "The basis of the State", writes Hegel, "is the power of reason realizing itself as will." (Ibid., 260) By becoming a member of the State, the individual reaches a free and rational existence. "The State is the reality in which (the individual) finds his freedom and the pleasure of his freedom. .... Only in the State does man lead an existence in conformity with his Reason." (Hegel, 1988: 135-136) In response to the arbitrariness that prevails in the State of Nature, the law objectively expresses the requirements of universal reason, and consequently, the citizen, freed from his particular instincts, recognizes the requirements of his own reason in the law. "Only that will which obeys the law is free, for it obeys itself." (Ibid., 140)

States, which each have their own individuality, behave like particular "individuals" with each other, that is to say they compete with each other while defending particular interests and pursuing particular goals. "Since the relations between States", writes Hegel, "have as their fundamental principle their respective sovereignties, they are to that extent opposed to one another in the State of Nature." (1989: 330) From then on, war is inevitable: "When the particular wills of States can come to no agreement, the controversy can be settled only by war." (Ibid., 331)

The protagonist of history is not the individual and solitary man, but the people which—in order to assert its individuality, cannot avoid confronting other people. In this necessarily conflictual relation, the people must face up to the ordeal of war if it wants to safeguard its freedom. The peoples who fall into slavery are those who did not have the courage to make war: "their freedom died from the fear of dying" (Hegel, 1989: 325). For Hegel, war is therefore a vital necessity for a free people; more than that, it is an ethical necessity, a spiritual necessity. War is the privileged moment when the people's spirit shows itself in history because, at this instant, all individuals turn away from their private interests and pleasures in order to pursue a common, more universal, goal.

The duty of the individual is to defend the State against the enemies that threaten its sovereignty. It is first of all in his own interest, since the State ensures his safety, through its laws and institutions. But above all, by consciously taking the risk of dying while defending the State, the individual fulfils his destiny as a free man. The individual only attains freedom by accepting "the life and death struggle": "It is solely by risking life that freedom is obtained. .... In the same way, each individual must aim at the death of the other, as it risks his own life thereby." (Hegel, 1992: I, 159) But war is not the work of hate, it is that of honour. "Giving death is devoid of wrath. .... Firearms are the discovery of a universal death that is indifferent, and nonpersonal; and the moving force is national honour, not the desire to injure a single individual." (Hegel, 1989: 328) The death that the individual meets at war is a heroic death; it is not the natural death of animals, it is the sensible death of a man who sacrifices his worldly goods and his own life in order to defend universal good.

While the individuals of a community are tempted to pursue particular goals—"those of acquisition and pleasure"—and they thus tend to distance themselves from everything, it is the government's duty to be careful "not to let the whole break up into fragments, and the common spirit evaporate" (Hegel, 1992: II, 23). And the best way to restore the unity of the whole is war. "In the state of war", writes Hegel, "the vanity for things and temporal goods is taken seriously—a vanity which in peacetime is a theme of edifying rhetoric." (1989: 324) It is through war that "the ethical health of peoples is preserved": "Just as the movement of the winds preserves the sea from stagnation which a lasting calm would produce—a stagnation which a lasting, not to say, perpetual peace would also produce among nations." (Ibid., 324-325)

All citizens must be ready to sacrifice their life in order to defend the sovereignty of the State: "If the State requires the sacrifice of life, the individual must consent to it." (Hegel, 1989: 123). However, in reality, there is a particular class whose role it is to ensure the preservation and the independence of the State: it is "the military class". It is the "universal class whose duty it is to sacrifice itself". It is the "class of courage" par excellence. (Ibid., 327)

In the front line of peoples who make war so as to safeguard their freedom, are "the great men" who are heroes. In Hegel's eyes, the great man is represented throughout history by Alexander the Great, Caesar, and Napoleon. This shows how much the Hegelian hero is, above all, a warrior. Of course, great men, carried away by their passion, have not always respected the principles of morals: "In pursuing their great interests, great men have often treated other venerable interests, and even sacred rights, lightly and inconsiderately. This conduct undoubtedly deserves moral blame. But their position is altogether different. So mighty a form must trample down many an innocent flower, and crush many an object in its path." (Hegel, 1988: 129) Hegel mocks school teachers who claim that great men have been "immoral men" (Ibid., 127): they only stoop to the point of view of manservants, for whom heroes do not exist. Great men have certainly had their own interests at heart, but, as if in spite of themselves, they "have had the happiness of being the agents of a goal which is a step forward in the progressive march of the universal spirit" (Ibid., 123). Thus, while letting their passion guide them, they have accomplished the work of reason: "One can call the cunning of reason the fact that the Idea makes passions work for it." (Ibid., 129) Wars are therefore still meaningful, and contribute to the progression of history, towards its realization; they "only take place where the course of things renders them necessary; anyway, seeds germinate once again, and mere chatter fades away in the face of the seriousness of the cyclical movement of history" (Hegel, 1989: 326).

World history is "the necessary development of the moments of reason", and is therefore "the realization of the universal spirit" (Hegel, 1989: 334). The Hegelian philosophy of history is fundamentally optimistic, but his optimism is precisely what raises questions, insofar as he ends up justifying the unjustifiable. War itself, with its evil and misfortunes, is considered to be a necessary moment of history which moves towards its end, despite the crisis and contradictions that can momentarily hinder its course. Hegel's idealism basically resembles cynicism. He does not see violence and all its horrors, he does not look at war and all its devastation, he wants to see beyond war, he always considers history in its evolution, and in it he sees the way forward for the spirit of the world. Killing is not a crime, as long as it is consistent with history, and it would be pointless to sympathize with innocent victims in their misfortune. In this perspective, history could not care less about the virtue of the individual man, of his moral requirements and claims for happiness; the only thing that counts is the effectiveness of the action which hastens the course of events. The law of history is well and truly the law of the strongest, that is of the most violent. The victor is always right, since he is the victor.

In reality, there is nothing original in Hegel's discourse glorifying the courage of men who accept to sacrifice their particular goods and interests in order to defend the State. Hegel basically only makes the ideology that has prevailed for centuries his own, but in doing so, he sanctions it, and reinforces its hold on minds and mentalities. For all that, truth in the Hegelian discourse must be recognized when he asserts that the attitude of the man who takes the risk of dying to defend the freedom of his community is highly moral. It is true that in numerous historical circumstances, war has been the opportunity for man to show the greatest courage and highest morality, even if this should not erase the fact that the man of war can show—and often shows—the greatest viciousness and the greatest baseness. "War", wrote Alain, "is dreadful in that it feeds off seemingly beautiful feelings, a few of which are honourable." (1939: 93) But the subjective morality of the warrior cannot hide the objective immorality of war.

Whoever understands the full extent of history cannot deny that for centuries, the participation of individuals in wars has played a part in consolidating the sense of community, and that in such a context, all the virtues shown by man have themselves been linked to war. Challenging war does not require the denial of these virtues, obviously. Such is history and we are all its heirs, and therefore its beneficiaries. Probably it was not fated to be that way, even if, most often, at the precise moment when history was being determined, the pressure was too high for things to be different. It is after all rather pointless to dream of a history which would not be our own. What counts today is to try and change things. With the hindsight that is ours, and the reflection it offers us, we can, and so we should.

The heroism sometimes shown by the warrior cannot erase the lethal nature of war. The warrior is not always a criminal, but war is always a crime. Instead of war being legitimized by the courage of the warrior, it must be de-legitimized by the crime of violence. The fact that history is violent should only teach us that men are unreasonable, and that it is an insane trick of the mind to want to reconcile history, therefore violence, and reason. In this respect, the glorification of war which Hegel indulges in, when he claims that it is the highest expression of the spirit in history, is more than an error of thought: it is an offence against the spirit. And it must be denounced as such.

In the best-case scenario, war is deeply ambivalent: it can be the expression of courage, but it is always the expression of lethal violence. If one is honourable, the other is criminal. It is for philosophy to overthrow the reasoning which ideology has made to prevail across the centuries, and according to which war is honourable, even though it teaches killing: war must be exposed as criminal, despite being the work of courage. The rhetoric on courage and self-sacrifice must be released from war, so that it can be linked to nonviolent resistance. Everything is then in order, and the philosopher can assert that indeed, an individual who overcomes his private interests and desires by accepting to sacrifice his worldly goods and even his life, taking the risk of dying for the defence of freedom, is pursuing universal good, is realizing the work of reason in history and is accomplishing his destiny as a spiritual being.

After recalling that a humorist, apologizing with the words "I have to make a living", received this reply: "I do not see why it is necessary", Hegel formulates this maxim: "Life is not essential, compared to the superior requirement of freedom". (1989: 165) This maxim which, in Hegel's eyes, dictates the conduct of the violent hero, dictates the conduct of the nonviolent wise man even more so.

Max Weber and the two ethics

The theory that Max Weber developed in 1919, in his short essay *Politics as a vocation*, clearly illustrates the ideology according to which violence is an absolute necessity for whoever intends to engage in politics; its immediate consequence being that he who wants to challenge violence must necessarily renounce political action. "The decisive means for politics, he categorically asserts, is violence." (Weber, 1979, 173) "He who wishes to engage in politics, he specifies, enters in relation with the satanic powers that lurk in every act of violence." (Ibid., 180) The essential requirement of love and goodness forbids killing but thereby forbids us to take the path to politics: "If the a-cosmic ethic of love tells us: "Resist not evil by force", for the politician the reverse proposition holds: "Thou shalt resist by force, or else you are responsible for the evil winning out." " (Ibid., 170)

Weber then establishes a distinction—destined for a great future—between two "totally different and implacably opposed" ethics: all of man's actions "can take a different direction according to *the ethic of responsibility* or according to *the ethic of conviction*" (Ibid., 172). He who acts according to the ethics of responsibility intends to "bear the ascribed consequences of his own actions" (Id.), while "the believer in an ethic of conviction feels "responsible" only for seeing to it that the flame of pure intentions is not quenched" (Ibid., 173). "But", he insists, "the absolute ethic just does not ask for consequences !" (Ibid., 171) Max Weber certainly does not scorn the attitude of he who intends to adjust his attitude according to the commandment of "absolute ethics", which require for the other cheek to be turned "immediately, without questioning the source of the other's authority to strike". Such an attitude "makes sense and expresses a kind of dignity" for he who wishes to be a saint and intends to "live like Jesus": "Except for the saint it is an ethic of indignity" (Ibid., 170).

Max Weber's reasoning thus becomes caught up in the antinomy between the lack of realism of an absolute refusal of violence, and the realism of its acceptance. But speaking of the result in terms of the absolute, introduces an error of reasoning in the premises, which will necessarily be found in the conclusions. One can of course imagine a man whose rule of conduct is to remain faithful under all circumstances to the commandments of absolute ethics, without worrying about the consequences of his actions. But that is purely theoretical. To then claim that this man is a saint, is to have a rather strange idea about saintliness. Following Max Weber in saying that this man intends to "live like Jesus", is to judge the attitude of the wise man of Nazareth strangely. If the latter had been religiously careful not to become involved in the politics of the society in which he lived, he certainly would not have been sentenced to death by the coalition in power. And when he is slapped in the face by a soldier who accuses him of insolence towards the high priest, he does not turn the other cheek "immediately, without questioning the source of the other's authority to strike". On the contrary, he calls out to him directly: "If I said something wrong, testify as to what is wrong. But if I spoke the truth, why do you strike me?" (Jn 18, 19-24) At no point is Jesus of Nazareth shown as a man who acts with no care for the consequences of his actions, and who only cares about maintaining the purity of any doctrine.

Obviously, he who refers to an absolute which is not part of this world ignores the reality of this world, and abandons all responsibilities towards it. Indeed, he becomes irresponsible. But it is pointless to hold forth about such an attitude. A man who evades his responsibilities can only be said to be irresponsible. But such an attitude cannot serve as reference in defining the conduct of he who has opted for nonviolence, determined to take on all his responsibilities in this world. Max Weber formulates a truism when he sets out to challenge the lack of realism of he whose only preoccupation is to apply the commandments of an absolute ethic of a-cosmic love, without thinking about the consequences of his actions. Man can indeed refuse all acts of violence and ignore the consequences of his actions, but this neither makes it possible to claim that the responsible man is inevitably violent, nor to conclude that a nonviolent attitude is necessarily irresponsible.

He who chooses nonviolent action—but Max Weber ignores the category of nonviolent action—does not aim to maintain the flame of the pure nonviolent doctrine alight, but to seek justice through means which do not contradict it. He intends to take full responsibility for the consequences of his actions. He who has opted for nonviolent action realizes that it is insane to claim to experience ab-solute (that is to say, according to the Latin etymology of the word, dis-connected from reality) nonviolence, and that he must constantly learn to experience relative (that is to say, still according to the Latin etymology of the word, re-connected to reality) violence. To speak of absolute nonviolence is necessarily to challenge nonviolence as an unrealistic attitude. Albert Camus himself did not manage to avoid this trap as he wrote, in *The Rebel, an essay on Man in Revolt:* "Absolute nonviolence is the negative basis of slavery and its acts of violence." (1951: 349) If nonviolence does not claim to be absolute, it wants to be radical (from the Latin *radix* which means *root*), that is to say it wants to up-root violence, it wants to extirpate it (from the Latin *stirps* which also means root), it wants to endeavour to make violence fade away by destroying its cultural, ideological, social and political roots.

For Max Weber, "(the modern state) can only be defined sociologically in terms of the specific means peculiar to it, as to every political association, namely, the use of physical force" (1979: 100). Violence certainly is not the unique means which the State can resort to, but it is its "specific means". In other words, violence is "the normal means of power" (Id.). Hence physical force is the very basis of the order that the State has to establish within the political city of men: "the State is a relation of men dominating men, a relation supported by means of legitimate (i.e. considered to be legitimate) violence. If the State is to exist, the dominated must obey the authority claimed by the powers-that-be." (Ibid., 101) The reasons for which men accept to obey other men are numerous and varied but, among them, Max Weber cites the fear of punishment, and the hope for a reward here on Earth or in the next world.

Once again, the thoroughness of Max Weber's analysis and reasoning cannot be doubted. As soon as he defines the political order which needs to be established among men as a relation of domination by which those who rule maintain those who obey in submission, it is natural that he should have violence down as the specific means for the exercising of political power. There are indeed no doubts as to the means of violence being coherent with the end of domination. It is therefore not right to question the choice of the means rather than that of the end. The question is to know whether men can have no other ambition together than to establish relations of domination-submission and of command-obedience, whether they do not have the vocation to conceive another political project, by founding a social order which would not be based on violence? It seems to us that these questions call for other answers than those which, under the pretext of realism, Max Weber resigns himself to.

7

The State as Institutionalized Violence

The State is made up of all the political, administrative, legal, police and military institutions which organize government and the public service. The specific mission of the State is to establish, maintain and restore civil peace in order to ensure the security of citizens. Public order can only result from the restricting organization of a society that rests on obligations and interdicts. The State exerts a power of constraint. It would indeed be illusory to claim to manage a society only through means of persuasion; should that happen, means of constraint should make it possible to force individuals to respect the "social contract" that is the basis for the city's order and cohesion.

There is a right and a duty to defend society against those who disturb public order. A society based on law cannot do without an institutionalized justice and police force, capable of neutralising, through "public force", the individuals and groups who threaten civil peace. A just and free society could therefore not be organized without the acknowledgment of the legitimacy of law enforcement and legal constraint.

But we must then answer a question whose political stakes are decisive: if social constraint and the use of "public force" are necessary to ensure civil peace, what are the legitimate means of this constraint? The States answer this question by claiming the monopoly of legitimate violence as theirs. "The modern State", writes Max Weber, "is a compulsory association which organizes domination. It has been successful to monopolize the legitimate use of physical force as a means of domination within a territory. To this end the state has combined the material means of organization in the hands of its leaders." (1979: 108).

Of course, legal restraint (as defined by criminal law) that may imply physical violence is not the only means to which the State can resort in order to organize society. However, the State rarely uses persuasion; it seeks dissuasion, which implies a threat and is already restraining. Restraint, and as a last resort, violence, are thus the specific means of the State. There is an organic relationship between the State and violence. This link is implacable: it constitutes the State.

"The State", asserts Nietzsche, "is the coldest of all cold monsters. It also lies coldly; and this is the lie that creeps from its mouth: "I, the State, I am the People"." (1963: 61) The concept of popular sovereignty is indeed the basis for that of state sovereignty, but popular sovereignty is a synthetic concept which carries the seed of that of the totalitarian State. From then on, to build a democracy, it is not only important to challenge State sovereignty, but also popular sovereignty. When Jean-Jacques Rousseau—whose influence was decisive in the doctrine of the State developed following the revolution of 1789—asserts that the clauses of the "social contract" "may be reduced to one—the total alienation of each associate, together with all his rights, to the whole community" (Book I, Ch. VI); he bases the dictatorship of "the community" on "each associate". Rousseau truly is the "prophet of the doctrinaire State" which Bakunin saw in him (Bakunin, 1965: 56). Jacques Maritain, who drew his philosophical inspiration from other sources than Bakunin, makes the same judgment (1965: 41-43): "Rousseau, who was not a democrat, injected in nascent modern democracies a notion of Sovereignty which was destructive of democracy, and pointed towards the totalitarian State. .... In order to think in a consistent manner in political philosophy, we have to discard the concept of Sovereignty, which is but one with the concept of Absolutism."

Hence popular sovereignty is more of a threat than a guarantee to the freedom of citizens: it implies that they should give up on their autonomy and submit to an alleged "general will", which can force them to die by sacrificing themselves for "the general interest". "It is a principle of all governments", writes Jean Guehenno painfully, "that a soldier should be docile and easy to kill." (1968: 23) It is indeed in the organization of military service that the State's hold on citizens is the most powerful. Compulsory conscription and universal suffrage were significantly established at the same time in modern societies. "Like a contagion, observed Taine at the end of the 19th century, conscription has spread from State to State; at the present time, it has reached Western Europe, and here it reigns along with its natural companion which always precedes or follows it, it twin-brother, universal suffrage. Each more or less incomplete and disguised, both being the blind and formidable leaders or regulators of future history, one thrusting the ballot into the hands of every adult, and the other putting a soldier's knapsack on every shoulder's back." (Taine apud Jouvenel, 1977: 30) Everything therefore happened as if the State had come to an arrangement with citizens by swapping the right to vote, for military duty. But, as Georges Bernanos pointed out (1948: 108), the State benefitted the most from this arrangement: "Compulsory conscription was a real, concrete benefit for the State. Whereas the right to vote had hardly—in the hands of the individual deprived of his rights— become the property of the nation in the same way as the rest of the war booty, than an illusion." Bernanos asserts that this arrangement was a fool's bargain for citizens: "The French wanted freedom, they wanted it with all their heart, they wanted it for all. They believed that, called upon to elect their masters, they thus became masters of the State and that, from then on, strengthening the State, they were strengthening themselves. …. Universal suffrage does not make men freer than the lottery makes them rich. What makes people free, is the spirit of freedom." (Id.) The State has indeed cared much more about forcing individuals to do their soldier's duties, than about forcing making itself respect their citizen's rights. "Amongst other numerous initiatives", Bernanos says sarcastically, "democracy has only succeeded in establishing the institution of democratic war—the "rule of all by all" remains in the clouds of the future, but you've made a great job of "war on all by all". …. The "war on all" is incompatible with the "rule of all", to the point that democratic war remains the business of dictatorships, and particularly of the essential kind of dictatorship that is the dictatorship of consciences." (Bernanos, 1948: 108)

In order to avoid the totalitarian trap, it is important to strongly refute any organic notion of society, according to which the function of each individual is defined according to the needs of the community. For then, the person ceases to exist by himself and for himself, and lives according to society and for society; he must submit to the laws which control the good working order of the social body. The order, the harmony and the unity of the whole justify the submission of each and every one of us. He who refuses to submit must be eliminated in order to avoid any contagion. Such a vision of society, which has inspired many a political doctrine, gives society every right, and man every duty. It destroys the autonomy of a person and only allows the power of a monolithic State to subsist. "It is man who is an organism, of which society is an organ, and not the reverse" asserts Nicolas Berdyaeff. (1963: 121)

The ideology of unity, which at the same time is the ideology of totality, naturally generates an ideology of power, domination and violence. The man of State or, more precisely, the man of The State, is obsessed with the unity of the whole, and thus acquires the obsession for violence. "For the violent man, writes Roland Sublon, everything comes from the One and everything must return to the One." (1979: 14) Sublon reflects on the meaning of the myth of Narcissus and its relation to power and violence. Narcissus is that young man in the Greek legend who, because he despises others, can only fall in love with his own image: "It is Him or nothing and He is Everything; the other, at best, is the enemy." (Ibid., 15) The powerful man cannot resist the temptation of becoming similar to Narcissus. He only loves himself, only listens to his own truth, and consequently, does not hesitate to use violence towards anyone who does not love him and does not submit to his truth. "Let one single alteration appear anywhere, and hidden violence is brought out into the open. The manoeuvres aiming to return to the same are now set in motion, and the strategies deploy their reductive processes.

The other must be reduced, differences must be erased, speech must be silenced, those who wander must be brought back, those who are wrong must be rehabilitated, those who prevent us from going round in circles must be eliminated. Narcissus contradicts, and his smile turns into a scowl. He takes handcuffs and gags out of their hiding places, prepares his torture racks, and cannot wait for Truth—once called into question—to come. The violent man defends Equality and Fraternity; he runs after the Same, but death is what haunts him." (Ibid., 15-16)

Number One is the symbol of violence, and number Three symbolizes nonviolence. In other words, violence is the triumph of the One, while nonviolence is the union of the Three—number Two, that expresses the face-to-face between two individuals who will probably only combine their individualisms, is too poor to symbolize true union.

A free society is pluralist; only a totalitarian society is one. Moisei Ostrogorski claims that the fundamental principle of the new political order established by the democratic revolution is "the principle of union instead of unity" (1903: 221). "Neither in the religious sphere, he writes, nor in society, nor even in the State, has unity been possible since the era of freedom—in which ideas and interests seek to assert themselves in all their diversity—started. Diverse social elements can only be maintained in unity through tyranny, whether it is the armed tyranny of the broadsword, or moral tyranny which started with theocracy, and has continued in the form of social conventions" (Ibid., 218). To prevent tyranny from causing the disappearance of such a variety of ideas and interests, disagreements and conflicts must be allowed to express themselves. The task of political power is to manage conflicts, and not put an end to them. Democracy is conflictual, for conflict allows the acknowledgment and respect of differences.

The foundation of a democratic government lies not in the general will of the people defined as an unchanging entity exerting absolute power over individuals, but in the agreement that citizens reach through the free confrontation of their particular wills. This agreement cannot be obtained for all things and once and for all; its very nature causes it to be constantly challenged, and it must continually renew itself according to the evolution of facts and ideas. Furthermore, in all likelihood, for each question that is debated, the agreement reached will only be that of a majority. So this partial agreement must not put an end to the debate; those who stand outside this majority must be guaranteed the freedom to continue to put their ideas forward. The point, for that matter, is not to look for a majority of ideas that, throughout an entire mandate, would have total power to decide on all matters—this would yet again amount to imposing an apparent unity on all citizens—but to look for a majority of ideas for each matter to be debated. The original social contract must guarantee the effective possibility of producing several different social contracts, i.e., as Ostrogorski pointed out, it must stipulate that "members of society, all equal in rights, shall not use force in their relations, but shall negotiate an understanding each time social life raises a problem of common interest, and that the agreement reached shall stand as law." (Ibid., 226) Obviously, contractual union is more difficult than forced unity, but democracy precisely rests on the respect for this difficulty and the refusal to eliminate it by resorting to violence.

The State bases the legitimacy of its own violence on the necessity to efficiently oppose the violence of individuals and social groups who disturb public order. Of course, there are borderline situations in which it proves difficult, or even impossible, to restore public order without resorting to violence. But political thought suffers a serious distortion, using these borderline cases in which violence can be necessary as a pretext, to build a doctrine that confers on the State the right to resort to physical violence normally in order to ensure civil peace. As soon as citizens have once and for all granted the State the right to resort to violence so as to maintain public order, it will be easy for the State to invoke this right for the defence of its own "safety" against citizens in the exercise of their duties. Once this limit has been overstepped—and history shows us that this is not merely hypothetical—the State does not constitute a guarantee for the security of its citizens anymore, but a threat. For the state-controlled order tends to standardize opinions too. The State is continually tempted to criminalize dissidence, and to repress it as delinquency. The State's official history, like that of war, is written by survivors and victors; it writes off the innocent victims of the State, who are thus condemned to anonymity and oblivion.

Every society, however, must acquire a police force, responsible for "maintaining order" and "enforcing the law". The word "police" has the same etymology as the word "politics" and refers to the government of the "city". The aim of policing, like that of political action, is to pacify social life, i.e. to build a society free from the grip of violence. The function of the police is to work to guarantee the freedom of citizens, to make sure their rights are respected, and to ensure their safety. Police officers must be literally "agents of peace", i.e. they must "make peace" between the individuals and groups living in the same city. The police's essential job is to prevent and, whenever necessary, to resolve conflicts by resorting to the nonviolent methods of interposition, mediation and conciliation.

The police may be required to use methods of "bodily restraint"—in the literal sense of the expression—in order to neutralize violent trouble-makers and to make sure that they can do no further harm. There are particular situations in which it is difficult, or even impossible, to neutralize one or several armed individuals threatening the life of others without resorting to violence. However, even in such circumstances, everything must be attempted to disarm and capture the criminal or criminals, while avoiding hurting or killing them. If despite everything, someone is killed by the police, it is considered a failure, which forbids all "victory communiqués". If the police fails to restore social peace without using lethal violence, the whole of society shares the responsibility for this failure. A democracy is beginning to deny itself when it refuses to acknowledge its own violence as a failure. It would be interesting to ask ourselves whether it would be possible to establish a public ritual during which, each time the use of public force causes the death of a man, a representative of the Republic (for example the Prefect) would recognize that the exercise of lethal violence, even if it was necessary, is always a tragedy, a failure—and that it should be a cause for mourning.

The existence of borderline cases, in which the need to resort to violence becomes essential, cannot be used as a pretext for the rehabilitation of violence as a regular means to ensure public order and restore social peace. In order for the exception not to become the rule, but on the contrary to confirm it, it is crucial to respect the latter even more rigorously. And the rule must be the nonviolent resolution of conflicts.

The violence of the penal system

One of the functions for which the State claims responsibility, in the name of the legitimate defence of citizens, is to arrest, judge and condemn those who have disobeyed the law and undermined public order. But at the same time, the State claims for itself the right to resort to violence to punish violence. The history of the repression of crime by the State may be more frightening than the history of crime. Simone Weil denounced the violence with which the State carries out its role as righter of wrongs. Very often, she asserts, a condemnation pronounced by the criminal justice system is "a crime against humanity" (Weil, 1956: 319): it is then "the basest vengeance" (1957: 41). Claiming to condemn the crime, society scorns the criminal who is crushed by misfortune. The man who has fallen into the hands of the penal system becomes "in the eyes of everyone and in his own eyes, a vile thing, an unwanted object" (1963: 142).

According to Simone Weil, one of the greatest malfunctions of punitive repression is that it shows the greatest severity towards those whom society has treated unfairly, and the greatest indulgence towards those it has favoured. True justice would require quite the contrary: "For faults as well as crimes, the degree of impunity should not increase as one goes down, but as one goes up the social ladder." (Weil, 1962: 34) One of the most difficult political problems to solve is therefore to prevent "a conspiracy to establish itself at the top, in view of obtaining impunity" (Id.). Simone Weil advocates several men being in charge of preventing such a conspiracy, but the important thing is that they should be sufficiently honest so as not to be themselves tempted to be part of it.

In a theocratic society in which penal law is inspired by religious law, in which the tribunals of men claim to give the rulings of a god "righter of wrongs", sanction seeks to be a punishment inflicted on the guilty man as an expiation of his fault, and the history of religions shows us how cruel such principles can be. In his book *The Gospel of life*, Karol Wojtyla confines himself to such an expiatory notion of justice when he writes: "Governments should do something about the violation of personal and social rights, by imposing an adequate <u>expiation</u> of a person's <u>fault</u> (we choose to underline), the necessary condition to be granted his freedom back. In this sense, authority also reaches the goal of defending public order and the safety of people". (Wojtyla, 1995) In a democratic, and therefore secular, society, governments should have no other goal than "defending public order and the safety of people". The function of justice is not to punish a fault, but to make a dangerous man harmless. Penal sanction must therefore involve no punishment, no corporal violence towards the delinquent. Yet prison, as it exists in our societies, remains a corporal punishment which should have been abolished by democracy a long time ago (is prison not considered as a "penitentiary", i.e., literally, as a place where one repents?).

Penal sanction which deprives the delinquent of his freedom by detaining him in prison aims to prevent further offences, on the one hand by preventing the delinquent from committing a second offence, and on the other hand, by dissuading potential delinquents from criminal acts. Indeed, society has the right and the duty to exercise legal restraint—literally a "bodily restraint"—towards individuals who disturb public order, thus neutralizing their ability for social nuisance. It is not possible to organize a litigious society without defining offences and establishing sanctions. But as well as allowing society to defend itself, the penal sanction must allow the delinquent to reintegrate society. If the delinquent loses some of his rights in society, the latter loses none of its duties towards him. The point is not to discuss whether the delinquent deserves to be treated with humanity; society owes itself to treat him with humanity. The inhumanity of the offence must be met with the humanity of the sanction. If it is a good idea to judge a crime according to the rigours of justice, it is also important to treat criminals according to the requirements of goodness. It is not about being indulgent towards the criminal, but about being good.

The aim of the sanction, especially detention when it proves necessary, must be the rehabilitation of the delinquent into society, i.e. his re-socialization. Yet everything leads to turning prison into a place of social exclusion, i.e. de-socialization. Detention conditions in prison have numerous perverse effects on the personality of the prisoner. By forbidding him all communication with others and depriving him of all responsibility, he is forced into regressive attitudes which tend to disintegrate his person. Prison is an inhuman structure which dehumanizes the prisoner. Once he is released, he will have a lot of difficulty in finding his place in society. It has been duly proved by investigations and verified by statistics: prison is a school for criminals; prison sentences do not have the sought-after dissuasive effect on the delinquent. For all that, it is relatively natural for those who are not at all tempted by delinquency to be impressed by prison. From then on, if the incarceration of "petty delinquents" indisputably increases the probabilities of a second offence, why do tribunals keep sending them to prison? Of course, they simply apply the law, but are they not free to create a precedent? In reality, everything happens as if the judges themselves were prisoners of the prison ideology, and that they dreaded the accusations of laxity which public opinion is ready to throw in their direction.

When faced with the manifest failure of the prison centred repression of delinquency, society is challenged to bring its social treatment into play. Detention must only be the last resort when it is necessary to neutralize "major criminals" who are considered to be a real danger to the public. For the others, and they are clearly far more numerous, it is certainly possible to avoid the vicious circle of the penal system thanks to what the Anglo-Saxons call the "judicial diversion". It does not only consist in avoiding prison, but also the tribunal through the suspension of penal action. It is then up to "mediators" to try to reconcile the authors of an offence with its victims. Thus, for infractions against material goods (theft or damage), the objective is their restitution or repair, and compensation for the damage done. If the mediation fails, penal action then becomes necessary, but in most cases, sentences that do not involve imprisonment—such as the obligation to do community service—can still make it possible to avoid incarceration.

For those whose detention proves necessary, the goal must still remain social rehabilitation. It would be better to give up large prisons with several hundred prisoners. The only criterion that is maintained for the organization of such penitentiaries is the efficiency of surveillance and the only goal is to prevent prisoners from escaping. Under these conditions, the prisoner's entire life depends on the logic of repression, and nothing prepares him for his rehabilitation. It would be better to move towards the creation of small units which would allow safety measures combined with socio-therapy measures. But such a program implies that citizens do not persist in avoiding their responsibilities by asking the State to make delinquents disappear behind the highest walls possible, and that they agree to take care of their rehabilitation.

The justification of the death penalty is consistent with the "expiatory" logic of penal justice. It is remarkable that, even in societies where the death penalty has been abolished, public opinion is generally in its favour. It continues to respond to "criminals" following the logic that justifies capital punishment and calls for the lex talionis: "a fracture for a fracture, an eye for an eye, a tooth for a tooth" (Lv 24, 20) and therefore "death for death". It brandishes the respect for the victim in demanding the murder of the assassin. It calls for vengeance and is outraged when it considers that the criminal benefits from a merciful treatment, i.e. humanity. This passionate reaction is prompted by a true desire for violence which foils the "humanist" proclamations of civilization. To justify the death penalty, is to decide to deny once and for all the transcendental and sacred character of human life. If a criminal's life is not sacred, man's life is not sacred at all.

The point is not to try and prove that the death penalty is not dissuasive; nor to consider the sentence that should be substituted for it. The d*eath penalty is impossible because it is unthinkable.* It is unthinkable, because to imagine the death penalty, is to accept the killing of a man who has become "innocent", i.e., literally, who has become harmless. Not even necessity, which is cited in cases of self-defence, can serve as pretext in order to accept killing.

Keeping violence "outside the law"

By institutionalizing violence as a normal—which serves as a norm—and regular—which serves as a rule—means of dealing with the conflicts that inevitably arise within society, the State installs it within the system. From that point onwards, the whole of social relations is contaminated by the logic of violence. In a democracy, the prime goal in politics is to cast violence outside the law; hence the State goes against this goal by including violence within the law.

Naturally, the democratic State and the totalitarian State do not show the same features, and do not deserve the same judgment. But if their relationship with violence differs in practice, this is not the case in theory. Between the doctrine of the liberal State and that of the totalitarian state there is a strong continuity. One proceeds from the other: not only does it borrow most of its arguments, but also most of its technical arsenal. "It is of Power's essence not to be weak", writes Bertrand de Jouvenel. .... "Then comes the time when whoever has taken hold of Power, whether it be a man or a gang, can make fearless use of its controls. .... The power house was there before them: they do no more than make use of it. .... The claws and talons which he then makes felt grew in the season of democracy. It is he that mobilizes the population, but the principle of conscription was founded in a democratic time. .... Even the police state, that most intolerable attribute of tyranny, has grown in the shadow of democracy." (Jouvenel, 1977: 35-36) The liberal State itself is underpinned by an ideology of necessary and legitimate violence which already bears within it the ideology that will help the totalitarian State to assert its own legitimacy. "The cancer of the State", write Emmanuel Mounier in his *Personalist Manifesto* published in 1936, "is formed within our very democracies,

.... "Democratic" state control flows into the totalitarian state like the river to the sea." (1961: 614) "Every centralized and sovereign State", writes Simone Weil, "is powerfully conquering and dictatorial and becomes as such as long as it thinks it is strong enough." (1960: 58) The bureaucratic machine which the liberal State has manufactured is always ready to serve a totalitarian regime. The constitutional and legal guarantees may stay, as long as they go unheeded. History often shows us that democracy is harshly and enduringly mistreated by the violent acts of State agents against citizens, while they claim to act in order to guarantee civil peace.

Reasons of State too often choose to ignore the reasons of democracy. Did not the Minister of the Interior of an extremely liberal French government assert on television, on February the 26th 1987: "Democracy stops where the interest of the State begins"? Of course, statesmen are generally more discreet but, saying that, did the French minister, Charles Pasqua, not reveal a hidden rule of practice among all States? When the security-based ideology clears the State of its acts of violence in the name of a necessary order, then can tyranny arise. The ideology of legitimate violence generates and feeds the doctrines of the totalitarian State. To fight these, that ideology must first be challenged as soon as it appears, quiet and well-intentioned, within the doctrines of the democratic State. The political philosophy of nonviolence refutes the doctrines of the State, in the sense that they by themselves generate a process of ideological legitimation of the violence which constitutes a threat for democracy.

Nonviolence assumes a deep and constant transformation of the State insofar as it seeks to solve conflicts without resorting to violence. However, such a process cannot lead to the disappearance of all political power based on restraint. Wanting to build a government-less society, without laws, police force and justice is a truly utopian vision. Such a society, if ever established, would immediately become de-structured under the effect of the dissolving force of individualism and particularism. Therefore the idea of a society that is inspired by a philosophy of nonviolence aims to establish a political power based on regulation, coordination, mediation, arbitration, and if necessary, on constraint, which would be a "functional equivalent" of the State, but that we consider preferable, so as to ensure the rigour and clarity of concepts, not to call a State. Such a political power would indeed be profoundly different from the State in its relation to violence. Rather than put an end to conflicts by using violence, it would endeavour to take them on and solve them by using nonviolence. This effort should become rooted in a tenacious political will and be embodied in the technical solutions arousing from a vigorous institutional inventiveness. These solutions could not be found in any text-book; they would have to be carried out progressively through multiple social experiments which would not take place on the edges of society, but would constitute a prime institutional investment.

Political nonviolence cannot be absolute, it is necessarily relative, i.e. linked to men, to situations and events. The point is therefore not to start from the pure idea of a perfect society and try to paste it onto reality. The point is, starting from the reality of acts of violence, to create a dynamic process that aims to limit, reduce, and, as far as possible, eliminate them.

There is a chain reaction of economical, social, cultural, police and military acts of violence which is impossible to interrupt as soon as, at one point or another in the process, violence is made legitimate by an ideology. The only way to break the logic of violence, is the pursuit of a momentum in order to reverse the process of the violent development of conflicts. This momentum is that which political philosophy encourages us to implement.

8

Nonviolence as a Political Requirement

The foundation of the Greek city according to Aristotle

To define the characteristics of the political city, Aristotle formulates two propositions: "man is by nature a political animal" (*Politics*, 1253, a 1) and "man alone, among the animals, has speech" (Ibid., 1253, a 5). To begin with, a community is formed "solely for the satisfaction of daily needs", but its true goal is to allow men to "live well" (Ibid., 1252, b 25), that is to say, to live happily by conforming to the requirements of virtue.

Speech allows men to communicate with each other on the subject of that which is useful or harmful and, especially, on the subject of that which is just or unjust. The political city is formed by the association of men who not only wish to meet the needs of their animal existence, but above all, the requirements of their human life. "The city", writes Aristotle, "is a community of equals, aiming at the best life possible." (Ibid., 1328, a 35) All citizens are alike and equal and therefore all have the same rights and the same political duties. "Freedom and equality can only be fulfilled if all citizens, equally and without exception, play the same part in the government and without restrictions." (Ibid., 1292, b 35)

In order for the government not to deteriorate into a domination of the few over the others, but for it to remain a form of service to the community in view of common use and common good, Aristotle advocates that all citizens should exercise power in turn. "When the State", he writes, "is founded upon the principle of equality and likeness, the citizens think that they ought to hold office in turn." (Ibid., 1279, a 5) "It is just", he continues, "that no one should command more than he obeys, and that each citizen should take his turn in commanding and obeying." (Ibid., 1287, a 15) On the subject of the election of the elders, Aristotle is shocked that a citizen should declare himself a candidate by publicly displaying his ambition. "It is for the most worthy citizen", he writes, "to have that responsibility, whether he likes it or not." (Ibid., 1271, a 10)

Therefore, according to Aristotle, the power that rules the city must be equally shared between all the citizens who are all free and similar. Political power as such implies no violence, it is exercised through the deliberation and vote of assembled citizens. But let there be no misunderstanding about that: if in the Greek city, actual political power is not exercised through the use of violence, the life of the city-dwellers is by no means violence-free. First, many of these dwellers—starting with slaves— are excluded from citizenship, and therefore play no part in the ruling of the city. They must devote all their time to "domestic" chores. Only those who are free from those chores can deal with philosophy and politics. Violence is then necessary to maintain order in the city, and defend the community against external threats. "There must be arms", asserts Aristotle, "for the members of a community have need of them, and in their own hands too, in order to maintain authority both against disobedient subjects and against external assailants." (Ibid., 1328, b 5) But Greek thought deserves credit for it has been able to distinguish the exercise of political power from that of violence; if resorting to violence is necessary for the exercising of power, power can be exercised without violence.

The nonviolence of power: Hannah Arendt

Hannah Arendt refers to Greek thought in order to show that violence really is the antithesis of political power. "Political relations in their normal course, she writes, do not fall under the sway of violence. This conviction we find for the first time in Greek Antiquity, insofar as the Greek *polis*, the city-State, defined itself explicitly as a way of life that was based exclusively upon persuasion and not upon violence." (1992: 11)

According to Hannah Arendt, political power arises when men gather to "live together" and decide to act together in order to build their future within one single city. "Power", she writes, "corresponds to man's ability to act, and to act in a concerted way." (1972: 153) The power that arises from common action has no need to resort to the instruments of violence in order to be exercised. "Power and violence are opposites; when the one rules absolutely, the other is absent. .... It is tautology to speak of nonviolent power. Violence can destroy power, but it is completely unable to create it." (Ibid., 166) Hence Hannah Arendt strongly challenges the main theory formulated by Max Weber, from his point of view of a sociologist observing social facts, according to which political power would be a relation of men dominating other men and supported by means of legitimate violence. Man, because he is essentially a being in need of relations, cannot be free alone, he becomes free only in the company of others. He becomes free when he is able to establish relations as free beings with others, that is, relations that present neither threat nor fear, neither domination nor submission. Wherever relations of domination-submission between men prevail, the reign of violence establishes itself, and it signals the failure of political power.

When power fails the men who govern, because their fellow citizens do not trust them, then they have to resort to instruments of constraint, or even violence, in order to force them to obey. Such violence allows them to be feared by men and to dominate them for a certain time, but it gives them no power. And when citizens are able to overcome their fear, when they once again dare to assemble, to speak and act together, then can they resume power and force the men who govern to leave.

Hence political power is based on words and actions that reinforce each other. Once again, Hannah Arendt refers to Greek thought: "To be political, to live in a *polis*, meant that everything was decided through words and persuasion, and not through force and violence. In the eyes of the Greek, restraining, dominating instead of convincing were pre-political methods of dealing with men." (Arendt, 1992: 64) If political action is based on speech, it becomes free from all violence in as much as violence and speech radically exclude one another. Speech can certainly be violent, but violent words become acts of violence and are not speech anymore. Furthermore, "violence itself", as Hannah Arendt writes, "is incapable of speech" (1985: 21-22). Of course, political power owes it to itself to act in order to realize itself in history, but it must act through an action which prolongs the words that brought it to life: "Power is actualized only where word and deed have not parted company, where words are not empty and deeds not brutal, ..., and where deeds are not used to violate and destroy but to establish new relations and create new realities." (Arendt, 1992: 260)

For men, to live a human life together, is to speak and act together; this "speak together" and that "act together" form political life. The words that pass between citizens, free discussion, public deliberation, democratic debate, con-versation, all these things launch and found political action. The latter happens when men turn (the Latin verb *versare* means to turn) towards each other to speak, decide and act together. Violence is therefore not the basis for politics, but its absolute opposite: human speech. A totalitarian regime is characterized by the total destruction of all public space where citizens would be at liberty to speak and act together.

The key to the political city is a public space where men, all equal and alike, freely exchange words in order to make decisions concerning their future together. This "wanting to live together" leads men to build a society by forming an alliance with one another (*societas* means alliance in Latin). To build a society is literally to create an association. The latter expresses itself through a constitution, that is to say, a social contract through which citizens decide on the political project they intend to realize together. Along with Hannah Arendt, it is a good idea to challenge "the vertical version of the social contract" which submits the individual to the domination of the government, and to advocate "the horizontal version of the social contract" through which individuals decide between themselves to conclude a pact that is based on a "relation of reciprocity", which unites them through "mutual commitment" (Arendt, 1972: 93).

The very essence of politics is the dialogue between men. The success of politics, is therefore the success of this dialogue, that is, the agreement between men to decide on their common future. Because the appearance of violence between men always means the failure of their dialogue, violence also always means the failure of politics. The essence of political action is not to act against one another, but to act alongside one another. Of course, the life shared by men within one single city can be disturbed at any moment by conflicts caused by individuals who do not respect the original alliance. It is important to solve these conflicts in order to restore social peace and make the dialogue between citizens possible once again. The resolution of conflicts is a condition of political life, but it does not constitute it. The individuals who resort to violence in order to realize their passions, satisfy their desires or have their particular interests prevail have already left the place where the political project of the community to which they belonged is being developed and realized. Their action is not consistent with the public space that is the political city anymore. They will certainly need to be joined so that they can be fought and their ability for violence neutralized. This struggle is necessary in order to preserve the possibility of political action for the community, but it does not constitute political action for rational men.

For all that, speech still offers possibilities in the fight against violence, like the palaver tradition in certain African societies. "In these traditional societies", writes Jean Duvignaud, "when faced with an act of violence, the solution was not vendetta, but a discussion which would bring the group together and through which violence would transmute into speech" (1980: 7). It is then possible to develop a solution for the conflict, and to reintegrate the delinquent or delinquents into the community of men who speak to each other.

It is therefore always advisable to define politics in relation to the projects that it bears within itself; not only does this project—which is to bring people together in a common action—leaves no room for violence, but it can only be carried out through nonviolence. In its end as well as its modalities, political action is organically in tune with nonviolence. Only the philosophy of nonviolence puts the political city back in its true perspective, and gives it its true dimensions back. Indeed, if political action is characterized by the fact that it is nonviolent, violence, in its very nature, is "anti-political", whatever its necessity may sometimes be. At best, it could perhaps be conceded that it is pre-political in so far as it precedes, and under certain circumstances, prepares and makes political action possible.

Violence, whose goal is always death, thus finds itself in fundamental contradiction with the essential requirement of politics, which is to build a society that is free from the grip of violence. In order for the respective rights of all citizens and all people to prevail, the government of the city must endeavour to solve peacefully the inevitable conflicts that arise between members of one single society, and between different societies. The government must therefore pacify social life in order to make political life possible, which not only implies the will to establish peace, but also the will to establish it through peaceful, i.e. nonviolent means.

Philosophical reflection does not allow us to assert that nonviolence is *the answer* that offers the technical means to face political realities under all circumstances, but it leads us to assert that it is *the question* which, in the face of political realities, allows us to look for the best answer under all circumstances. If, straightaway, we wanted to consider nonviolence as *the* right answer, we would only see the difficulties of its implementation, and we would probably rapidly convince ourselves that they are insurmountable. However, if we consider nonviolence to be *the* right question, we can then look upon it as a challenge to be taken up, and set ourselves to look for the best answer for it. Until now, men have generally not asked themselves the (right) question of nonviolence, and they have accepted the (wrong) answer that violence offered straightaway. Asserting that nonviolence is always the right question should prevent us from believing that violence is the right answer too quickly. For, if it is true that the right question does not immediately give us the right answer, it directs our search in the direction where we are most likely to find it. And this is already decisive. For the act of asking the right question is a necessary condition—even if it is not enough—to find the right answer.

As soon as violence is legitimized for the sake of reasons of State, it is given free reign within history. This is precisely what history teaches us. When faced with all the irreparable harm which violence causes when it becomes the specific means of politics, it is not necessary to seek out complex moral considerations in order to refute it. The reasons to do so lie in political action itself. And they are imperative.

Every act of violence, especially if it is the government's deed, must be seen as a failure of political action in its attempt to control conflictual situations without resorting to violence. The very fact that it was not able to solve a conflict other than through violence shows a malfunction in society; it must not be trivialized as if it were functioning normally. In the face of the necessity to resort to violence, the urgency is not to justify it, but to look for nonviolent means which in the future will allow, as far as possible, to prevent such a situation from happening again.

Democracy and citizenship

It is generally admitted that democracy is the political project that is most suited to a just and free society. But the very concept of democracy finds itself covered in a fundamental ambiguity. According to its etymological sense, the word democracy means "government of the people, by the people and for the people", to take up the expression used in the French Constitution to define the principle of a Republic. But the word democracy also stands for a government that respects human rights and liberties, for each and every man. These two meanings might not contradict each other, but in order to realize democracy, the people must be the bearer of an ethical requirement that is the basis for the democratic ideal. Democracy is a gamble on the wisdom of the people. Unfortunately, the people's democratic wisdom is not always present in political events. A people can become a crowd, and passion can seize hold of a crowd more easily than reason does.

In reality, true democracy is not popular democracy, but citizen democracy. Democracy wishes to be the government of citizens, by citizens and for citizens. The citizenship of each woman and man in the city is the basis of democracy. The exercise of citizenship gives the life of the individual a public dimension. Of course, man needs to have a private life, but this private life away from others is not enough to allow him to become himself. For that purpose, he must venture outside his house, enter the public space, and go to meet others. Man is essentially a being in need of relations, able to form alliances with others through words and actions. He only comes into being through this relationship of mutual recognition and respect. From then on, it becomes possible to build a society based on freedom and equality. The citizen's freedom must not be defined negatively due to the fact that he is not subjected to the abusive restraints of political power, but positively, due to the fact that he effectively takes part in this power. The democratic ideal implies an "equal" distribution of power as well as possession, and knowledge, between citizens. This ideal is perfect, but it has one major inconvenient in that it is unachievable. However, it shows a direction, it allows a method and creates dynamics.

In order to create citizenship, it is important to refer to universal principles that recognize and guarantee the inalienable rights and liberties of every human being. As soon as specific criteria such as race, ethnic origin or religion are referred to in the creation of citizenship, democracy is already being denied. For division and opposition are thus caused between men, and are very likely to degenerate into acts of violence one day. Citizenship is only possible between men who recognize each other as equal and alike, beyond all their differences. However, the universal should not be attempted through the standardization of cultures, but through their convergence. Every culture tends to assert its superiority over other cultures and to assume for itself the privileges of universality. The concept of "universal culture" is totalitarian; it justifies conquests, war and domination. It is not Culture that shows the characteristics of universality, but political ethics creating respect for mankind, i.e. the respect of others in their uniqueness.

Thinking about the universality of beauty leads us to a better understanding of the universality of truth. Truth, like beauty, must address the freedom of man, without ever seeking to impose itself through restraint. Truth, like beauty, must reconcile man with himself, thus paving the way for the reconciliation of all men with each other. The universality of ethics, which is the basis for the wisdom of the rational man, thus presents a deep analogy with the universality of art. Art manages to transcend the culture that it is born in, all the while expressing its uniqueness. Art attains the universal, whereas no work of art is similar to any other. Through different forms that are linked to the differences between cultures, art—whether it be poetry, literature, music or painting—achieves a meaning which speaks to every human being. In every culture, art expresses the same questioning about man's fate, and through this questioning, it formulates the same quests and requests. Hence ethics must successfully express human universality.

In reality, the people does not express itself and decides nothing. Only citizens can express themselves, and only a minority of them decide. But this decision is democratic in so far as it results from a broad public discussion in which all can take part. Yet, in representative democracies, the words of citizens have but little importance and this during elections, and maybe referendums. The public space in which the citizen exercises his right to speak tends to amount to the size of the polling booth. If public discussion is the essence of democracy, then nothing is less democratic than a society in which the citizen only truly has the possibility of expressing himself in the isolation of the polling booth. Obviously, we cannot fail to recognize the decisive role of the organization of free elections in the long walk of peoples towards their liberation from tyranny and despotism. We simply wish to highlight the fact that free elections may be necessary for democracy, but they are not enough. Citizen participation in elections cannot be a sufficient participation in the re-public, i.e. a sufficient participation in the decisions that direct the course of public affairs. The citizen does not exercise his power by voting, but in fact delegates it to a representative upon which he will have no further control until the next election. The citizen does not "express his opinion" by voting, but in fact "gives" it to one of those who demand it loudly. The principle of delegation is not that which must be challenged—it is necessary whenever direct democracy is not possible—but its practical modalities, which make it seem like a relinquishment of power.

Ultimately, democracy's claim that it allows citizens to rule is broadly speaking deceptive and misleading. It is not true that in democratic regime citizens take part directly in the decisions of political power. According to Karl Popper, the philosopher of Austrian origin, the idea that democracy is "the power of the people" is dangerous. For in reality, "every member of society knows that he does not rule, and so he feels that democracy is a fraud" (Popper, 1993: 131). He therefore believes that democracy should be less pretentious: its goal should not be to give power to the people, but to prevent power from becoming tyrannical and depriving the people of its freedom. In other words, "democracy is a way of preserving the Rule of Law" (Ibid., 190). For Karl Popper, the main question for democracy is not as much that of power, but that of its limitation: "The main thing", he asserts, "is that the government should not have too much power" (Ibid., 106). He wants a State but he wants as little of it as possible: he wants a "minimal State" (Ibid., 114).

Democracies do not allow the people to exercise power, but they grant citizens the right to control power. The most important thing is that citizens should be able to remove the government as soon as they consider its politics to be contrary to the interests of the city, and above all when they do not respect the Rule of Law. In order to define democracy, Karl Popper therefore rules out the idea of "power for the people" and replaces it with the idea of "judgment by the people" (Ibid., 108): "We cannot all govern and rule, but we can all judge the government, we can all play the part of members of a jury." (Ibid., 133) However, the judgment of members of a citizen jury itself is fallible, and cannot constitute an absolute guarantee against the violation of a person's rights by the government. Members of a jury can be tempted by "the fashionable (and nearly always stupid) ideologies that turn true into false even when the truth is there before our eyes" (Ibid., 142). That is why Karl Popper thinks that the most important task is to develop a culture of nonviolence among citizens, in order to eliminate violence from people's minds.

The number and the law

Democracy claims to base its legitimacy on majority rule; but the latter does not guarantee respect for the law. Majority rule does not guarantee respect for the ethical requirements that are the basis for democracy. The dictatorship of the many can be more implacable than the tyranny of one single person. Antidemocratic forces have always leaned on majority rule in their attempts to impose their power on the whole of society. What should happen when the will of the majority, that is to say "the will of the people", opposes justice? For the democratic citizen, there can be no doubt: ethical requirements must take precedence over the will of the majority, the law must prevail over the majority. In a true democracy, respect for the law is much more restrictive than respect for universal suffrage.

Citizenship cannot be based on the collective discipline of all individuals, but on the responsibility, and therefore personal autonomy of every man. In the name of his conscience, every citizen can and must oppose majority rule when it generates blatant injustice. A dissenting sense of citizenship thus exists, a civic dissent which, in the name of a democratic ideal, refuses to abide by majority rule.

Democracy is not guaranteed by a powerful State, but by the Rule of Law. The latter is not composed of the *values* of democracy, but of the *institutions* of democracy that embody and historicise these values. The Rule of Law is a fragile institutional balance that always runs the risk of being broken. The threats to democratic order are initially generated by ideologies based on discrimination and exclusion. Whether it is nationalism, racism, xenophobia, religious fundamentalism or economic liberalism exclusively based on the quest for profit, all these ideologies threaten democracy. From then on, promoting and defending democracy—these two approaches reinforce each other and must be undertaken together—initially consists in fighting against those ideologies whose seeds are spreading inside as well as outside society. Indeed, these ideologies know no borders.

Anti-democratic ideologies are all linked to the ideology of violence. They never hesitate to proclaim that violence is necessary and legitimate as soon as it becomes theirs to use. That is why, ultimately, the threat against democracy is always that of violence and, the defence of democracy is consequently always a struggle against violence. But it is only possible to challenge anti-democratic ideologies, which assert the legitimacy of violence when it supports their cause, efficiently, by opposing them to the political philosophy of nonviolence as a basis for democracy.

The threats to democracy do not only express themselves through the spreading of perverse ideas that undermine the principles of democracy; they are also, and above all, present in the organization of actions which aim to destabilize the institutions of democracy. The struggle against these ideologies can therefore not amount to a theoretical debate, it has to be a combat. All citizens who remain attached to democracy must then rise up, gather and get organized in order to resist. But, then again, it is essential that the means of the struggle for the defence of democracy be consistent with the values and principles of democracy, that is to say that they be nonviolent.

The great acts of violence in history—wars, massacres and genocides—are not natural or spontaneous, they have been thought through and organized. The hatred and passion that came with them were generated by ideological propaganda and political constructions. The irrational part, which has lead individuals towards killing, was prepared by rational constructions. Because no political force has been able to oppose these constructions in time, that what became inevitable has come to create the irreparable.

Ideologies based on discrimination and exclusion flourish on the fertile ground of emotions and passions which, most often, direct mens' collective behaviour more strongly than reason does. Racism, xenophobia, and more generally, any attitude of hatred towards others do not only rest upon false ideas, but also upon a set of fears and sufferings. In order to fight these ideas efficiently, we must both understand these fears and sufferings and endeavour to heal them. In this respect, nonviolent action appears rather like a form of group therapy.

Every political philosophy, every social project and every strategy of struggle that does not take into account the irrational and affective factors which strongly affect human relations, would be doomed to failure. When passion is the main drive for collective behaviour, it is not enough—when seeking to appease social and political life—to address individuals with logical and rational arguments. Not that it is pointless to appeal to reason, but even the best philosophy could not do without the support of social psychology, that can help individuals to become reasonable. Faced with a social pathology which affects individuals, of course, but as members of a specific group, it is a good idea to try and develop that which Charles Rojzman calls a "social therapy" (1992: 35). This method of intervention aims to train individuals to develop a "democratic spirit". "This training", Charles Rojzman specifies, "must essentially rest on a diagnosis concerning the needs, desires, fears and hates of individuals, groups and institutions, and a therapeutic treatment which by nature can only address individuals. A new form of civic education will have to teach us to know these needs, emotions, passions, and give us tools to control them." (Ibid., 43-44)

The religions have made a pact with the empire of violence

Until now, the great historical religions have played a vital part in the emergence of cultures and civilizations, and have left a deep mark on the construction of political cities. However, there is no choice but to admit that they have failed to understand the philosophical requirements of nonviolence, and have joined forces with the prevailing ideologies of necessary, legitimate and honourable violence. By making a pact with the empire of violence, they have ignored the ethical, spiritual, metaphysical—probably also theological—and political stakes of nonviolence. They have not only recognized that violence was a natural right of man as part of the legitimate defence of his interests, but, on many occasions, they have also sacralized violence by offering it the support of their God. When religion gave violence its blessing, violence did not become sacred, but religion became sacrilegious. Religion then found itself deeply tarnished, but it must have been tarnished before, to be able to make such a pact with violence.

Religions have often inclined men to intolerance rather than benevolence towards others, through the rigid teachings of an exclusive and dogmatic speech. They have thus sustained the exclusive communitarianism groups that profess discrimination, exclusion and violence. How many times has history not proved Freud right when he claims that: "A religion, even when it calls itself the religion of love, must be hard and unloving towards those who do not belong to it. Fundamentally indeed every religion is in this same way a religion of love for all those whom it embraces; while cruelty and intolerance towards who do not belong to it are natural to every religion." (Freud, 1981: 160) Throughout history, the certainty that God was "on their side" has convinced many groups that it was just and necessary to fight other groups to the death. Even today, all over the world, believers—idolizing their own religion—rise up in arms to fight infidels.

The doctrinal body of religions has therefore been corrupted by the ideology of violence. This religious sacralization of violence has often been a decisive factor in giving it free rein within the history of men, peoples and nations. Religions have therefore strongly contributed to the confinement of peoples' political culture to the ideology of violence. More precisely, Western history bears the mark of innumerable crusades, wars of religion, colonial wars and "just" wars, which have all been legitimized by Christianity. The symbol of the cross, the symbol of the non-violent death of Jesus of Nazareth against whom the established powers had united, has taken the shape of a sword and symbolizes the violence of Christians.

It is probably not for philosophy to pronounce itself on the existence of God; but if philosophy does not make it possible to know the true God, at least it allows us to identify the false gods—and this is decisive in itself. Indeed, reason teaches us that the gods who make a pact with the violence of men, who support it and sometimes order it, most certainly live in the pantheon of false gods. The "god of armies" is thus certainly a false god. The real God can only be a "disarmed God". When man claims that a god is supportive of violence, these are not the words of God. These are the words of a man about God; these are the words of a man who is mistaken in what he says about God. Man always needs to justify his own violence and, when he believes in a god, he needs to convince himself that this god justifies his violence. So, not only were the authors of many allegedly sacred texts wrong in believing that God justified the violence of their people, but they have misled and continue to mislead all those who draw inspiration from their texts to justify their own violence.

Simone Weil regretted that "the philosophical cleansing" of the Catholic religion had never been undertaken (1953: 264). In reality, the philosophical cleansing of all religions has never been undertaken and must be undertaken. It is indeed for philosophy to judge religion, and if the principle of nonviolence is indeed the basis of philosophy, this cleansing must be undertaken by asserting the primacy of this principle over all "religious" considerations. It must necessarily lead to a radical break with all the religious doctrines of just wars and legitimate violence. But will "religious" men have the courage to bring about such a break and question their "tradition"? It certainly would not be reasonable to be sure of a positive answer.

Political parties

One of the characteristics of parliamentary democracy is to be dominated by the control of political parties. These are one of the chief expressions of the freedom of association that is granted to citizens by the Rule of Law. In theory, their function is to allow members of society to play a direct part in political life according to the diversity of their opinions. The French Constitution of the 5th Republic (instigated by Charles de Gaulle) was the first in France to acknowledge the role of political parties who "shall contribute to the exercise of suffrage" (article 4). The role played by political parties in favour of democracy can be assessed by observing what happens in societies when the State refuses their existence: it is the start of an immediate totalitarian spiral.

The organization of political parties should be questioned as to whether they allow citizens to exercise their own power fully within the city. Right at the start of modern democracy, Moisei Ostrogorski, one of the pioneers of political sociology, highlighted the limits and insufficiencies of political parties. Analysing the creation and development of political parties in Great Britain at the beginning of the century, Ostrogorski notes their tendency to force their members by letting conformism prevail. "Party membership", he writes, "to a large extent became an object of devotion, a faith with an orthodoxy, and almost a cult. .... The followers of the party were all provided in a lump with a stock of convictions, which spared them the trouble of all personal exertion. "We now think in battalions", as a shrewd observer, a Northumberland workman, remarked on this subject. .... Every attempt at asserting the freedom and independence of political thought was now repressed; for every difference of opinion was a blow struck at the unity of the party." (Ostrogorski, 1979: 45-46) Ostrogorski considers that the organizational and functional methods of parties, by fabricating and imposing a stereotyped opinion on every subject, "have caused the dwindling of individuality and the growth of formalism in political life in all aspects, culminating in the highest sphere of political relations, that of leadership" (Ibid., 47). He also denounces "electoral methods which consist in hypnotizing the voter"; from then on, national consultations do not really express the will of citizens (Ibid., 71). Furthermore, he points out that the councillor, instead of representing his voters, is more of a delegate for his party. "The elected representative", he notes, "sits in Parliament less for a particular constituency than for one party or the other" (Ibid., 74).

Ostrogorski asks how it is possible to "put right the moral drive of citizens", which finds itself "compressed by the rigid party as if by a vice" (Ibid., 101). It is only possible, he answers, by putting an end to the party system, since experience has shown that it does not meet the requirements of democracy, and that it ultimately impoverishes political life. For that purpose, members of the sovereign people must first of all reappropriate their "power of social intimidation", that is to say instead of being intimidated by rulers, they should themselves intimidate them (Ibid., 181). To achieve this end, Ostrogorski suggests that the existence of rigid and permanent parties—whose goal is the seizure of State power—should be put an end to, and replaced by associations of citizens specially formed in view of a specific political claim. According to him, such a method of organization and action is able to revitalize democracy, and give individuals the practical possibility of exercising their power as citizens.

Many years later, Simone Weil, in a text which she wrote in London in 1943 for the "Free French" administration, also radically criticized the party system, and agreed with many analyses previously made by Ostrogorski. According to her, the political party is the very example of a social group in which "the collective dominates thinking beings" (Weil, 1957: 132). She gives it two different definitions which, for her, are equivalent: "A political party is a machine for fabricating collective passion. A political party is an organization built in order to exert collective pressure on each of its members' thoughts." (Id.) This pressure exerts such influence on the individual that he has great difficulty in resisting it. This requires incredible strength of character which the majority of citizens lack. The political party which is, by nature, but a means, becomes its own end in itself. It has no other objective than its own development. From then on, "every political party is totalitarian—potentially, and by aspiration" (Ibid., 131). Simone Weil is indignant about the fact that a party member who would be determined to listen to the inner voice of his own conscience, in the face of any political or social problem, would probably be excluded from the party; or the party would at least not invest him for any election, and he would therefore never be elected by the nation. In fact, considering the quasi-monopoly of parties in politics, that man would suddenly be unable to intervene in public affairs efficiently. As for those who wish to take part in running the city, they must resign themselves to "going through the mill of parties" (Ibid., 141). But in most cases, men accept to submit to party discipline, for it ultimately allows then not to think, and "nothing is more comfortable than not having to think" (Ibid., 143).

Simone Weil considers that the renunciation of autonomy of thought, of judgment and of action on behalf of those who are elected is contrary to the spirit of the French Revolution. The people of 1789, she claims, "would never have thought possible that a representative of the people could have abdicated his dignity to the point of becoming the disciplined member of a party" (Weil, 1962: 42). In a real democracy, candidates should appear in front of voters and assert their convictions, their analyses and their suggestions. Then, "those elected will join forces or not according to the natural game of affinities" (Weil, 1957: 144). Of course, such a decision and management process in the running of public affairs would be quite complex, much more difficult than the one resulting from the game of parties; but might not the latter, by dint of simplifying democracy, eventually put an end to it? Democracy is never simple. So Simone Weil sees only advantages in the suppression of parties which enslave minds and eventually establish a true "spiritual and mental oppression" (Ibid., 141).

She lays down two conditions in order that an "association for promoting ideas" should exert no constraint on its members thinking: on the one hand, "that excommunication may not be applied", and on the other hand that, "ideas must really be put into circulation" (Weil, 1962: 46). The environments in which men gather and exchange ideas must thus be kept "fluid" (Weil, 1957: 145). This fluidity is that which distinguishes a group of ideas that can be source of improvement for all, from a political party that weakens the individual by depriving him of his autonomy of thought and action.

Ultimately, if Simone Weil's proposition to put an end to political parties does not seem very realistic, her analysis of their malfunction is not any less perceptive. There is no doubt that the monolithism which parties adopt sterilizes the reflection within them, and, indeed, in the whole of society. There is a strong tendency within parties—by virtue of the very structure of their organization—according to which discipline eventually jeopardizes freedom of thought. Democracies suffer from this lack of intellectual democracy within political parties.

Vaclav Havel—while he was still but a dissident facing up to the totalitarian regime of Czechoslovakia, and was thinking about the best political model for the development of democracy—challenged the party system with similar arguments to those of Ostrogorski and Simone Weil. "This static conception, he writes, of rigid, conceptually sloppy and politically pragmatic mass political parties run by professional apparatuses and releasing the citizen from all forms of concrete and personal responsibility .... can only with great difficulty be imagined as the source of humanity's rediscovery of itself." (Havel, 1989: 217) He saw in the party system which "offers privileges as a reward for obedience to a group fighting for power", the beginning of "bureaucratization, corruption and anti-democracy" (Havel, 1989: 21). In order to revivify the connective tissue of democracy, Vaclav Havel envisages the creation of "structures that are open, dynamic and small" which "should derive from a living dialogue with the genuine needs from which they arise; and when these needs are gone, the structures should also disappear" (Havel, 1989: 154). Contrary to formalized political parties, these structures should allow citizens to think—not about the technical solutions which must be brought to political problems—but about the ethical values that ought to be the basis for the political project needing to be undertaken. "The issue", states Havel, "is the rehabilitation of values like trust, openness, responsibility, solidarity, love. I believe in structures that are not aimed at the "technical" aspect of the execution of power, but at its significance." (Ibid., 153)

Refusing the primacy of economics over politics

Nowadays, the public space where men tend to gather, is the market, or the trade fair; however, citizens do not gather there, but producers, salesmen and consumers do. According to Hannah Arendt, individuals are drawn to the market place by "the desire to see products, and not to see men" (1988: 271). This fact clearly expresses a primacy of economics over politics which characterizes our societies.

First of all, man must face the necessity to satisfy his vital needs: food, clothing and shelter. These needs are in no way contemptible, and man cannot claim to be free from the necessity to satisfy them. He would be deluding himself in hoping one day to be free from the necessity to work. For that matter, inactivity and idleness generate boredom, and the latter is already a downtime. The daily obligation to satisfy vital needs is an essential structure of human existence, and the necessity to work which results from it gives meaning to time. But man's economic activity has become the prisoner of a "commercial order" which fundamentally denies the citizen by reducing the individual to being a mere producer/consumer. Until now, work has taken up the essential of individuals' lives, and has deprived ordinary citizens of philosophical reflection and political action. The worker has dominated the citizen so much, that the city's political life has become seriously atrophied. As a consequence, and paradoxically, individuals who are not engaged in gainful employment do not enjoy social recognition. This is particularly true for women.

Homo faber—who makes tools—has supplanted *homo sapiens*— who thinks and seeks to become wise. The latter can certainly not despise the former: not only would he not exist without him, but the man who invents tools to improve his life conditions already shows great intelligence. But *homo faber's* labour ought to allow *homo sapiens* to take time to think not only about the efficiency of tools, but especially about the meaning of life. Yet, precisely, the fabrication of tools still takes up so much of man's time today, that he does not have time to look for the wisdom which gives his life meaning and transcendence.

The great preoccupation of politicians themselves too often is to organize the economic space, and rarely to develop the political space. The primacy that is given to economics over politics has caused society to fall into the clutches of essentially economic conflicts of interest. Political action is thus perverted, since it serves economic interests. Yet political action is fundamentally different from economic "making". Political discussion does not only seek to decide on the necessary means of living together, but also to clarify the reasons to live together. But then, political debate has neglected the question: "why act?", to focus mainly on the question: "how to do?". Therefore, because of the primacy of economics over politics, political power has deteriorated into administrative and bureaucratic power. In order to bring new life to democracy, political action and debate—mistreated by economism—must be rehabilitated.

One of the major challenges with which we are confronted today is to imagine a new way of organising and structuring our time, so that the latter would not mostly be taken up by work. On account of scientific and technological discoveries, the satisfaction of mens' vital needs does not require them to devote most of their time to work. But the individual is then faced with "free time", which often worries and frightens him. This "free time" appears to him as "empty time" which he does not know how to fill. And the solution is not to invent new forms of leisure, new distractions that would only serve to "pass the time", i.e. to "kill" it. The very concept of "leisure civilization" must be challenged. This spare time should allow men to gain better access to the freedom of citizens through philosophical reflection and political action. Nothing would be worse than for men to be simultaneously both workers without work and citizens without citizenship.

One of the most harmful consequences of time structuring in societies where economism prevails, is that workers-citizens have little or no time to read. Yet reading is one of the main cultural vectors. A people whose citizens do not read, while oral traditions weaken, becomes a people without culture, vulnerable to ideologies. Images, and notably televisual images, could certainly play an important part is the access of individuals to culture, but it would be necessary to uphold criteria in order for television programmes not to be purely commercial. For all that, we do not think that an image-based culture should substitute for a book-based culture. In our societies, the decline in citizens reading is somewhat frightening. The majority know nothing about the great literary and philosophical works which constitute, according to Tolstoy's expression, "the intellectual and moral treasure that humanity has accumulated" (1923: 103). This decline in reading is such an important shortfall that it would be a serious error to resign ourselves to it; it is therefore important to try and make up for it. The philosophical culture of citizens is one of democracy's essential foundations. Karl Popper thought that "the cultural miracle of fifth century Athens was the result of the emergence of a free market in books, which was also due to Athenian participatory democracy" (1993: 97). The fact that philosophical debates should be the privilege of a circle of initiates ought to be considered as a serious malfunction of democracy. One of the most useful tasks would be to create times and places which would allow each and everyone to become familiar with the reading and discussing of great literary and philosophical works.

The requirements of ecology

There is a profound connection—which is not just symbolic—between the wrong done to "nature" and the violence done to man. Man owes it to himself to respect nature. Man is part of nature, but, more so than that, nature is part of his humanity. When he inflicts "violence" onto his environment, he himself suffers its after-effects. The destruction of his "living environment" has a direct effect on his "quality of life". Man becomes literally ill from the damages he inflicts on nature. The pollution of air, water and earth does violence to man, and this violence can be fatal. Hence the need to respect and protect nature does not proceed from sentimentalism, but from an ethical requirement, that is the basis for a political imperative.

Respect for nature starts with having a good knowledge of it, and eco-logy allows us to acquire it. Ecology is above all the study of natural environments and systems in which living beings live. This study then makes it possible to research and formulate the rules and norms to which man's activities—notably economic activities—must submit, in order to respect the natural rhythm and balance of these systems.

Prevailing economic doctrines have let themselves become blinded by the tyrannical logic of productivism. They have not understood the full extent of the contradictions and dead ends which technical progress—left to its own devices—has led us into. They have not been able to turn away in time from the end of the 18th century scientific illusions, following which continuous social progress has been hoped for, as the inevitable consequence of linear technical progress. We must now acknowledge the failure of the scientific conception and the realization of industrial progress. This does not mean that all technological innovation should be banned, through a fallacious apology of the "good old days". But it does mean that it has become urgent to control the industrial development of our societies, and to redefine the criteria according to which we must control it. Limits have been overstepped, thresholds have been crossed, and it is not possible anymore to assert the idea of punctual excess and abuse. The industrial production system itself must be challenged, and submitted to the imperatives of ecology. Producing differently implies working differently, consuming differently, and ultimately, living differently, i.e. enjoying a better life.

For a long time, a very long time, men have had to protect themselves from all sorts of dangers that nature threatened them with; today, through the technical power that they have gained, men are the ones who pose serious dangers to nature. This, as the German philosopher Hans Jonas highlighted in his book *The Imperative of Responsibility*, is a radically new situation which requires that the very foundations of the ethics controlling man's power to act be reconsidered. The radically new fact is that the power which man has acquired over nature is "above all a power of destruction" (Jonas, 1993: 190) and that, consequently, "the promise of modern technology has turned into a threat" (Ibid., 13). We now know that Earth is mortal. Obviously, the worst may not happen, but it has become a possibility. This possibility really must therefore be taken into account. "The solidarity of man's and nature's destinies—of which we have become aware through danger—also makes us rediscover the autonomy of the dignity of nature and commands us to respect its integrity beyond its utilitarian dimension." (Ibid., 188)

From now on, man must face the state of vulnerability which his power to act has caused nature to be in, and he must realize that nature has become his responsibility. Man's responsibility through his actions only used to concern an immediate future, whereas today it stretches across time, and concerns a more distant future. He must therefore act so that human life on Earth may still be possible in the future. "An imperative responding to the new type of human action and addressed to the new type of agency that operates it might run thus: "Act so that the effects of your action are compatible with the permanence of genuine human life"; or expressed negatively "Act so that the effects of your action are not destructive of the future possibility of such life"." (Jonas, 1993: 30-31)

Faced with his new power to act, man is under the obligation to define the rules of a new ethic which must take the long-term consequences of his actions into account, of an ethic which must be an "ethic of the Future" (Ibid., 50), or more precisely, an "ethic of responsibility towards the Future" (Ibid., 133). However, in order for will to meet its ethical obligation, the latter cannot only be based on reason, but also on a feeling: "It is, Hans Jonas claims, the feeling of responsibility" (Ibid., 123). According to him, "it is a metaphysical responsibility in and of itself, since man has become dangerous not only for himself, but for the entire biosphere" (Ibid., 187).

Hence men are obliged to make a deal with nature, allowing them to live in symbiosis with it: it is what Michel Serres calls "the natural contract". "That means we must add to the exclusively social contract a natural contract of symbiosis and reciprocity. .... An armistice contract in the objective war, a contract of symbiosis, for a symbiont recognizes the host's rights, whereas a parasite—which is what we are now—condemns the one he pillages and inhabits to death, not realizing that in the long run he is condemning himself to death too." (Serres, 1992: 67) Such a contract turns nature into a "subject of the law" (Id.), which ought to be respected as such.

9

The Nonviolent Resolution of Conflicts

Halting mimetic rivalry

Through the simplification that it introduces into reality, violence breaks the complexity of existing links between things and men. A conflictual situation always results from a tangle, a most complex overlapping of numerous causes. To solve a conflict, it is necessary to try to act simultaneously on all the causes which have generated it. Violence is incapable of conducting these different actions; because of its simplifying mechanism, it only retains one cause, and acts in one single direction.

It is said that Alexander the Great, king of Macedonia, stopped in Gordium, capital of Phrygia, at the start of his campaign against the Persians. There he learned that an oracle had promised the Asian Empire to the one who would undo the intricate knot tying the yoke to the pole on the chariot of Gordium, king of Phrygia. But, since he was not able to untie the knot, Alexander cut it loose with his sword. Alexander's gesture symbolizes the violent act perfectly: it cuts the knot when it should be untied. In doing so, it irreparably destroys the rope that constituted the knot, and renders it definitely useless.* As for violence, it is incapable of contributing to the outcome of a conflict. Only nonviolent action can undo the Gordian knot of a

---

* Translator's note. In French, the word *dénouement*—which means "the outcome", but literally is "the untying"—refers precisely to the resolution of a conflict.

conflict, thus making its resolution possible. Cutting the knot rather than taking time to undo it shows impatience. Violence is always im-patience. Violence is precipitation; it is action breaking the speed limit. It does violence to time, which is necessary to the growth and maturation of all things. Not that time acts by itself, but it grants action the period it needs in order to become efficient. Hence the virtue of patience is at the heart of the requirement of nonviolence. It is not made of resignation, but of determination; it takes all the time it needs in order to reach its ends. Patience has the strength of perseverance.

Let us consider René Girard's theory, according to which the origin of a conflict between two adversaries lies in the mimetic rivalry that opposes them, for the appropriation of one single object. The strategy of nonviolent action intends to put an end to the mimicry by which each of the two rivals imitates the other's violence, returning blow for blow, fracture for fracture, eye for eye, tooth for tooth. The very principle of nonviolent action lies in the refusal to be pulled into an endless spiral of violence. Jesus of Nazareth challenges the old *Lexis Talionis* which is based on the imitation of an adversary's violence, and teaches us not to use violence to resist it. "On the contrary", he states, "if someone strikes you on the right cheek, turn to him the other also." (Mt 5, 38-39) What he also teaches, is to break the endless spiral of mimicry by refusing to imitate the violence of the one who took the initiative of aggression, of he-who-started-it. To turn the other cheek after the first has been struck, is not to submit to the adversary, but to face up to him; it is not to submit resignedly to the logic of violence, it is on the contrary to fight against this logic with all one's strength.

To decide not to imitate the violence of our adversary, is to wish to avoid being contaminated by his cruelty. "The existence of an enemy", write Edgar Morin and Anne Brigitte Kern, "fosters both their barbarousness and my own. Even when resulting from a one-sided blindness, enmity becomes reciprocal as soon as felt enmity makes us hostile in turn. .... We must jam the infernal machine that, always and everywhere, makes cruelty out of cruelty." (1993: 200-201)

In order to break this logic, the conflict must constantly be refocussed on the object of its cause, and not allowed to degenerate into pure people rivalry. Jesus opts for a radical solution, and claims that it is best to give up on the object rather than to start a war with whoever covets it. And he goes even further: in order to be sure to break the logic of violent confrontation, he suggests that the rival should be offered a second object which he does not covet, or at least not yet. He therefore advises his friends to give their coat to whoever wishes to take their tunic as well (Ibid., 5, 40). He thus intends to highlight that the possession of an object cannot justify a man's death. Would it not be absolutely unreasonable, not only to risk killing, but also to risk dying in order to defend an object? Jesus ultimately advises simple prudence over heroism. It is indeed not prudent to risk one's life in order to defend one's purse.

Ownership and violence

It is a good idea here to consider the existing link between ownership and violence. Does not man most often resort to violence for the defence of the object of his ownership? "Ownership", writes Tolstoy, not only implies that I shall not give up my possession to whoever wishes to take it, but that I shall defend it against him. And that which one considers as one's own can only be defended through violence, i.e., through struggle, and if necessary, even with killing. .... Without violence and without killing, ownership could not be maintained. .... To admit ownership, is to admit violence and killing." (Tolstoy, 1901: 98) However, is ownership not a right for every individual so that he and his family may simply live? Is ownership not one of the freedom's conditions? Is it not, ultimately, a human right? Indeed, this seems undeniable. Moreover, when Tolstoy denounces ownership, he specifically condemns the ownership of Russian land, which is entirely in the hands of a few landlords, and whose very hard-working peasants are thus dispossessed. And so Tolstoy does not condemn the ownership of goods, but the accumulation of goods by a few, that deprives others of that which they need to survive. "The man", he writes, "who does not only seek to help himself, but also others .... must only possess to the extent that other men do not have to ask for a share of his possessions." (Ibid., 383) Laozi also sees cause for war in the accumulation of goods. He thus writes in book 9 of the Tao Te Ching: "There may be gold and jade to fill a hall, but there is none who can keep them." Similarly, among the "things that dwindle like the sparkle of a coin", Buddha cites "the pleasure in accumulating goods" (1991: 80). And among the "evil friends" which the well-advised man should be wary of, he places "those who claim the necessity of growing richer and richer" (Ibid., 81).

In Plato's *Phaedo*, Socrates asserts that for true philosophers, truth must be the only object of their desire. And in order to acquire the necessary time and freedom to the quest for truth, they must renounce the objects that their body desires, but which are but clutter to the mind. Violence precisely arises from the attachment to objects. "Only the body and its desires cause war, civil discord and battles", says Socrates, "for all wars are due to the desire to acquire wealth." (Plato, Book XI, 66a)

To say that the accumulation of wealth generates violence: is this to establish a link between nonviolence and poverty? No, if poverty is synonymous with destitution, but it is to establish a link between nonviolence and justice. Justice indeed requires that everyone possess the objects and goods allowing them to live. Justice does not require that I deprive myself of that which I need; but at the same time it requires that others may not be deprived of that which they need; and I am liable for that. In that sense, justice does not require poverty, but sharing. There is no possible justice without an equal sharing of objects and goods.

The fact remains that man is entitled to the acquisition and possession of objects which are of vital necessity to him; the resulting corollary is that he can rightfully defend them against whoever would seek to take them from him. The resolution of a conflict must therefore establish relations of justice between the two rivals; they must guarantee the mutual rights of each rival over the object, and in order for this to happen, it is necessary to refer back to the object constantly; a negotiation focusing on the object might thus be possible.

Rivalry between people can only make conflict worse, and lead it into the dead-end of violence. Furthermore, violence is highly likely to destroy the very object that is at stake in this dispute. Violence is often a question of deliberately worsening the situation to further one's own ends, that is, the scorched earth policy. It is not uncommon for each of the two rivals to prefer to have the object destroyed rather than to have it become the other's property.

It is therefore best to negotiate about the object by examining who has rights over it, and what these rights are. Both adversaries may very well assert their legitimate rights to the object. Might these rights possibly be reconciled? Might the object possibly be equally shared? Might there be other objects likely to satisfy the claims of both protagonists? In all these cases, it seems very probable that an agreement can only be reached insofar as each party accepts to make some concessions, as long as the latter protect the best part of their rights. Nonviolent struggle has no other goal but to create the conditions of a negotiation about the object; this negotiation would allow both rivals' rights to be respected. But in order to reach an agreement, any unjustified claim to the object would have to be abandoned. And for that, real restraint ought probably to be exerted onto whoever unduly asserts their claim. Nonviolent struggle must be able to exert such restraint.

Mediation

Mediation is the intervention of a third party, a third person, who steps into the space between the protagonists of a conflict, who stands between the two ad-versaries (from the Latin *adversus*: that which is set opposite, which is opposed), i.e. between two persons, two communities or two peoples facing each other, and turned against each other. Mediation seeks to encourage the two protagonists from ad-versity to con-versation (from the Latin *conversari*: to turn towards); it seeks to bring them to turn towards each other, to speak and understand each other, and if possible, to find a compromise which paves the way for reconciliation. The mediator endeavours to be a "pacifying third party". Through his intervention, he tries to break the "binary" relation—that of two adversaries confronting one another blindly and deafly—in order to establish a "ternary" relation, thanks to which they will be able to communicate, with the help of an intermediary. Two discourses, two reasonings, two logics confront one another within the binary relation that two adversaries have, and no communication can make mutual recognition and comprehension possible. The point is to pass from a logic of binary competition to a dynamic of ternary cooperation.

The "third party" mediator endeavours to create an "intermediary space"[1] that produces distance between the adversaries, so that they may both stand back in order to assess themselves, each other, and the conflict hurting them. The creation of this space separates the adversaries—just as two men fighting are separated—and this separation can allow communication. The intermediary space is meant for "re-creation"; the two adversaries will be able to rest, away from their conflict, and re-create their relations, peacefully and constructively. Mediation therefore seeks to build a society in which adversaries may learn or re-learn to communicate, in order to reach a pact which would allow them to live together, if not in absolute peace, at least in peaceful coexistence.

Mediation can only be undertaken if both adversaries wilfully agree to become involved in this reconciliation process. Mediation can certainly be suggested, advised, recommended, but it cannot be imposed onto them. By choosing mediation, both adversaries show that they understand how the development of their hostility can cause them harm; it is therefore in their best interest to attempt, through an amicable agreement, to find a positive outcome for the conflict that opposes them. They also show that they realize how legal intervention—which would use its authority to impose a decision on them—would only make it worse. Most often, legal decisions cut the knot of a conflict by naming a winner and a loser—one wins the trial and the other loses it—and both parties leave the court more adversarial than ever. Mediation does not care so much about judging a past act—which the legal institution does—than about leaning on it in

---

[1] On the notion of "intermediary space" [*espace intermédiaire*], see Duval (1993).

order to overcome it, and allow yesterday's adversaries to invent a future that is free from the weight of their past.

It is not the mediator's function to sit in judgment or to pronounce a verdict. He is neither a judge who finds for one side against the other, nor an arbiter who awards damages to one party against the other, but an intermediary who tries to re-establish communication between the two in order eventually to reconcile them. The mediator has no power to force agreement or impose a solution onto the protagonists; and the primary precondition on which mediation is based is that the resolution of a conflict must be mainly the work of the protagonists themselves. Mediation aims to enable the two adversaries to take possession of "their" conflict, so that they might cooperate in tackling, mastering and resolving it together. The mediator is a "facilitator": he facilitates communication between the two adversaries, so that they can express their own points of view, listen to each other, understand each other and reach an agreement.

The mediator must, as François Bazier stresses, "side with one, then side with the other, not be impartial" (1993: 20). This observation leads us to reject the notion of "neutrality" which has often been used to describe the mediator's position. The mediator is not, in fact, "neutral". According to its Latin roots (*ne*, "not" and *uter*, "one of two"), the word neutral means "not the one or the other, neither of the two". So, in the case of an international conflict, a neutral country is one which joins neither of the two opposing sides, which gives its support and assistance to neither of them and stays out of the conflict. Now a mediator is precisely not someone who joins "neither of the two adversaries", but someone who joins both, giving support and assistance to both the parties involved, and taking sides first with one, then with the other: committed twice over, two times involved, and on two sides. However, this double partiality is never unconditional; on each occasion it is a partiality of discernment and fairness. In this sense, the mediator is not neutral but *equitable*, striving to give to each side its due. This is how the mediator can win the confidence of both adversaries, and foster the dialogue between them.

Mediation can take place at the level of community relations as well as of social or political relations. "Community mediation" concerns people who become involved in daily conflicts such as neighbourhood disputes or family feuds. Mediation generally starts with separate preliminary meetings with each of the two parties. These meetings allow the people involved in the conflict to put their point of view in a climate of confidence. The mediator does not conduct a cross-examination, but asks questions respectfully, with the aim, not just of understanding the party but also (and above all) of reflection and self-understanding in terms of her own attitude to the conflict. The mediator practices, in a sense, the art of maieutics (from the Greek *maieutikê*, "the art of midwifery"); for they assist their clients in "giving birth" to their own truth. The quality of the mediator's listening proves the determining factor here in the success of the mediation: a person who feels listened to is well on the way to feeling understood, and can then confide and not only give the facts (or at least one version of them), but also, which is more important, convey their own subjective experience. To disentangle a knotty conflict, it is not enough to establish the objective truth of the facts; it is above all necessary to grasp the subjective truth of the people involved, with their feelings, frustrations and sufferings. Then all parties can put a name to the feelings that are motivating them, and the mediator's active listening has already, by itself had a therapeutic effect which begins to heal the confiding party's pain, assuage their fears, calm their anger and mitigate their latent violence: it can then proceed to disarm the hostility to the adversary which that party has been nourishing.

These preliminary interviews have the function of preparing the two parties to accept the notion of embarking on the mediation process. Once they have understood and accepted the principles and rules of mediation, the mediator, or generally, the mediators, can then suggest that they meet. The commencement of mediation implies that both parties should conclude an armistice (from the Latin *arma*, arm, weapon and *sistere*, to stop, to cease): each of them makes a commitment to renounce all acts of hostility towards the other throughout the mediation. There again, the mediator's essential role is to facilitate expression and ensure both adversaries' ability to listen, in order to re-establish communication, clear up misunderstandings, and allow mutual comprehension. The mediator can resort to reformulation techniques in order to clear up any misinterpretation of each person's words. Such a confrontation—in the presence of a mediator—aims to substitute the confrontation between two monologues—in which each person hears nothing but himself—for a true dialogue—in which each person listens to the other. Little by little, and if everyone agrees to proceed, this dialogue—several encounters might be necessary—must bring out the possibility to undo the knot of the conflict, by finding a compromise that essentially respects the rights and protects the interests of both parties. The mediator, as Jean-François Six puts it, succeeds when he "allows each of the two distant parties to come closer, to reach towards the middle, where they will be able to shake hands without either of them being humiliated and losing face" (Six, 1986: 118). A successful mediation must lead to a written agreement, signed by both parties. This "peace treaty" equals a pact which requires all signatories to accept responsibility. The mediator can thus ensure that the pact is respected by all.

Any mediation may naturally fail, due to one or the other of the protagonists. In all probability, the conflict would then resume, and justice might have to put an end to it, according to its own procedures.

Community mediation mainly takes place within civil society on the initiative of citizens who have formed a private voluntary association. Community networks must remain one of the privileged places where mediation takes place; furthermore, the majority of mediators should be citizens who intend to actively play their part in community life. But mediation must not be a mere "social experiment" left to private initiative. It must be considered as one of the very first ways to regulate social conflicts, as one of the essential elements constituting a sense of community. In this perspective, the mediator must be seen as one of the main social actors that contribute to the establishing of social peace. In terms of the requirements and aims of democracy, the stakes of mediation are truly political, and highly important. That is why it is best to institutionalize mediation in the different sectors of society, by trying hard to combine citizen initiatives with those of governments.

In order for mediation to carry out its social function, public authorities must directly take part in the development of its institutionalization. Because mediation is in the public interest, it is normally for public authorities to participate in the funding of associations which exercise mediation activities. But public authority itself, whether legal or political, must acquire mediation services. When the mediator is appointed by public authorities, his independence and autonomy must be fully acknowledged and guaranteed. Furthermore, according to the very nature of the mediation, he must not be granted any power of decision or constraint. His only power must be that of recommendation; the power of decision remains in the hands of the authority that appointed him. And since prevention is always better than cure, it is the mediator's role to approach public authorities with the administrative, statutory or even legislative reforms that are likely to prevent conflicts.

Hence the practice of mediation in the different sectors of society can become one of the main methods of nonviolent resolution of conflicts between individuals and groups. By avoiding the recourse to the State's repressive methods, and allowing citizens to become directly involved in the management of conflicts between other citizens, mediation encourages the self-regulation of societal violence.

The principles and rules of mediation can equally be applied to strictly political conflicts, whether on the national or the international level. Conflicts, crises and wars could thus be defused through the practice of mediation by a third country offering its "good offices". Mediation can be one of the most efficient "weapons" of peaceful diplomacy.

Karl Popper and "teaching nonviolence"

"Civilization", according to Karl Popper, "essentially consists in reducing violence." (1994: 33) Individual liberty can only be guaranteed in society when every member gives up the use of violence: "The Rule of Law calls for nonviolence, which is one of its essential elements." (1993: 72) If any given individual uses violence against another, it becomes necessary for the government to step in to restore public safety and social peace. Popper, however, believed that the Rule of Law must be based not on state repression, but on individuals being public-spirited enough to give up violence of their own accord. Before that can happen, a culture of nonviolence needs to be fostered among citizens, and the first step to take is to teach children about nonviolence. The more "the duty of teaching nonviolence" (Ibid., 73) is neglected, claims Popper, the greater the hold of the culture of violence over society and the greater the government's need for recourse to restrictive and repressive measures.

Education "consists not just in teaching the facts, but also, and above all, in showing how important it is to eliminate violence." (Popper and Condry, 1994: 33) Through his experience as an educator, Karl Popper has reached the conviction that "children do not like violence" (1993: 70), but he supports the theory that "we educate our children to violence" (1994: 26-27). According to him, the most powerful instrument of this education to violence is television, which tends to play a prominent part in children's environment. Sat for hours in front of the small screen, children contemplate violence day after day, and this violence becomes an example for them. Thus, "children and young people are in real danger: that of getting used to violence" (Popper, 1993: 77). It is therefore important to "avoid breaking down the natural resistance that most people have to violence" (Ibid., 71) by taking the necessary steps in time. As we have previously highlighted, Karl Popper essentially conceives of democracy as being a control over power by citizens. In this perspective, he asserts that the very survival of democracy absolutely relies on the submission of television's power to a strict control. For "when we allow the general aversion to violence to be broken down and superseded, we really undermine the Rule of Law and the general agreement that violence is to be avoided. We undermine our civilisation." (Id.)

For a nonviolent education

"The Republic", writes Blandine Barret-Kriegel, "needs men and women who prefer goodness." (*Libération*, March 25, 1992) But if it is virtuous men and women who make up the Republic, who is going to educate the Republic's children in goodness? In a democratic—and therefore secular—society, no institution of political society is meant to define the philosophical and moral requirements which should yet be at the basis of the Republic. Schools and universities, as a general rule, only teach "dead philosophies", in the same way that they still teach dead languages. Philosophy teachers are above all historians of philosophy; their teachings essentially come from books. The teaching of living philosophies is left to the initiative of individuals who have no other authority than that which other individuals grant them. For all that, it cannot be otherwise in a field where the ultimate rule must be respect for everyone's freedom of conscience. We know from experience that States which seek to impose "moral order" are not democratic. It is for civil society, which comes before political society, to define the "values" that are the basis for culture and civilization. "Moral authorities" precede political authorities in saying what is right, but they have no other power than their ability to convince. Indeed, no "value" could be imposed through restraint, but as a result it admittedly becomes extremely difficult to establish—in a democratic society—the ethical rules on which all citizens' behaviour must be based.

To destroy the seeds of ideologies that legitimize and honour violence, it is necessary to supply the whole of society with a "culture of nonviolence", and culture begins with education. The latter plays a decisive part in the child's introduction to responsible citizenship. Unfortunately, the prevailing education system does not have political citizenship on its horizon, but economic competitiveness. In the design of the education system generally prevalent in societies described as modern, instruction has a far bigger place than education. The primary objective is to allow young people to arrive on the labour market with the technical skills needed for the best chances of finding a job. It goes without saying that school must enable the young to gain an occupational qualification, with which they can find work or, better still, be able to choose the occupation which best suits their aptitudes. But the role of education cannot be limited to this without betraying its mission. School should above all be aimed towards public-spiritedness.

Children's "civic education" must try to foster autonomy rather than submission, a critical mind rather than passive obedience, responsibility rather than discipline, cooperation rather than competition, and solidarity rather than rivalry. Children, when all is said and done, must be educated in nonviolence. For that to happen, however, the education itself must first of all draw on the principles, rules and methods of nonviolence: *nonviolence in teaching is the first step to teaching nonviolence*. Adults must respect the child's world and not seek to invade and brutally occupy it, imposing their laws and ideologies. Nonviolent education certainly does not imply that the authority of adult should be erased. The child needs to be confronted with this authority in order to build his personality, but it is in the very nature of an educator's authority to exercise itself through nonviolence. Eric Prairat, echoing Georges Gursdof's assertion that violence is "akin to a below-the-belt blow to the honour of philosophy" (1960: 84), considers violence to be "akin to a below-the-belt blow to the honour of education" (Prairat, 1988: 45-46).

Educators must themselves try to make "object lessons" out of the inevitable conflicts which arise among children, so as to enable them to discover that these occasions of opposition to others have to take their place in the process of their personal development. "Once we accept", writes Eric Prairat, "that conflict is not coterminous with violence, but that violence is only one possible issue for conflict, then we open up between the two an ideal opportunity for the educator: not, of course, to obfuscate or dress things up, but to teach children, or rather learn alongside them, how to live through the confrontations that are bound to crop up in our social life, and resolve them in a positive way." (Ibid., 46)

To initiate children into citizenship, they must be taught the proper use of the law. The obedience required of citizens is not a passive, unconditional submission to the orders of a higher authority, but the considered and consenting observance of a rule whose legitimacy they themselves recognize. One essential dimension of education must be to arrange for the children to take part in the setting up of the community rules which they are going to have to keep, by providing the opportunities for them to learn by experience that these are necessary if they are to be able to live together in mutual and general respect. "To turn children into autonomous beings is to give them access to all three aspects of rules for life in common: making the rules, applying the rules, and rendering justice." (Bisot and Lhopiteau, 1993: 213)

School must be the place for eliminating the prejudices that fuel discrimination against "others", against those who belong to other communities, other peoples, ethnic groups or religions. When enemy stereotypes are passed on to children, it means that their minds, feelings and bodies are already being primed, that they are already learning how to make war. "Enemy stereotypes", writes Bernadette Bayada, "incite hostile behaviour. Then, in a vicious circle, they become self-justifying and give the misleading impression of truth and certainty." (1993: 139) A crucial requirement of education, then, is to defuse the children's perception of "others", especially those whose social identity is marked by differences. Their sense of perception must be educated in such a way as to enable them to abandon all hostility towards "those others who are different", and to learn to look kindly upon them; they must not, however, lose their ability to judge critically what may be criticized in their behaviour. Between hard racism and soft ecumenicism lies the space for the quest for a lucid and equitable judgment that does "others" justice, without betraying the requirements of truth.

10

Nonviolent Alternatives to War

War poses a major problem for philosophy: not only does it contradict but it also rescinds the essential requirement of the ethic: "Thou shalt not kill". To declare war is to give men the imperative order to kill other men. "The state of war", writes Emmanuel Levinas, "suspends morality; it divests the eternal institutions and obligations of their eternity and rescinds ad interim the unconditional imperatives. In advance its shadow falls over the actions of men. War is not only one of the ordeals—the greatest—of which morality lives; it renders morality derisory." (Levinas, 1992: 5) War is not only the failure of philosophy; it is its negation and its renunciation.

Clausewitz and a reflection on war

Carl von Clausewitz offers us a "philosophy of war" (1955: 52); he introduces his reflection as a "philosophical elaboration of the art of war" (p. 44). According to him, the essence of war is to be a "duel" (p. 51) and "its immediate purpose is to shatter adversaries, and thus render them incapable of further resistance" (p. 51). War is therefore the confrontation of two wills through violent means, each of the two adversaries deliberately intending to impose their will on the other.

But war results from a political conflict between two governments, and its objective is therefore political. "War", asserts Clausewitz, "is merely the continuation of politics by other means." (p. 67) The Prussian general did not mean by this—as it was sometimes implied—that politics were already war, but on the contrary, that war was yet another political action. "If we reflect", he writes, "that war has its root in a political object, then naturally this original motive which called it into existence should also continue the first and highest consideration in its conduct." (p. 66) "War", he specified, "is not merely a political act, but also a real political instrument, a continuation of political commerce, a carrying out of the same by other means. .... The political intention is the object, war is the means, and the means must always include the end in our intention." (p. 67) More precisely, war is a continuation of politics by other means than those of diplomacy: the government "fights battles instead of writing notes" (p. 705). "The conduct of war in its great feature", Clausewitz continues, "is therefore politics itself, which takes up the sword in place of the pen, but does not on that account cease to think according to its own laws." (p. 710) War's new means must be but "subordinate acts", for "political intercourse does not cease by the war itself" (p. 703). In this perspective, Clausewitz believes that in framing plans for a war, the major preoccupation of governments must be that "the political point of view should give way to the purely military point of view" (p. 706).

But is it possible to follow Clausewitz in stating that war is merely a means of continuing politics? In fact, when he says that on the one hand "war is an act of violence" (p. 53), and on the other hand "war is a political act" (p. 66), Clausewitz formulates an implacable contradiction. For the recourse to violence can only signify the failure of politics, whose entire project is precisely to build and maintain—first within the city, but also beyond its gates—an order which would owe violence nothing. Politics and war are fundamentally anti-nomic (the word anti-nomy, from the Greek *anti*, anti, and *nomos*, law, refers to a contradiction between two laws): the laws of war are contrary to the laws of politics. For all that, Clausewitz is aware of that antinomy, and he speaks of the "contradiction that distinguishes the nature of war from every other human interest, individual or social" (p. 703). But from then on, war cannot be the continuation of politics; it is an interruption of politics. As soon as war is declared, politics give way to violence, which will occupy the centre-ground as long as the battle lasts. In the best case scenario, politics only reasserts its rights at the time of Armistice, once arms cease to speak and adversaries sit down at the same table to negotiate.

Analysing "the pure theoretical concept of war" (p. 55), Clausewitz defines what he calls "the law of the extreme" (p. 58): in the abstract, "war is an act of violence and there is no limit to its manifestations" (p. 53). The outcome is that "a sort of reciprocal action arises, which logically must lead to an extreme" (p. 53). But in fact, Clausewitz asserts, war is different from what it should be in theory, because its conduct essentially depends on men, who do not act according to the imperatives of pure logic: "Theory must also take into account the human element" (p. 65). That is why, in all probability, the law of the rise to extremes does not apply in reality. "Any act of war", Clausewitz concludes, "ceases to be subject to the strict law of forces pushed to the extreme." (p. 58) And he is happy that it should be so, for otherwise war's political objective would be "engulfed by the law of the extreme" (p. 58) and "we would be dealing with something devoid of meaning and intention" (p. 704). If war "was a complete, untrammelled, absolute manifestation of violence, as the pure concept would require, war would of its own independent will usurp the place of politics the moment politics had brought it into being" (p. 66). If the law of the rise to the extreme did indeed apply in reality, if we reached the "utmost extremity of exertion", "regard for the discussion of political demands would be lost, and the means would lose all relation to the object" (p. 678).

Clausewitz's requirement that "the political point of view should give way to the purely military point of view" does indeed impose itself from a theoretical point of view in order for his theory of war to remain coherent; but the question is whether in practice, such a principle does not meet more obstacles than he allows? Another question is whether in fact, the objective contradiction between the nature of war and that of politics—in other words, whether the antinomy between war's (violent) means and politics' (nonviolent) end—is not the strongest, and whether ultimately, however the subjective intention of the political men leading operations may be, the military point of view should not give way to the political point of view? Of course, violence's manifestation is never limitless, but does it not always overstep the limits below which the political point of view could give way to the military point of view? Is this "human element", which Clausewitz says theory must take into account, not more often passion than reason? And is it not in the nature of passion to incite men to express their violence well beyond the limits imposed by political reason? Clausewitz would certainly not fail to challenge "total war" by emphasizing that the military means employed then "totally" eclipse the political end which claims to justify it. But as soon as it becomes impossible in reality to overcome the contradiction between the means of war and the end of politics, it is highly likely that the means eclipse the end. At the very least, this likelihood is too important that we may not ask ourselves whether other means than war exist—means which themselves are political, i.e. nonviolent—in order to continue politics when diplomacy has failed to solve a conflict? And we can probably attempt to answer this question by building on Clausewitz's reflection.

When he asks the question: "how to influence the probability of success?", Clausewitz answers: "In the first place, naturally by the same means which we use when the object is the subjugation of the enemy, by the destruction of his military force" (p. 73). Without a doubt, the choice of nonviolence totally deprives us of these means. But Clausewitz then sets forth "a particular means of influencing the probability of the result without defeating the enemy's army, namely, upon the expeditions which have a direct connection with political views" (p. 73). And he puts forward that if we thus manage to "raise political powers in our own favour", it is likely to "become a shorter way towards our object than the routing of the enemy's forces" (p. 73-74). He then asks the question "how to act upon our enemy's expenditure in strength" and answers that the solution "lies in the wearing out of his forces" (p. 74). He points out that "we choose this expression not only to explain our meaning in few words, but because it represents the thing exactly, and is not so figurative as may at first appear. The idea of wearing out in a struggle amounts in practice to *a gradual exhaustion of the physical powers and of the will by the continuance of exertion.*" (p. 74).

Is it not possible here, in the very light of the Clauswitzian principles of confrontation of enemy forces, to define the concept of a civil defence based on a strategy of nonviolent resistance? This strategy, if it cannot claim to exhaust the enemy's physical strength, can seek to wear out his political will until he renounces his undertaking. If the aim cannot be to destroy enemy forces, it is "the defeat of the enemy's intentions, that is to pure resistance, of which the final aim can be nothing more than to prolong the duration of the contest, so that the enemy shall exhaust himself in it." (p. 81) If we concentrate our resources in the perspective of pure resistance, "then the mere duration of the contest will suffice gradually to bring the loss of force on the part of the adversary to a point at which the political object can no longer be an equivalent, a point at which, therefore, he must give up the contest" (p. 75). So the point is to "overcome the enemy by the duration of the combat, that is to wear him out" (p. 75).

Along with duration, another factor also has a determining effect on the efficiency of popular resistance: the space factor. The efficiency of resistance is directly proportional to the duration of the action, but also to its area. Speaking about "the people's war", Clausewitz notes that "the act of resistance, whose effect is like that of the process of evaporation, depends on how much surface is exposed." (p. 552) Forces of repression in particular will find it all the more difficult to neutralize resistance as the latter stretches further: "The spirit of resistance which spreads everywhere becomes impossible to capture anywhere." (p. 553)

"Hostile operations" (p. 70) are over and war comes to an end when the will of one or the other of the two adversaries is suppressed, and he resolves to sign the peace agreement. "As soon as the actual expenditure of strength has exceeded what they had first anticipated, they should make peace." (p. 72) Hence must nonviolent civil resistance opt for a strategy which leads the adversary to note that the hiring of his soldiers and civil servants requires disproportionate expenditure of strength compared to the original political objective; and that from then on, it is clearly in his interest to negotiate a peace treaty.

When thus referring to Clausewitz' words, borrowing several of his formulas and applying them to the strategy of nonviolent resistance, we do not in any way claim that the Prussian general could have unconsciously made a plea for the defence of nonviolent action. For him, there is no doubt that "the decision by arms" (p. 82) is the supreme law of the confrontation between two States. "*The bloody solution of the crisis*", he asserts, "and the effort needed for the destruction of the enemy's forces, is the firstborn son of war." (p. 83) For him, it would therefore be an error of principle to "prefer a bloodless solution" (p. 82). Should this method be chosen, it is at the risk of not being the best one.

We only assert that several of the categories defined by Clausewitz in building his theory of war make it possible to develop a coherent and pertinent theory of nonviolent civil defence. It goes without saying that both theories remain largely antagonistic in many of their assumptions and conclusions. But this does not seem to prevent us from borrowing what we have, and establishing the correspondences that we have established.

Nonviolent civil defence

By itself, disarmament does not offer any solution to the problem of war. In fact, armament is not the cause of wars. Arms do not create wars, but on the contrary, wars create arms. The solution is not therefore to seek to eliminate arms in order to eliminate wars, but to eliminate wars in order to eliminate arms. Yet wars cannot be eliminated simply by wishing to eliminate conflicts. These form the very thread of the history of men, communities and peoples. Wars can be eliminated by wishing to solve conflicts by other means than arms. So the point truly is to imagine means other than violence in order to solve inevitable human conflicts humanely.

It is not as much about calling for disarmament as about creating the conditions that make it possible. In view of this, it is best to set oneself a goal which takes into account reality and the necessity to create a process that is able to change it. The concept of "transarmament" seems the most appropriate to designate this objective. It expresses the idea of a "transition" during which the means of a nonviolent civil defence—guaranteeing as much as military means but without the same risks—must be prepared. While the word "disarmament" expresses nothing but rejection, the word "trans-armament" seeks to convey the idea of a project. While disarmament evokes a negative viewpoint, trans-armament suggests a constructive approach. Security is a fundamental need for any human community; and insofar as the other members of a society have the feeling that their security requires the possession of arms which can efficiently fight back an aggression, disarmament could only cause them to feel insecure. Before it is able to disarm, war must be prepared for through other means than violent ones. For all that, the trans-armament and disarmament concepts are not antagonistic, for one of the purposes of the trans-armament process is to make the effective measures of disarmament possible.

Trans-armament aims to create an alternative to military defence, i.e. to organize nonviolent civil defence so that it may substitute for armed defence. But this can only be a long-term objective. Before nonviolent civil defence can be considered by the majority of the population and by public powers as a functional alternative to armed defence, its feasibility must first be established, and its true credibility acquired.

Clausewitz highlights the fact that one of the factors affecting war is the "theatre of operations" which is composed of "the territory, with its surface area and its population" (p. 57). In the context of the strategy of nonviolent civil defence, the theatre of operations is composed of society with its democratic institutions and its population. In reality, the invasion and occupation of a territory do not constitute the *goals* of an aggression; they are but the *means* for establishing the control and domination of society. The most likely objectives that an adversary seeks to reach through the occupation of a territory are ideological influence, political domination and economic exploitation. In order to reach these objectives, he must occupy society; to be more specific, he must occupy society's democratic institutions. From then on, the borders which a people must defend to protect its freedom are those of democracy. The territory whose integrity guarantees the sovereignty of a nation is not geographical, but that of democracy. As a result, in a democratic society the defence policy must not be based on the defence of the State, but on that of the Rule of Law.

It is therefore a good idea to reframe the debate on defence around the concepts of democracy and citizenship. If democracy is the object of defence, the citizen is the protagonist of defence, because he is the protagonist of democracy. So it is important to consider the relation which a democratic society must establish between defence and citizens. Until now, beyond the rhetorical statements according to which defence is "everyone's business", our societies have not managed to enable citizens to take on an effective responsibility in the organization of the defence of democracy against the aggressions—whether they be internal or external—that it endures. The law-and-order ideology of military dissuasion has caused the whole of citizens to be deprived of responsibility towards their obligations of defence. As soon as technology precedes, supplants and eventually eliminates political reflection and strategic investigation, the citizen is no longer the protagonist of defence: the technical instrument, the military machine, the weapon system have been substituted for him.

Citizens must therefore duly re-appropriate their role in the defence of democracy. In order for citizens to take part in the defence of society, it is not enough to seek to instil a "spirit of defence" into a civil population; a true "defence strategy" ought to be developed, which should mobilize all citizens for the "civil defence" of democracy. Until now, the awareness of citizens towards defence imperatives—including that of children—has been strictly limited to the organization of military defence. This restriction can only hinder the development of a real will to defend the institutions that guarantee the workings of democracy. In order for the spirit of defence to really spread across society, it is necessary to "civilize" ["make civil"] defence and not to militarise civilians. The mobilization of citizens can be all the more effective and operational if the suggested tasks are indeed being suggested within the political, administrative, social and economic institutions in which they work on a daily basis. The preparation for civil defence is perfectly in line with the life of citizens within the institutions in which they carry out their civic duties. The required spirit of defence becomes deeply rooted directly in the civic spirit that drives them in their daily activities.

In the face of every attempt by an illegitimate power to destabilize, control, dominate, attack or occupy society, it is therefore essential for the civil resistance of citizens to become organized on the front of democratic institutions that allow executive, legislative and judicial powers—whose function is to guarantee the freedom and rights of each and every one—to be exercised freely. It is the responsibility of citizens who work in these institutions to make sure that the latter continue to function according to the rules of democracy. They must thus refuse allegiance to any illegitimate power which, inspired by an anti-democratic ideology, would seek to divert these institutions from their duties for its own ends.

The ultimate objective of any illegitimate power seeking to take control of a society is to obtain—through the conjunction of means of persuasion, pressure, constraint and repression—the objective collaboration and complicity of citizens, or at least of most of them. From then on, the main focus of a strategy of civil defence must be the organization of a general yet selective and perfectly targeted refusal of this collaboration. Civil defence can thus be defined as a policy of defence of democratic society against every attempt at political control or military occupation; it mobilizes all citizens into a resistance which combines—in a prepared and organized manner—nonviolent actions of non-cooperation and confrontation with any illegitimate power, so that the latter can be stopped from reaching the ideological, political and economic objectives by which he justifies his aggression.

It is essential that the organization of this defence should not be left in the hands of individuals. It is for public authorities to prepare for civil defence in all the institutional spaces of political society. The government must therefore develop official instructions as to the obligations of civil servants who would be confronted with a major crisis and have to face the orders of an illegitimate power. These instructions must highlight the fact that public administrations have a strategic role in the defence of democracy: to deprive usurping power of the means of implementation that it needs in order to carry out its policy.

While it is being prepared within political society, civil defence must simultaneously be prepared within civil society in the different organizations and associations that citizens themselves have started, in order to gather according to their political, social, cultural or religious affinities. The networks formed by these associations of citizens which occupy the whole country's social space—and which include mainly political movements, unions, associations and religious communities—ought to be able to turn into as many resistance networks in a crisis situation threatening democracy. On the specific role of associations, Alain Refalo writes: "The civic responsibility of citizens involved in associations must extend to the defence of civil society when it is being attacked. Associations, protagonists of democracy, must also be the protagonists of the defence of democracy." (1989: 28)

The institutional implementation of nonviolent civil defence by public authorities comes up against considerable sociological obstacles—and in all probability, will continue to come up against these for a some time to come. In fact, the State first needs the army for itself, in order to ensure the maintenance, and if necessary, the re-establishment of its own authority. If military mysticism proclaims a religion of freedom, military policy practices a religion of order. Furthermore, the State worships obedience too much not to feel strong disgust towards citizens being taught to refuse to obey illegitimate orders. "It is highly likely", writes Gene Sharp on that matter, "that this faith in the omnipotence of violence, and the ignorance of the power of nonviolent popular struggle have been absolutely compatible with the interests of prevailing elites in the past, which did not wish the people to realize its potential power." (1980: 72)

Hence, today as yesterday the implementation of nonviolent civil defence remains a true challenge. It would not be reasonable to expect public authorities to organize it in the same way that they organize military defence, through a process which would be imposed from the top of the State to the bottom of society. Citizens ought first to become convinced themselves that it is necessary for the defence of democracy, i.e. ultimately for the defence of their own rights and their own freedom. Here as elsewhere, each time democracy is first and foremost in question, it is for the citizens to speak out.

11

Violence and Nonviolence in History, According to Eric Weil

Man, between reason and violence

Eric Weil's philosophical works are unanimously considered to be "one of the masterpieces of our times" (Lacroix, 1968: 83). The characteristic of Eric Weil's philosophical work is to be entirely based on a reflection on violence and nonviolence. It therefore particularly serves our purpose to explore his work and endeavour to demonstrate the reasoning behind it.

We would like to read Eric Weil in the same way as he himself explains he sought to read Kant (1990: 9-10). First of all, we wish to adhere to his text as much as possible, "not to do it violence", to try and understand his discourse while revealing its coherence. But after this effort of demonstration and comprehension, we will seek to show appreciation and evaluation, that is to say judgment and criticism. Indeed, "the will to remain faithful to thought, to any author's thought, does not exclude criticism or opposition". The point is to establish a dialogue, a discussion with the author with whom we share the path. It then becomes legitimate to point out some weakness, imprecision or ambiguity in our interlocutor's thought, and to express our disagreement with him on one subject or other. This disagreement seems inevitable.

Among all the definitions of humanity on offer, Eric Weil chooses the one that is most widely used: "humans are animals with reason and language, or, more precisely, with rational language". (1974: 3) Admittedly, man does not naturally express himself or act in compliance with the requirements of reason; but he must strive to do so if he is to become fully human. It is this human effort to think, speak and live rationally which is the characteristic of philosophy. But at the same time as our philosophical man decides to opt for reason, he becomes aware of that within himself which prevents him from becoming rational. The philosopher is not afraid of external dangers, not even death, but of "the unreason within himself" (1974: 19); he has a "fear of violence" (1974: 20). This violence discovered by the philosophical man within himself, this impulse towards an irrational attitude, is an obstacle to the realization of his own humanity. This violence within is what "is not in agreement with that which makes us human" (1974: 47). The philosopher fears violence, therefore, because "it is the obstacle to becoming wise" (1974: 20).

So the would-be philosopher, at the very moment of wanting to become rational, stands self-revealed as a creature of needs, interests, desires, and passions, and, as such, naturally impelled towards violence to others. But we can only discover that we are violent because we are endowed with reason. Violence is only understood upon re-flection; that is to say, after we have turned back from our own violence. We only discover and comprehend violence (in ourselves, but also in society and its history), because we "already have the idea of nonviolence" (1992: 20). Man is violent, but understands that he is so only because he bears within himself an imperative of nonviolence which is the imperative of reason itself. "Reason", writes Eric Weil, "is one possibility for humans. .... But only a possibility, not a necessity; and it is a possibility offered to a being which has another possibility open to it. We know this other possibility is violence." (1974: 57) But violence is not merely "the other possibility" for humans; it is "the possibility realized in the first instance" (1974: 69).

The choice of nonviolence

Man is therefore capable of reason *and* of violence, and must choose between these two possibilities: "Freedom chooses between reason and violence" (1992: 47). Philosophical requirements, though, lead man to choose reason over violence:

"Violence, violently felt", asserts Eric Weil categorically, "must be driven out *once and for all.*" (1974: 75) This, then, is the "secret of philosophy": "The philosopher wishes violence to disappear from the world, but recognizes needs, acknowledges desires, agrees that man remains an animal, albeit a rational one: what matters is to eliminate violence." (1974: 20) This established, the philosopher can proclaim a moral rule—for himself, but also for others—which shall determine the attitude to be taken in all circumstances: "It is right to desire that which lessens the quantity of violence in human life; it is wrong to desire that which makes it greater." (1974: 20)

Because reason is a defining feature for humanity itself, both in each individual man and in all, "it is the main duty of (moral human being) to respect the rational in every other human being, and to respect it in themselves as they respect it in their fellows" (1984: 31). And this immediately implies that they must forbid themselves any violence to any person: "They may not forget .... that they have no right to will certain consequences (of their actions); for instance, those which would turn other people into *things.*" (Id.)

Someone who has chosen reason, in order that the coherence of their inner commentary may inform and transform their life, submits their decisions to the "test of universality" (1992: 52): "Each person must behave in such a way that their manner of acting and deciding can be thought of as a manner of acting for anyone and everyone; in other words it must be such that it can be universalized." (1982: 269) Now the "primary contradiction", which destroys all coherence of inner commentary and of life, is "that between violence and universality" (1992: 53). This is why no-one can ever make progress towards universality except by choosing nonviolence, for "this is the universal." (1974: 64)

Violence always remains, however, another option for those who have chosen reason, universality and, accordingly, nonviolence. The philosopher will never, therefore, come to an end of this self-transformation through reason. Furthermore, and above all, the man who chooses reason does so in a world where others have chosen violence; he must therefore also make efforts to educate those others in reason, and to transform the world so as to put an end—so far possible—to the rule of violence. For this reason "nonviolence is philosophy's point of departure, as well as its final goal." (1974: 59)

Confrontation with others

The philosophical man is not a solitary being; he belongs to a historical community which therefore leads him to confront his own discourse with that of others. He is not certain that this confrontation totally avoids violence. A person who chooses rational speech over violence can come up against the "violence of the man who does not accept the discourse of another man; he seeks satisfaction by fighting for his own discourse that he wishes to be unique not only for himself, but for everyone; he tries to make it unique through the real elimination of all those who hold other discourse". (1974: 57) Dialogue may therefore prove impossible, and it then gives way to violent struggle. But this will be "against the will of men whose common fundamental principle is that of nonviolent discussion—a strong enough will that it can have them agree on their disagreement, thus neutralized." (1992: 45-46)

Hence dialogue is truly the "domain of nonviolence" (1974: 24), but the rational man himself is soon confronted with its limits. "Dialogue is lying in its assertion that it can eliminate violence." (1982: 280) Discussion, or "the nonviolent confrontation of those who are opposed" (1992: 43), is only possible between those that Eric Weil calls "real men" (1974: 25), that is to say those who have chosen rational discourse. Admittedly, even within the community of "real men", violence remains a possibility, but those who use it exclude themselves from it. So the first fact which "real men" must establish "is that violence among themselves is unacceptable" (1974: 26).

However, as Eric Weil points out, "real men" have not completely excluded violence. On the contrary, it seems necessary to them: on the one hand, to neutralize and incapacitate the irrational men who refuse dialogue and choose violence within their own community; on the other hand, to fight and overcome the barbarians who could attack them at any time. To defend itself against this double threat, the community of real men "has acquired a political and military constitution" (1974: 25).

Every historical community must indeed organize itself so as to constrain individuals and groups who "refuse to be subjected to reason" (1984: 132). This organization constitutes the State, and the latter has to resort to violence in order to constrain and neutralize the individuals and groups who disturb social peace and public order. Eric Weil makes his the most widespread definition of the modern State according to which its characteristic is that "it has the monopoly of the use of violence" (1984: 142). Thus, in a modern society, "no one can be constrained into anything except by the State" (1984: 142).

The violence of the State is justified by the necessity to make the individuals who resort to violence in their own interest, and to satisfy their own desires, see reason. "The first crime—the fundamental crime in the modern State—is the use of violence (even indirect) by an individual, acting as an individual." (1984: 142) The State always considers the individual as a virtually violent being, who could at any moment really become violent.

In order that the action of the State may not itself become arbitrary, it must be decided upon in accordance with the law. Eric Weil completes the first definition that he gave of the modern State by specifying that its essential characteristic is to be a "Rule of Law": its action—as well as the action of every citizen—"is controlled by laws" (1984: 143). Thus, "the State .... through the law, controls the use of violence" (Id.). The State's function is therefore to constrain the individual—by forcing him to obey the law—to have a rational behaviour; it is to bring man to reason. That way, the State ensures and guarantees the safety of rational individuals by protecting them against the violence of those who are not.

Admittedly, Eric Weil is aware that every State—despite all the guarantees that have theoretically been established by the law and the constitution—can turn into an "instrument of oppression" (1984: 132). "He who thinks ....", he writes, "has to be aware that every State is composed of violent beings, that every ruling group is made up of passionate individuals, and that, consequently, every State runs the risk of betraying its concept, the concept which justifies it" and that the constraint he exerts then becomes an "unjust constraint" (1984: 261). But the philosopher has no alternative but to accept that risk by doing everything in his power to overcome it, for ultimately, "he knows that the existence of a rational being that justifies the State is only possible and can only last within the rational State" (Id.).

The necessity of counter-violence

Therefore, paradoxically, philosophy, which is essentially the refusal of violence, does not entirely refuse violence. Philosophy itself, Eric Weil concedes, "recommends the use of violence, because it has to admit that it must rise up against violence" (1974: 58). "But", he immediately points out, "this violence is then but the necessary means (technically necessary in a world that is still being governed by violence) to create a nonviolent state." (1974: 58-59)

Someone who has chosen reason and nonviolence must face up to the violence that arises in history; they cannot stop themselves from entering the field of political action; they must strive for the advent of a world in which reason and nonviolence will prevail in human relationships. "The choice of nonviolence takes on concrete meaning in relation to history." (1991b: 214) But at this point Eric Weil insistently asserts that, in order to achieve this end, the means that are reason and nonviolence prove radically insufficient. "Violence in itself is the negation of all meaning; it is pure absurdity; but we will fall into the most violent (and the most inevitable) external conflicts if we convince ourselves that it is enough to speak of nonviolence and good life in society." (1984: 233) Whenever the irrational man cannot be convinced by the arguments of reason, he must then be constrained by those of violence. "If offering men reason", writes Eric Weil, "instead of imposing it, was enough for them to become rational, violence would have ceased to govern us a long time ago." (1984: 21) The rational man cannot rely on "the force of good" to fight against the violence of evil-doers: "As far as reality and realization are concerned, good has no force, since all force is on evil's side." (1984: 45)

According to Eric Weil, "no other process but persuasion would be allowed for whoever would not wish to sacrifice the purity of their will for utility—as it is defined in every day life" (1984: 21). But as soon as means of persuasion—such as they are carried out within a discussion—prove ineffective in convincing those who have chosen violence against reason, the rational man—should he indeed wish to take on his responsibilities in history—must then use violent means to constrain them. For Eric Weil, there is no other alternative—in the face of irrational men—than the already existing one between, on the one hand, the failure of nonviolent means (that leads to a failure of nonviolence in history) and, on the other hand, the success of violent means (that makes possible, or at least preserves, the success of nonviolence in history).

Wisdom in the world

So, someone who would seek to base their behaviour in the world on the sole principles of pure morality, would probably come to refuse all action, precisely in order to preserve the purity of their will. "It is probably possible", notes Eric Weil, "to reject any form of violence; but those who make that decision, and take it seriously, thus leave the field of politics; they may reach saintliness, they will act no more." (1984: 232) But in acting no more, they abandon the world to the actions of violent people. The moral man must therefore refuse to give in to "the temptation to rest comfortably on pure—but purely negative—moral conscience" (1984: 18).

As it happens, this period of rest will probably not last very long, for the man of pure morality runs a high risk of becoming the victim of the violence of irrational men. He can then "accept to sacrifice his own life in order to avoid being violent himself" (1982: 273), but, in that case, he will also have to "accept, according to the principle of the universalization of his maxim, the sacrifice of the survival of every moral being and thus of morality itself" (Id.). It is therefore the moral man's duty to defend his life so that he may continue to defend morality. This leads Eric Weil to formulate this formidable paradox: "The defender of morality" can be driven to "the use of violence while seeking to defend the possibility of nonviolence within himself" (1992: 39). Yet Eric Weil recognizes that "some situations may occur .... in which death—wilfully accepted, and sometimes sought after—can be willed as the only means allowing the new concrete morality to seep into the conscience of contemporaries and future generations". (1992: 117)

The philosophical man must therefore experience the wisdom which he aspires to, in the world. "It is not about being dead to the world, detaching oneself from it, cutting oneself off from it, it is not about being wise outside the world, or alongside it, but within the world." (1974: 438) Philosophy indicates the path to "practical wisdom", this "ability of man's to discern that which leads to the desired result, thanks to experience and reflection" (1992: 191). If such wisdom is only practical, it can probably inspire as well as direct the behaviour and actions of the immoral and violent man; from this point of view, it is morally neutral. But as soon as the individual understands that "violence is evil for man and for all men", "practical wisdom and living morality cannot be separated: the will of nonviolence acts as a guide for this wisdom which, without it, would be but an arbitrary instrument" (1992: 191). The rational man must show prudence to be able to discern what his conduct should be in a given concrete situation. "Prudence is this practical form of wisdom that determines the execution and leads to the success of the moral individual's initiatives." (1992: 126) But prudence does not recommend inaction to the rational man, it advises him which actions to undertake.

Someone who has chosen reason must therefore act in order to be the incarnation of reason in the world. "Hence the philosophy of the philosophical man only achieves its end through action. …. Philosophy is carried out and ends in action. …. Flight is strictly forbidden." (1974: 417-418) And, according to Eric Weil, action must often be violent in order to be efficient. He does not consider it reasonable to refuse violence entirely, because such an attitude can only cause to reinforce violence's hold over the world, and to hand the latter over to irrational forces. From then on, "when everything has been said, reason has no other means than violent ones." (1991b: 217). At times, violence can be "noble and just" (1984: 233).

Violence as a means to carry out nonviolence

Eric Weil, however, does not forget that it is the choice of nonviolence which is the basis for man's rational behaviour in the world. Nonviolence is not only a philosophical requirement, it is also a political requirement. It cannot only be a concern for the philosopher who re-flects on history, but also for the politician who acts in history. "Nonviolence in history and through history has become history's goal, and is conceived as its goal. .... Progress towards nonviolence defines the meaning of history for politics." (1984: 133) But it is precisely in order to carry out nonviolence in history that it is necessary—technically necessary—to use the means of violence. "Nonviolence as a fundamental choice is—and is only—fundamental in the strict sense of the word: reflection derives from it as well as from sovereign political good; it only finds its end within it because it has originated from it. Between the starting and ending points nonviolence remains to be realised, in the middle of violence, and therefore also through the use of violent means." (1991b: 410)

Violence must therefore be used to serve nonviolence. Nonviolence as an end to history, justifies violence as a means to act in history. "The choice of nonviolence is not a choice for the "non-use" of violence; on the contrary, the choice only makes sense if it is admitted that in the world of violence, and whether or not violence it is aware of its own nature, only violence can efficiently serve nonviolence's interest against violence." (1991b: 409-410) Eric Weil is formal: only violence's striking arguments are likely to be heard by the violent man, and only they can consequently assist nonviolence's progress in history. "The historian learns to see this obvious—and confusing—fact: that unless history is refused and violence and death are accepted, the will for nonviolence must fight against violence through violence—the only "argument" which violent people can understand." (1991b: 252) Similarly, Eric Weil also writes: "Violence exists between ourselves; and nonviolence, if it does not want to give way to violence, is forced to use the only means which its adversary recognizes." (1991a: 171)

The politician who bears the responsibility of the future of the community could not care less about the lessons in morality of those preaching nonviolence to him. "If he wants to succeed, he will have to use the means—the only means—which violent people respond to, and which are their own. When one carries the burden of politics, one does not fight violent people through an attitude of refusal of any form of violence." (1991a: 165)

According to Eric Weil, "violence has been, and still is, the *driving cause* of history", despite the elimination of violence being its *"final cause"* (1984: 232). So in the eyes of history, therefore of the historian, and consequently of the philosopher, violence—despite being considered negative—has played and still plays a positive part in the advent of freedom in the world. Violence must be "understood positively, as a spring without which there would be no movement; being negativity in every aspect, it is, in its totality, the positivity of the Being that rationally recognizes itself as freedom." (1974: 55)

The end justifies the means

For Eric Weil, there is no doubt that "the end justifies the means" (1991a: 169). He is even surprised that this principle may have a bad reputation and that moral men may be scandalized by it. "Yet, this principle is not only true, it does nothing but formulate a truism. Indeed, how else could a means be justified, if not by its end?" (1991b: 209) Admittedly, the means of violence contradict the moral requirement of nonviolence; considered in themselves, they are immoral and therefore bad, but they are necessary as soon as they alone make it possible to efficiently fight against the violence of evil-doers.

Yet Eric Weil is aware that the principle according to which the end justifies the means entails the risk of any means being justified by any end. "Too often", he notes, "the most noble promises—deserving every man's collaboration in their realization—only act as a cover for moral laziness, for the basest instincts, for cowardice, for coldness of the heart: the goal then justifies any means, simply because the invocation of the goal must silence any objection, any discussion, on the subject of moral values, perhaps even of the technical appropriateness of the processes." (1992: 67) Eric Weil is therefore aware of the risk that this principle—as real as it may be—could pave the way for arbitrariness. "If politics", he asks, "can rightfully use violence and ruse, do we not grant it the right to arbitrariness? .... Do we not expose ourselves to most serious risks once we allow violence and lies?" (1991b: 167) "How can we avoid ", he continues, "consciously or not—unawareness is no excuse—becoming the henchmen of a form of violence that does not serve reason or fight against private, arbitrary, selfish violence, violence that does not aim for the universal?" (1991b: 168) Who indeed does not claim that their cause is a just one, and that their struggle is that of good against evil, of truth against error? "Once violence has been introduced into politics, whatever the side that invoked it may be, it is extremely difficult to send it back to the arsenal of available arms that do not get used." (1991b: 383) However, while he asserts the truth of this principle, Eric Weil cannot hide his concern for the way in which it may be used. "It is not necessary", he writes, "to look for illustrations which prove that, more than once over the course of history, the risk that is inherent to the principle has turned into a disaster." (1991a: 169)

The greatest risk is to forget that the means of violence are only necessary, and that they do not necessarily become good. The politician, writes Eric Weil, "must never forget that these means are dangerous, not only because they can foster tensions, conflicts, passions between nations and groups, but also, and above all, because they can be considered—and they often are—to be admirable actions in themselves, precisely where they succeed." (1991a: 171-172) Eric Weil strongly refutes the historians, philosophers and political leaders who preach "the gospel of violence", for, "against them, abstract morality .... is simply right". (1991b: 252)

Eric Weil does not forget either that the men who are responsible for executing the politician's decision to resort to the means of violence, themselves have to suffer from the wrong means they put into practice. "Violence, even if its immediate use seems necessary, pushes citizens into actions and habits that are contrary to rationality" and "they thus receive a sort of counter-education" (1984: 238). From then on, the moral man is tempted to refuse to recognize the need for such immoral means, in order to keep a clear conscience. But Eric Weil constantly sees this abstention on behalf of the moral man as shirking his responsibilities. True moral obligation does not involve evading this necessity, but taking it on, by trying hard to overcome it. That is why, while he recognizes the political necessity to use the wrong means of violence, Eric Weil claims that their only true justification is to build a society in which they will not be necessary anymore. "The wrong means are imposed (onto the politician) by evil-doers. But in a positive way—and this is decisive—his goal remains to make the use of these means superfluous and really wrong, that is, technically ineffective, technically unjustified." (1991a: 170) "If (the statesman)", he insists, "must fight evil with evil, it is for him to prove, for him to show that he has been forced into it, and that he has obeyed necessity, for the sole purpose of eliminating this very necessity." (1991a: 172)

Overcoming the necessity for nonviolence

Ultimately, Eric Weil thus reasserts the necessity to realize nonviolence in history, by overcoming and surmounting the need to resort to violence. He also thinks that humanity has already made considerable progress in that direction. "The mere fact that we now consider violence—whether open or hidden—as evil proves this, while for millennia, humanity sincerely admired the strong and the cunning." (1991a: 170) Eric Weil is convinced that violence has indeed contributed to nonviolence's progress in history. "There is", he asserts, "no absolute historical contradiction between violence and nonviolence: to an extent (great in comparison to the past), nonviolence now exists in the world, and it comes from violence—it is still its goal." (1984: 233)

Above all, Eric Weil thinks that humanity today has reached a new phase of its evolution; it has become possible for it to take a decisive step towards its accomplishment in nonviolence: "From now on, humanity can consciously want that which it has entirely unconsciously pursued. It can think nonviolence and honesty, and can act towards their ever-developing realization." (1991a: 171) Nonviolence can now increasingly be substituted for violence in order to realize the meaning of history. "It is now important to build a world in which morality may live alongside nonviolence; a world in which nonviolence may not be mere absence of meaning—that meaning which violence sought to find in history without knowing that which it was looking for, which it created violently, and which it continues to look for by violent means. The task is to build a world in which nonviolence may be real without being suppression *both* of the non-sense of violence *and* of all positive meaning in the life of men." (1984: 234) He eventually believes that society today can catch a glimpse of the realization of the ideal which it has been assigned from the beginning of time, by the man who has chosen reason, and therefore nonviolence: "In modern society, the law always tends to diminish the role of historical factors; ideally, it seeks to achieve a purely rational system, controlling the relations between individuals so that violence may be excluded from them." (1984: 83)

12

Dialogue with Eric Weil

Deciding on nonviolence

Having walked alongside Eric Weil at length, having made him speak, and having carefully listened to him, it is now time to establish a discussion with him, in order to highlight our agreements and disagreements.

First of all, Eric Weil has the great merit of clearly stating that violence radically contradicts the requirement of reason which man bears within him, and which is the basis for his humanity: in order truly and fully to become a man, the individual must freely choose reason over violence. He is aware that man is a being who has needs, desires and passions and that, as such, he is a violent being. But precisely, if man is able to understand himself as a violent being, it is because the idea of nonviolence is already a part of him. Violence is one of man's possibilities, and it always will be. But man possesses another possibility that corresponds to a constitutive requirement of his being: nonviolence.

To fulfil his humanity, man must set out to inform his desires and passions through reason, and to submit them to his will: he must decide on nonviolence. This decision gives sense to his existence, that is, both direction and significance. Eric Weil's philosophical reflection is thus entirely based on the concept of violence, and therefore, on the concept of nonviolence. Wishing to clarify that which lies at the very heart of his thought, Gilbert Krischer writes: "At the category level, violence is the concept of that which threatens man in his very humanity: the elimination of human relationships from man to man, to other men and to the man he is. It is the cause of his dehumanization. It is this other side of man within man, that which man is in conflict with; this conflict constitutes man in his very humanity. Man comes into being through the experience of violence." (1992: 123-124) Violence is unreason, contradiction, non-sense, because it is in-humanity. That is why the rational man must decide to rule violence out and to choose nonviolence for good, all the while knowing that this choice will need to be constantly renewed so as to ward off the ever-present possibility of violence.

Hence violence is discredited by Eric Weil's philosophy, and any "gospel of violence" is refuted: the requirement of nonviolence is the sole basis for the humanity of man. Nonviolence must not only inform man's thoughts, it must also determine his attitude in life, his behaviour with other men, and his commitment to history. Nonviolence is therefore a practical form of wisdom. For the man who has chosen nonviolence is not a solitary being: he lives in a historical community within which he is hand in glove with other men. There can be no question of his avoiding meeting and being with others in order to be true to his choice of nonviolence. He must stand by his community: he must move nonviolence forward within this community's life. For if it gives sense to the rational man's personal existence, it also gives sense to the collective history of men and peoples. It is therefore the rational man's responsibility to act in order that history itself may increasingly become nonviolent.

Provided that others have equally chosen reason, speech and nonviolence, it is then possible for him to establish a dialogue with them, to start a discussion with them. Together they form a community of "real men". If a disagreement arises between them, it must not generate violence, since they have commonly agreed not to resort to it. This disagreement must be overcome through discussion; and if they cannot reach an agreement, they should at least agree on the subject of their disagreement, and thus defuse the conflict between them. Nonviolence is the golden rule that will prevail in the relations between real men who have chosen reason over violence.

Choosing between killing and dying

But Eric Weil is aware that the rational man will inevitably come up against the violence of irrational men, both inside and outside his own community. What attitude should then have the man who has chosen nonviolence when he finds himself in a situation where he is compelled to choose between killing and dying? If we only consider the formal requirement of pure morality, there can be no doubt for Eric Weil that the individual must choose to die, so that he himself may avoid being violent. But he criticizes, contests and finally refutes this choice. He refutes it as a temptation which the moral man must not give in to. Accepting to die seems like an easy solution for Eric Weil. For ultimately, death lets the moral man escape all the difficulties he may encounter in life in order to remain true to morality. Death, in a way, makes his life simpler. That is why Eric Weil suspects the person who chooses to die of showing more cowardice than courage.

But, above all, he challenges this choice because in accepting to die, the moral man abandons the world to the violence of immoral men; he deserts history, whereas it is in history that violence must be defeated and reason made to progress. Eric Weil thus asserts that in the eyes of the requirement of concrete and historical morality, and not of formal and abstract morality, the moral man must choose killing rather than dying, in order to preserve the possibility of the realization of nonviolence, within himself and his community.

It is at this point that we must start a discussion with Eric Weil. First, the individual should be in an exceptional situation to have to consciously choose between dying and killing. In most cases, he has to choose between two *risks*—that of killing and that of dying—which is very different. For a priori it is not always clear, that in taking the risk of dying rather than killing, the probabilities that he may be killed may be higher.

Furthermore, we find it difficult to believe Eric Weil when he says that it is easy for the moral man to prefer dying to killing. We would rather be inclined to thinking that for the moral man, the fear of dying remains stronger than the fear of living, and that consequently, he himself is naturally more tempted to kill than to die. But above all, we do not believe that a person who accepts to die out of loyalty to his choice for nonviolence would leave history in the hands of violent, irrational men. Someone who dies on account of the violence of evil-doers—not because the latter caught up with them as they escaped or joined them in their retreat, but because they decided to confront it head on so as to stand in its way and prevent it from pursuing its headlong chase in history through its endless destruction—that person is more than ever present in history. They do not only exist and remain in history, but also act in history; they make history. They do not seek to protect their own purity, but to protect history against the impurity of violence. By refusing to become a party to violence, they build a new resistance front against it with their own body. They are aware that in accepting to resort to violence themselves, they would on the contrary make a breach and give way to it.

Someone who agrees to die so as to avoid killing can *hope* effectively and efficiently to contribute to the extinguishing of violence in the world. *Hope*, is indeed, at stake here, as a philosophical choice. It seems to us that ultimately, Eric Weil's thought on the subject of the necessity of violence must be understood in terms of *despair*. Whoever agrees to kill so as to avoid dying is very likely to contribute to the rekindling of violence in the world. Thus, in the eyes of history itself, and according to history's efficiency criterion, it is reasonable to hope that it is more operative to die in order to realize nonviolence within oneself today, than to kill in order to leave open the possibility to realize it tomorrow. Someone who agrees to die in order to realize nonviolence within himself, realizes it in history at this very point. Someone who agrees to die while opposing the violence of history with their entire being, and for that, refusing to be violent himself, offers hope in history: they teach reason and nonviolence more than someone who agrees to kill in order to defeat violence. The rational man's violence is indeed highly likely to serve as a pretext to the irrational man's violence.

It therefore seems essential to reverse the order of Eric Weil's rule and exception. According to him, the rule—when the moral man must choose between killing and dying—is to kill, even if he admits that there may be exceptions to this rule.

On the contrary, it seems to us that for the man who has chosen nonviolence, the rule should be to prepare to die so as to avoid killing—even if there may be exceptional situations in which he may have no alternative but to stand in the way of even greater violence, especially when it affects and is likely to kill his friends and relatives. Having said that, it would be rash to feign to forget that the very person who has chosen nonviolence as a rule of conduct may well, under such circumstances, not have the courage to die, and decide to kill because the fear of dying has become more powerful than the will not to kill. After all, who could then cast the first stone at him?

So generally, Eric Weil believes that real men must agree—in order to maintain cohesion within their own community, and thus to leave open the possibility for its members to live morally—to resort to violence to force reason upon individuals who have chosen violence. But he then reintroduces violence into the very life of the man who has chosen nonviolence. Admittedly, he is careful to reassert that nonviolence remains history's end, its final cause, but it is only in order to justify violence as a necessary means—technically necessary—to reach this end.

Does the end justify the means?

When Eric Weil establishes the dualism of the irrational man's violence and the rational man's violence, and he bases his line of thought on it, so as to assert the necessity of counter-violence to suppress violence, he exaggeratedly simplifies reality. For, in most violent conflicts, it is practically impossible to establish such a manifest and categorical cleavage between the behaviour of both adversaries. In most cases, each of them can legitimately justify being in conflict against the other. Each can have grounds for claiming that he does nothing but defend his right against the other. It is indeed noteworthy that both should resort to the same rhetoric of legitimation. The words by which they justify their own violence are indeed symmetrical, and often equally happen to be partially justified.

We cannot therefore confine ourselves to the defensive pattern according to which rational men may be forced to resort to violence to fight against the violence of evil-doers, criminals or the insane. History was and still is filled with lethal conflicts in which each of the two opposing communities can emphasize—with the same sincerity (but sincerity is not truth)—the fact that it is only defending itself against an enemy which threatens its right to exist.

For Eric Weil, it is obvious that the end justifies the means. Should there be a contradiction between nonviolence, considered history's end, and violence, considered the means to act in history, the rational man must come to terms with this contradiction; even if he might never resign himself to it, he must always endeavour to overcome it. It seems to us that Eric Weil's reflection on the relation between end and means represents a weak point in his line of thought. Admittedly, he is aware of the dangers and risks inherent in the principle of the justification of means by the end; but according to us, the slightly hasty manner in which he defends and legitimises this principle offers no possibility of efficient protection against one or another. For if it is indeed necessary that the end be just so that the means may also be, this is far from enough. The end does not justify any means. History itself shows us that the wrong means pervert the end in the name of which they are being used. There is, in actual fact, coherence and homogeneity, between the nature of the means employed and the nature of the end that is achieved. The necessity to use means that are coherent with the end that is wanted is not only a matter of morality, but also, and indissolubly, a matter of efficiency. Eric Weil does not seem to be paying enough attention to this organic link between end and means. He does not take the time to visualize the act of violence which he deems necessary to suppress the irrational man's violence, and to examine all its consequences, for whoever commits it as well as whoever endures it. This exempts him from noting that this act of violence itself is also a failure of reason.

Can violence be the antidote to violence?

Eric Weil constantly uses the postulate according to which the action against violence—whether it be the violence of criminality, injustice, oppression or aggression, and he generally does not distinguish these forms of violence—is necessarily violent as the basis for his argument, and without this postulate ever really being discussed. He makes this postulate seem unquestionable. Yet precisely, this postulate seems quite questionable to us. We would like to discuss it while pursuing the dialogue with Eric Weil.

Among the means likely to bring the irrational man to his senses, Eric Weil only distinguishes persuasion and violence. But in order for persuasion to achieve its end, the individual who has chosen violence ought to decide to give it up, choose reason and accept discussion of his own free will. This is not impossible, for the violent man remains radically capable of reason; but it is not the most likely. And as soon as persuasion has failed to convince whoever has chosen violence, Eric Weil claims that the rational man has no other alternative but to choose violence himself to constrain them, since violence's striking arguments may be the only ones they can hear. But those who believe that violence is the only language that can be understood by their adversaries, and that can make them see sense, necessarily learn and can effectively only speak that language. Hence they themselves become caught up in the fatality of violence.

Eric Weil leaves no room for a form of constraint to prevail which would not be violent, which would have other arguments than those of reason, but which would not enter the inhumane and dehumanising logic of violence. The notion of nonviolent constraint is entirely missing from Eric Weil's reflection. For him, nonviolence can only be carried out through dialogue and discussion; it can only be the nonviolence of words. He does not know the nonviolence of action. He knows nothing of the nonviolent action that can force an irrational individual to accept discussion, by exerting a force which is not an act of violence against him, that is to say, which does not violate his humanity.

According to Eric Weil, every action in history is necessarily violent and whoever renounces violence also renounces action in history on the pretext of protecting the purity of their will. Admittedly, this theory is unjustified. Its decisive error seems to us that it has not established a distinction between force and violence. He always speaks of violence in a general way, and includes all forms of constraint in this word alone. From then on, he leaves no space for a nonviolent force which would not only be based on the force of reason, but also on the force of action;

he leaves no space for nonviolent action which may carry out a real force of constraint, that would owe nothing to the destructive and lethal logic of violence.

"It seems quite clear", writes Patrice Canivez, "that Weil has in mind an intervention of the philosopher in history; one which would result in the birth of a nonviolent version of action, that is, in the strict sense of the word, of a specifically political version of action. .... This point must obviously be linked to the philosopher's Socratic attitude, that is to say his refusal of active violence." (1990: 43) But with such an assertion, Patrice Canivez transcends Eric Weil's thought. Admittedly, this transcendence follows the logic of his philosophy and, in that sense, he is true to his thought; but it has not been explicitly formulated by him. It is true that Eric Weil's entire philosophical reflection calls for a "nonviolent version of action", but he himself has clearly never felt the possibility of such an action. That is why he has always maintained the necessity of violent action. Patrice Canivez points out that Eric Weil himself has considered situations in which action can become nonviolent: "It is true", he then notes, "of the government since it acts through discussion." (Ibid., 60) But in fact, in this care, the government discusses more than it acts, and only seeks to persuade interlocutors who have not chosen violence. Yet the action that poses a problem, both to the philosopher and to the politician, is the one acting against violence. Ultimately, the effective quest for the possibilities of nonviolent action enables the realization of Eric Weil's philosophy, but it realizes it beyond its own vision. In order to be able to assert that which Patrice Canivez writes, it is necessary to stand on Eric Weil's shoulders: this offers a horizon which he himself has never discovered.

Violence knows no limits

In recognizing the necessity of violence, Eric Weil would certainly like to limit its use to the bare minimum. But, by its own entirely mechanical logic, violence does not acknowledge any limits. As soon as it finds space, it wishes to fill that space. Eric Weil senses this danger but it seems to us that he does not dedicate the necessary reflection to it, so as to control it and seek protection from it.

Although he feels the need to assert the necessity of violence, Eric Weil wants to believe that humanity will successfully eliminate this necessity. But such an expectation is very likely to be in vain, for it postulates that all men may have freely decided to choose reason over violence. Eric Weil may well require that the rational man—who uses violence to defeat the violence of evil-doers—firmly intends it, or even be tenaciously determined to do so, in order to create a world in which it will not be necessary anymore; but contrary to his assertion, this is not decisive. For this is not up to the rational man. It is up to irrational men and their tendency to choose reason. Yet, Eric Weil is aware that it can be required, but not expected of men who are in the hands of passions, to be rational.

If we strictly confine ourselves to Eric Weil's system, asserting that the action of the rational man must also seek to eliminate violence which fights against unjust violence, this is equivalent in fact to postulating a history that is free from unjust violence, which implies that history may be free from the unjust man. This is like postulating a *u-topia* which will never be realized *anywhere*. It must be acknowledged that Eric Weil's system is the prisoner of an implacable contradiction and that ultimately, it does not work.

When he attempts to assess history, and more specifically the action of violence in history, he seems to show great optimism which does not find confirmation in practice. The conclusions that he reaches refer to nonviolence's progress in history, and we remain somewhat sceptical about this. At the very least, this progress is not linear. Progress always comes at great cost, and it is never established for good. And above all, there are so many and such large steps backwards that we strongly doubt that the overall assessment may be positive. If the rule is to defeat violence through violence and thus to reduce the number of its victims, the exceptions to the rule—which highlight the fact that violence increases violence and raises the number of its victims—are too many, too often and too serious to be mere exceptions. They contradict the rule to such a point that they do away with it.

In reality, there will always be irrational men among us who will not be convinced by the force of reason and will have to be constrained through violence if, as Eric Weil claims, there is no other alternative to their being neutralized. That is why—despite his ultimate gamble on reason in order to reassert that nonviolence truly is the meaning and end of history—the logic of his philosophy does not make it possible to anticipate history outside the logic of violence. He himself has given violence too much credibility that men may be hoped to set history free from its hold. Admittedly, he does not confine history to the fatality of violence as do the ideologies of violence. He maintains the possibility of a nonviolent history to the end of his reflection. For men do not inevitably have to choose violence. They do so of their own free will. Furthermore, not all of them do, and Eric Weil even believes that less and less of them do. But if it is true that it may be enough for a few of them to choose violence in order that those who have chosen reason may become compelled to resort to violence themselves so as to neutralize them, then history is well and truly confined to the necessity of violence. It is of course pointless to accuse the gods or fate: irrational men are to blame. But should not the question that Eric Weil does not ask, indeed be asked: are not rational men also to blame, for they have not been able to invent other means than those of violence to defeat the wickedness of irrational men?

Emmanuel Levinas: ethical criticism of the State

Emmanuel Levinas notably refers to Eric Weil's work when he acknowledges the necessity of the State (see Levinas, 1993: 64). But he remains more vigilant than Weil and attempts to ward off the dangers inherent to the state-controlled management of society.

Relationships between men are not restricted to face-to-face encounters between one man and another. As soon as a third appears, justice needs to be reorganized, and this requires laws and institutions, that is to say, the State. Levinas does not deny that the necessity to administer justice demands "a certain violence" (Levinas, 1993: 124). The violent man who threatens his fellowman "calls for violence" (Ibid., 123). From then on, according to Levinas, "one cannot say that there is no legitimate violence" (Ibid., 124). However, he remains aware that any form of violence contains an implacable part of injustice.

The universal rules and laws according to which the State judges its citizens can only lead to an imperfect justice system that, ultimately, does not do justice to the person being judged; the latter is unique, but is not acknowledged as such. The State "does not untie the knots, but cuts them" (Levinas, 1990: 264) and repressive justice is always "at the limit of potential injustice" (Id.). The action of the State too often turns against the good it is supposed to aim for: "War and administration, that is to say, hierarchy, through which the State is instituted and maintained, alienate the Same, which they were supposed to maintain in its purity; in order to suppress violence, it is necessary to have recourse to violence." (Levinas, 1991: 55) According to Levinas, "left to itself, politics bears a tyranny within" (1992: 334-335). The State must therefore not be left to "its own necessities" (1990: 248). That is why "politics must always be able to be controlled and criticized on the basis of ethics" (1992: 75).

The State which refuses to become caught up in its own logic—Levinas calls it "the liberal State"—must always be "concerned about its delay in meeting the requirement of the face of the other" (1991: 238-239). The State must have a guilty conscience considering that it is never just enough. It must always feel remorse for its own harshness. The necessity of a justice system that is administered under the guise of State laws does not exempt man from his responsibility towards other men. "In the State where laws function in their generality, where verdicts are pronounced out of a concern for universality, once justice is said there is still, for the unique and responsible person, the possibility of, or appeal to something that will reconsider the rigour of always rigourous justice. To soften this justice, to listen to this personal appeal, is each person's role." (Levinas apud Poirié, 1996: 108)

For Levinas, the establishment of a social order based on hierarchy can only lead to an imperfect justice system: "For me", he claims, "the negative element, the element of violence in the State, in the hierarchy, appears even when the hierarchy functions perfectly, when everyone submits to universal ideas. There are cruelties which are terrible because they proceed from the necessity of the reasonable Order. There are the

tears that a civil servant cannot see: the tears of the Other. ....
The I alone can perceive the "secret tears" of the Other,
which are caused by the functioning—albeit reasonable—of
the hierarchy. Consequently, subjectivity is indispensable for
assuring this very nonviolence that the State searches for in
equal measure." (Levinas, 1991: 63-64) Analysing the conditions of a possible political order in Emmanuel Levinas' work,
Vincent Tsongo Luutu writes: "By showing how politics does
not always—as it should—carry out the noble objectives that
it sets itself, and by prompting it into a therapeutic guilty conscience, ethics rouses—as if by a prophetic action—the humanity within politics. .... Humanity, the basis of Levinas'
philosophy, is this ability to say no to inhumanity that is specific to triumphant totality." (Luutu, 1993: 131-132)

Gandhi ignored

Hence does Emmanuel Levinas criticise the State in a way that is
not found in Eric Weil's work. All things considered, Eric Weil's
State has a clear conscience. But Levinas does not ask himself
either whether it would be possible to oppose the violence that
threatens the other man by other methods than those of lethal
violence. Neither one nor the other refer to Gandhi in any way.
Ultimately, when all is said and done, it seems that Eric Weil's
mistake is to have ignored Gandhi and not to have learned anything from him. A question arises here, which does not seems to
have an answer: how is it possible that Eric Weil may not have
paid any attention to Gandhi's thoughts and actions? What can
explain the fact that he does not say one word about Gandhi
throughout his entire work? How is it possible that the philosopher who has thought about violence and nonviolence all his life
may not have found himself—at one time or another—in resonance with the person who, as early as the late thirties, history
had already elected as the "apostle of nonviolence"? For, obviously, it is not possible for Eric Weil not to have heard of the
nonviolent action undertaken by Gandhi in order to free his people from the violence of British colonial oppression. From then
on, how is it possible that Gandhi's testimony, which Albert Einstein described as "the greatest political genius of our times"

(1979: 52), may not have been considered by Eric Weil, that it may not have entered his reflection at any time? Of course, strictly speaking, Gandhi was not a philosopher. But he was more than that; he was a wise man, and in Eric Weil's very eyes, wisdom is the realization of philosophy. He also was a politician and as such, he became—at a decisive moment in the history of his people—the main author of its liberation. As for Eric Weil, following Hegel, he has not ceased to think about history, which has somehow been raw material for his reflection. He has thus thought about Machiavelli a lot, and has sought to do him justice regarding the accusations against him which he considered fallacious. Why has he not thought about Gandhi?

Let us be clear: our purpose is not to regret that Eric Weil may not have rallied to the principles and theories formulated by Gandhi on the subject of nonviolence. Our regret is simply that he may not have considered them and discussed them, that he may not have confronted the principles and theories of his own philosophy with the thoughts and actions of Gandhi. Without wishing to prejudge the conclusions that Eric Weil may have reached, it seems to us that such a confrontation would have been very fruitful.

Gandhi proved, contrary to Eric Weil's assertions, that it was possible to renounce all use of violence while remaining present and actively taking part in the history of one's own community. Very early on, the attention of many philosophers was drawn to the exceptional side of the Indian leader's undertaking. As early as 1927, Jacques Maritain writes in *Primacy of the Spiritual:* "The example of Gandhi should put us to shame." (1927: 131) In 1933, in a study entitled *On the purification of means*, Maritain examines "the testimony born of Gandhi" at length. Admittedly, he expresses reservations and criticism towards the Gandhian doctrine; he criticizes it for condemning every recourse to the means of violence both in principle and in the absolute. However, he wonders whether "Gandhi's approach", once it has been rectified and readjusted, "could not, as he himself often declared, be applied in the West as in the East, and renew the temporal struggles for human beings and freedom". (Maritain, 1933: 198-201)

The unexplored field of nonviolent methods

As for Emmanuel Mounier, he turns to Gandhi as early as 1933, and pays great attention to the nonviolent means of action that he advocates for the freeing of his people. "None of us have any doubt", he writes, "that violence is always impurity; that a practical ideal of nonviolence must be the limit which we must constantly seek to come closer to." In this light, he asserts his decision "to study and test all the yet unexplored field of nonviolent methods, without ever losing sight of their efficiency, and while seeking to make up for lost time so as not to defer our action in vain." Admittedly, Mounier does not absolutely rule out the necessity to use violent means, but he sets several conditions, and the first of these is: "That we should beforehand, in so far as we should have efficiently nurtured and armed them, have heroically tried all the nonviolent means that are at our disposal, and should not accept violence as a final and last resort." (Mournier, 1961: 325-326)

In February 1949, Paul Ricoeur published an article entitled "The nonviolent man and his presence in history" (1955: 223-233) in the magazine *Esprit*. He also takes Gandhi's contribution to history into account: "Inimitable as he may himself be, limited as his work may be, Gandhi symbolizes in our times more than hope, but a demonstration. .... Gandhi was not any less mercilessly present to India as Lenin was to Russia." What seems particularly exemplary to Ricoeur in the action campaigns carried out by Gandhi, is that they realize the reconciliation of ends with means. "Far from banishing the ends away from history and deserting the plan of means which it would leave to their impurity, the nonviolent being endeavours to join them in an action which would intimately be a spirituality and a technique." And he acknowledges that Westerners do not know anything about this technique of action and this method of resistance, and that they are wrong not to study them.

It is difficult not to think that, should Eric Weil also have paid attention to Gandhi's work, it would have led him to alter some of his words and recognize the possibility of nonviolent action in history.

13

Gandhi, the Requirement for Nonviolence

Gandhi's name and face have become familiar to Westerners, yet his thought and action remain widely unknown to them. They generally nurture a distant admiration for him in the way that one gladly admires those whom legend has given a saintly halo of wisdom, but they continue to keep their distance. They do not take the trouble to come closer to him in order to listen to and understand him. Gandhi thus remains for the most part ignored within his very celebrity.

Everyone associates the word nonviolence with Gandhi's name, but there again, Gandhi's nonviolence appears remarkable; there is nothing exemplary about it. Hence is there a prevailing idea in the West, that Gandhi's thought may be characteristic of an uncertain orientalism, which may not concern those who care about realism and efficiency, that is to say, those who wish to be "rational". Yet Gandhi's contribution is essential to the comprehension of nonviolence. There is a 'before' and an 'after-Gandhi', both in terms of the philosophical reflection on the ethical requirement of nonviolence that is the basis for man's humanity, and in the experimentation of the strategy of nonviolent action which allows the peaceful resolution of conflicts. But it is also true that Gandhi's thought is not easily accessible. His words and writing are countless, but they are always circumstantial, and in order to be understood correctly, they must be considered in the very context in which they were formulated. Gandhi left us no synthetic treatise clearly defining his idea of nonviolence. We must take the time to decipher it amongst all the things he said. Furthermore, Gandhi is a complex character. "This man", stated Pandit Nehru knowingly, "was an extraordinary paradox." (1952: 364) His thought often shows contrasts which go against our Cartesian reasoning and leave us disconcerted. We must therefore endeavour to go beyond these contrasts, even if it sometimes involves circumventing some of his assertions. We cannot limit Gandhi's thought to plain "Gandhi-ism", a doctrine that would be closed in on itself. Gandhi does not provide us with set, model answers; he nevertheless invites us to join him in asking essential questions in whose essence is the very meaning of our existence and our history. And, as he attempted to do in his own time, it is for us to invent here and now the best possible answers.

The quest for truth

When Gandhi writes his autobiography, he calls it: *The story of my experiments with truth*. For him, life has no other goal, no other meaning but the quest for truth. "Nothing", he states, "is or exists in reality except Truth. .... Devotion to this Truth is the sole justification for our existence. All our activities should be centred on Truth." (1960: 25-26) He is deeply convinced that man's truth lies within himself and that he must not lose himself seeking for it anywhere else. "What is Truth?", he asks. "A difficult question, but I have solved it for myself by saying that it is what the voice within tells you." (Ibid., 99) To choose his life, man's only option is to pay attention to this "still small voice" (1969: 137) that speaks within him. It is the only voice which may lead him on the path of truth. This "voice of conscience" is "the supreme judge of the legitimacy of any act and any thought" (1960: 125).

Hence must man fully accept his autonomy as a free and responsible being: he must himself promulgate the laws to which he has to conform his thoughts, words and actions (autonomous, from the Greek *autos*, himself, and *nomos*, law: who follows his own laws), without relying on any external authority—whether it be religious, social or political—that would tell him how to behave. Such submission would in reality be an abdication by which the individual would give up his freedom. Admittedly, this autonomy inevitably includes the possibility of being wrong, but he can only reach the truth by taking that risk. "We may be wrong", writes Gandhi, "in our efforts to move forward, maybe even greatly so. But man is a being that must rule himself; this autonomy implies a power to make mistakes and correct them as often as one makes them." (1969: 137) Gandhi is convinced that should he be wrong, it is impossible for the sincere man not to uncover his mistake in experimenting with that which he believes to be truth. "In such selfless search for Truth", he writes, "nobody can lose his bearing for very long. Directly one takes the wrong path, one stumbles and is thus redirected to the right path." (1960: 28) The individual would take the risk of persisting in his own error by promising obedience to an external authority.

A seeker of truth must convince himself that he is always on the move and that he will never reach the end of the road. The truth that he can make out is fragmentary, relative, partial and therefore imperfect. That is why man must never seek to impose his truth onto others. "The Golden Rule of our conduct", Gandhi claims, "is mutual toleration." (1960: 133) When it was pointed out to him that the quest for truth leads individuals to different opinions, he answered: "That is why nonviolence is a necessary corollary. Without that, there would be confusion, or worse." (1969: 282)

The truth which Gandhi seeks is not found in the register of abstract ideas, but in that of concrete attitudes. Since man essentially is a relational being, the most important thing is the truth of his relationship with others. In other words, man's truth is not so much in the soundness of his ideas as in the soundness of his relationships with others. Yet violence "distorts" this relationship. It is therefore only possible to establish a true relationship with others by taking care to avoid any form of violence towards them. As Joan Bondurant brought out, the entire Gandhian philosophy is centred in the idea that "the only way to test truth is through an action based on the refusal to harm others" (Bondurant, 1969: 25). The truth is not found in man as an individual, but in his relationship with others, in a relationship that respects the truth of others.

Gandhi imagines that nonviolence was discovered by some "wise old man in search of Truth" who understood that he who persistently seeks to destroy the beings who cause him difficulties is on the wrong track. He thus experienced that "the more he resorted to violence, the further he went from the Truth" (1960: 32). Because men are all part of humanity, to do violence to the humanity of others, is to undermine one's own humanity; and this double violence is destructive for the truth. "Nonviolence", writes Gandhi, "is the basis for the quest for truth. No day goes by when I do not realize that in reality, this quest is in vain, if it is not based on nonviolence. To oppose a system, to attack it, is good; but to oppose its author, and to attack him, this equals opposing oneself, to becoming one's own assailant." (Gandhi, 1964: 348) Hence Gandhi manages to convince himself that "violence is suicide" (1969: 254). Not only, not principally because the violence that man exerts against his adversary pulls him into a vicious circle in which he is very likely to be crushed himself; but above all because the violence that he commits, albeit allowing him to triumph, greatly undermines his own humanity. Man is the first to endure the violence that he practices; he is wounded deep within himself by his own violence, and perhaps fatally so.

Gandhi realizes that the requirement of truth merges with the requirement of nonviolence. "Without nonviolence", he writes, "it is not possible to seek and find Truth. Nonviolence and Truth are so intertwined that it is practically impossible to disentangle and separate them. They are like the two sides of a coin, or rather of a smooth unstamped metallic disc. Who can say which is the obverse, and which is the reverse? Nevertheless nonviolence is the means, and Truth is the end. Means, in order to be means, must always be accessible, so the practice of nonviolence is our supreme duty." (1958: 42)

Doing good

Gandhi is certainly aware that man has an instinct which drives him to do violence to others in order to satisfy his needs, fulfil his desires and defend his interests. But this instinct for violence corresponds to the animal side of human nature, and man also has in him the requirement of nonviolence that corresponds to the spiritual side of his nature: "Man as animal is violent, but as Spirit is nonviolent. As soon as he awakes to the spirit within, he cannot remain violent." (1969: 156) According to Gandhi, in order to achieve his humanity, man must therefore adapt his attitude towards others to the requirements of nonviolence. "Nonviolence", he claims, "is the first article of my faith. It is also the last article of my creed." (1969: 84) Hence Gandhi seeks a Truth which is not only the Truth of thought, but also the Truth of action. Truth is both just thought and just action, inseparable. If just thinking is necessary for just action, the quest for truth ultimately aims not for the understanding of the truth, but for the realization of goodness. Truth, when all is said and done, is not theoretical, but ethical. It is essential for man not to be right, but to be good. One can delude oneself in thinking that one alone—or alone with one's community, race, nation or religion—is right over others, one can only be good with others. The will to be right generates war; peace can only arise from the decision to be good. Goodness is the first and last expression of truth. This implies refusing once and for all to do wrong in order to defend the truth, which is precisely the contradiction that the ideologies of violence are caught up in.

The first requirement of truth is to abstain from all forms of violence towards all living beings. This requirement of nonviolence remains negative and is not self-sufficient, but it is essential. It does not achieve all of truth's demands, but it alone makes it possible to achieve them. However, Truth does not only demand that one abstain from harming others, it also requires that one wish them well, that is to say, that one show them goodness. "Nonviolence", writes Gandhi, "is the total absence of ill-will against all that lives. .... Nonviolence, in its active form, is goodwill towards all life. It is pure Love." (1960: 107)

During the course of his experiments, Gandhi finds that "the nearest approach to truth was through Love" (Ibid., 102). According to him, there is such a tight link, such a deep correlation, such essential coherence between Truth, Love and nonviolence that together they ultimately form a true identity. The prevailing ideologies deceive and mislead men by making them believe that it is possible to combine love and violence, thus overlooking the fundamental antinomy between them. "Love", Gandhi points out, "has many meanings, in the English language at least, and human love in the sense of passion becomes a degrading thing also." (Id.) And in order to clearly understand Gandhi's thought when he refers to love that turns into passion—and therefore does not hesitate to resort to violence so as to reach its ends—one must not primarily think of love between two human beings, but rather of the love of individuals towards their clan, their nation, their race, their religion, etc. For it is these forms of love that are likely to become murderous.

Gandhi refuses to believe that it may be necessary to resort to violence to fight against the violence of irrational men. In fact, the resulting effect is very likely to be contrary to the intended one. For then "the chain of violence becomes longer and stronger" (1969: 88). Violence, which is always an evil, cannot have a hold over evil in order to fight against it. It is only possible to fight against evil by offering it resistance which takes its roots in goodness. "Science teaches us", Gandhi very pertinently notes, "that a lever can only move a body if it has a supporting point outside the body it is applying itself to. In the same way, in order to overcome evil, one must stand outside it, on the solid ground of unalloyed goodness." (Id.) To meet violence with violence is to subject oneself to the logic of violence, and to reinforce its hold over reality. The only way to resist violence is therefore to break its logic, starting by abstaining from coming to reinforce it. "Nonviolence", claims Gandhi, "does not consist in renouncing all real struggles against evil. Nonviolence, as I conceive it, establishes a more active campaign against evil than the law of the Old Testament *Lexis Talionis*, whose very nature results in the development of perversity." (1969: 203)

The virtue of boldness or intrepidity

Gandhi places boldness at the top of the list of the virtues of the strong man. To be intrepid, according to the etymological sense of the word (from the verb *trepidere*, to tremble), means not trembling in the face of danger. "Intrepidity", he writes, "connotes freedom from all external fear—fear of disease, bodily injury, death or dispossession." (1960: 56) In order to testify to the truth, man must first overcome the fear within him which advises him to stay away from danger. "Strength", Gandhi asserts, "lies in the absence of fear." (Ibid., 125)

Someone who is free from fear will not feel the need to protect himself from danger by hiding behind arms. The violent person, in reality, is someone who is afraid. "The brave", writes Gandhi, "are those armed with intrepidity, not with the sword, the rifle, or other carnal weapons, which, strictly speaking are used only by fearful men." (Ibid., 55) Someone who wants peace must have the courage to defy the arms of those who prepare for war. "I am a man of peace", Gandhi asserts. "I want the peace which you find embedded in the human breast that is exposed to the arrows of the whole world, but which is protected from all harm by the Power of the Almighty God." (Ibid., 126)

The man who chooses nonviolence realizes that by refusing to kill, he takes the risk of being killed. He must therefore tame the fear which this risk generates: "Just as one must learn the art of killing in the training for violence, so one must learn the art of dying in the training for nonviolence. Violence does not mean emancipation from fear, but discovering the means of combating the cause of fear. Nonviolence, on the other hand, has no cause for fear. .... Training in nonviolence is thus diametrically opposed to training in violence." (1969: 153-154) When he frees himself from the fear of death, man frees himself from his desire for violence: "The strength to kill is not essential for self-defence; one ought to have the strength to die. When a man is fully ready to die, he will not even desire to offer violence." (Ibid., 272) When he overcomes the fear of death, man attains freedom: "Man lives freely only by his readiness to die, if need be, at the hands of his brother, never by killing him. Every killing or other injury, no matter for what cause, committed or inflicted on another is a crime against humanity." (Ibid., 153) When man dies while conforming to the requirement of truth within him, his death is not a defeat; on the contrary, it consecrates his victory over violence. "As for me", writes Gandhi, "nothing better can happen to he who chooses nonviolence than meeting death in the very act of nonviolence, that is to say while pursuing Truth." (1934: 288) Defeat would be to deny, to repudiate the requirement of truth, and to consent to the use of violence. Death met on the way of truth and nonviolence is the supreme victory of the intrepid man who did not tremble in the face of danger and suffering; it is the victory of he who refused to defend his own life and accepted dying in order to protect the meaning of his life. "I would not", writes Gandhi, "[for anything in the world], suppress that voice within, call it conscience, call it the prompting of my inner basic nature. .... That something in me which never deceives me tells me now: "Do not fear. .... Be ready to die to testify to that which you have lived for." (1969: 104)

Ultimately, refusing to imitate the violence of the adversary might well surprise, disconcert and finally, disarm him, when he thought that he deserved a reply. For, Gandhi notes, "there is no satisfaction in killing someone who welcomes death, and that is why soldiers like to attack the enemy when he returns blow for blow and meets violence with violence." (1934: 409)

The consent given to death by whoever takes the risk of nonviolence is contrary to passive acceptance, to resignation. "Nonviolence cannot be taught to a person who fears to die", writes Gandhi, "and has no power of resistance. A helpless mouse is not nonviolent because it is always eaten by the cat." (1969: 180) Someone who has chosen nonviolence does not die because death catches them from behind; they die while looking death in the face; they die because they resist the violence that attacks them. Their very death is an act of resistance. But man cannot swear to anything, and nobody knows how they will behave on the day of the ultimate ordeal. "Have I that nonviolence of the brave in me", asked Gandhi? "My death alone will show that. If someone killed me and I died with prayer for the assassin on my lips, and God's remembrance and consciousness of His living presence in the sanctuary of my heart, then alone would I be said to have had the nonviolence of the brave." (Ibid., 105)

Gandhi died exactly as he had foreseen it. We now know that which he himself ignored: he truly had the nonviolence of the brave in him.

The primacy of reason

One of the reasons for which philosophers have mostly ignored Gandhi, is probably that he gave a religious connotation to the expression of his conviction concerning nonviolence. The prevailing feeling is that his reflection on nonviolence takes its place in religion, and that somehow one ought to share his faith in God in order to agree with his conviction. This, it seems to us, is a misunderstanding, and there is no choice but to accept that Gandhi was largely responsible for this. He himself confused his message on nonviolence by referring to God most of the time, whereas in reality he is not a "religious" man, and he has no personal relationship with a personal God. According to him, "God is not a human being" (1971: 76), but a "living force that is changeless and supports all beings" (1969: 110). Hence the God that he worships is nameless and faceless. "I have not seen God", he confesses, "neither have I known Him. .... I have no words for characterizing my belief in God." (Ibid., 110-111) For Gandhi, God is ultimately nothing but the Truth etched deep within human beings. He thus comes to substitute the religious affirmation: "God is Truth" for the following suggestion: "Truth is God" (1958: 38). There is but a nuance left between the approaches implied by the two formulations. Someone who thinks that "God is Truth" considers that it is enough to have faith in God's words, revealed by religion—that is to say, by their religion—in order to possess the whole truth. They then easily persuade themselves that whoever refuses to believe in these words is in the wrong. And to defend the truth and fight wrongness, they make it their duty not only to combat heresy, but also to wage battle against heretics. The proposition that "God is Truth" is therefore highly likely to become a totalitarian affirmation that generates Holy War. Gandhi points out that indeed, "millions have taken the name of God and in His name committed nameless atrocities" (1960: 103).

To think that "Truth is God" involves quite a different intellectual and spiritual approach. For then, truth does not reveal itself to man by an external revelation, but by an internal requirement which expresses itself through the "still small voice" of his conscience, that is to say his reason. It therefore truly is reason which leads Gandhi to the discovery of the requirement of nonviolence. "Reason", he claims without hesitation, "is another name for nonviolence." (1970: 146) Gandhi thus asserts the primacy of reason over religion, and he himself intends to judge the truth of holy scriptures according to the requirements of his conscience. "Scriptures", he writes, "cannot transcend reason." (1959: 31) That is why he does not hesitate to challenge the aspects of religion which his reason does not approve. "I reject", he states, "all religious doctrine if it is in conflict with sober reason or the dictates of the heart. .... Error can claim no exemption even if it can be supported by the scriptures of the world." (1969: 139-140)

The decisive criterion by which Gandhi judges religious teachings is their conformity with moral requirements. "From my youth onward", he writes, "I learnt the art of estimating the value of scriptures on the basis of their ethical teaching." (1959: 29) Hence is Gandhi "convinced that there is no religion higher than Truth" (1969: 134). He wishes to serve "no other God than Truth" (1969: 45); he "worships God as Truth only" (1969: 86).

Under these conditions, it becomes legitimate to ask whether he would have given his message of nonviolence more clarity and power, should he have released it from its religious shell and expressed it with more philosophical rigour. By default, this is what we ourselves must do if we want to express the universal significance of his message.

Nonviolent resistance

For Gandhi, the quest for truth is identified with the struggle for justice. It is in South Africa, where he lived from 1893 to 1914, that he organized an act of nonviolent resistance for the first time. His objective was to allow Indian immigrants in that country to assert their rights in the face of the white racist government. "I came up with this method of nonviolence", he writes in 1942, "when dealing with this problem. The different steps that I took then were not the work of a visionary or a dreamer. They were the work of a man at grips with practical problems." (1969: 41) On another occasion , he explains how he got the idea of organizing the struggle of South African Indians, and presents nonviolence as a method of action that constitutes an alternative to violence: "Up to the year 1906, I simply relied on the force of reason. .... But I found that reason failed to produce an impression when the critical moment arrived in South Africa. .... There was talk of wreaking vengeance. I had then to choose between allying myself to violence or finding some other method of meeting the crisis and stopping the rot; and it came to me that we should refuse to obey the legislation that was degrading and let them put us in jail if they liked." (1969: 161-162)

When he started organizing the struggle, Gandhi used the expression "passive resistance" to refer to the movement that he had created. "Among English people", he noted, "whenever a small minority did not approve of some obnoxious piece of legislation, instead of rising in rebellion they took the passive or milder step of not submitting to the law and inviting the penalties of such non-submission upon their heads." (1934: 172) However, as the struggle developed, he realised that this expression "gave rise to confusion" (Ibid., 169) and "was apt to give rise to terrible misunderstanding" (Ibid., 171). More precisely, "passive resistance was conceived and is regarded as a weapon of the weak. Whilst it avoids violence, which is not available to the weak, it does not exclude its use if, in the opinion of a passive resister, the occasion demands it." (1986: 16)

It was essential for Gandhi to stress the fact that if Indian people renounced the recourse to violence, it would not be out of weakness, but on the contrary, because they were strong enough to overcome their desire for vengeance, and look for a peaceful solution to the conflict that opposed them to white people. From then on, he sought to invent a new word to refer to his struggle. He finally chose the Sanskrit term *Satyagraha*: "*Satya* (truth)", he explains, "implies love and *Agraha* (firmness) engenders and therefore serves as a synonym for force. I thus began to call the Indian movement *Satyagraha*, that is to say, the Force which is born of Truth and Love and nonviolence, and gave up the use of the phrase "passive resistance"." (1934: 170) Gandhi also describes *Satyagraha* as follows: "It literally means holding onto Truth and it therefore means, Truth-force. I have therefore called it love-force or soul-force." (1986: 16)

In actual fact, the expressions "Truth-force" and "Love-force" which Gandhi uses raise questions. In what sense can one talk about "Truth-force" when the point is to fight against a social injustice that is supported by a political ideology? Can "Truth-force" be enough to convince an adversary who is determined to defend his powers, interests and privileges? Can it be enough to efficiently oppose the force of violence of an unscrupulous enemy? Can "Truth-force" reach the conscience and convert an adversary who will stop at nothing to achieve his ends?

The power of suffering

For Gandhi, the support on which the lever of nonviolent resistance rests, is the suffering of the one who intends to remain true to Truth and refuses to be a party to evil. This is his reasoning: "In the application of *Satyagraha*, I discovered, in the earliest stages, that the pursuit of Truth would not allow violence to be inflicted on one's opponent, but that he must be weaned from error by patience and sympathy. .... And patience means the acceptation of suffering. But in politics, the struggle on behalf of the people mostly consists of opposing error in the shape of unjust laws. When you have failed to bring his error home to the lawgiver by way of petitions and the like, the only remedy open to you, if you do not wish to submit to error, is to compel him by physical force to yield to you; or by suffering in your own person, by inviting the penalty breaching the law." (1958: 6)

So, according to the pure doctrine defined by Gandhi, someone who chooses to resist by means of nonviolence does not seek to constrain their adversary, but to convert them to the acceptance of suffering. That is why they "must have faith in the inherent goodness of human nature" (Ibid., 88) and be convinced that "meek suffering for a just cause has a virtue all its own and infinitely greater than the virtue of the sword." (Ibid., 66) "To obtain a decisive result", Gandhi adds, "it is not enough to convince reason; one must also touch the heart and, consequently, appeal to the power of suffering." (1969: 108) That is why he is not afraid to face the tyrant without arms: "I seek to blunt the edge of the tyrant's sword entirely", he says, "not by putting up against it a sharper-edged weapon, but by disappointing his expectation that I would be offering physical resistance. The resistance of the soul that I should offer instead would elude him. It would at first dazzle him, and then compel recognition from him." (1960: 110)

In this perspective, according to Gandhi, nonviolent resistance does not seek to embarrass or humiliate an adversary so as to force them to give in. As a consequence, victory does not depend on the number of people who enter into resistance, but only on their ability to suffer for truth and justice: "I do not regard the force of numbers as necessary when the cause is just." (1958: 33) He even asserts that the victory of nonviolence over injustice is possible if one single man totally dedicates himself to truth, and expresses pure love towards his adversaries. Hence civil disobedience constitutes a peaceful rebellion that is more effective than armed revolt. It cannot be broken if the resisters are determined to face up to the greatest ordeals, for it is "based upon an implicit faith in the absolute effectiveness of innocent suffering" (Ibid., 172). "The hardest fibre", Gandhi finally states, "must melt in the fire of love. If it does not melt, it is because the fire is not strong enough." (1960: 115)

But then again, such assertions raise questions and it seems difficult to follow Gandhi's reasoning through to its conclusion. Admittedly, just as violence exacerbates an adversary's desire for violence, so can nonviolence defuse it. Contrary to violence, nonviolent resistance leaves space for the adversary to be able to realize the injustice that they are responsible for, and to decide freely to change their behaviour. The suffering of someone who has chosen not to fight back can indeed touch the adversary's heart, and disarm them. Every man can convert to evil as well as turn away from it. Nonviolence makes the conversion of an adversary possible; it even facilitates it, but it does not have the power to impose it. If this conversion is always possible, experience shows that in many circumstances it is not probable. When Gandhi asserts nonviolence's ability to convert the most hardened adversary by referring to the absolute power of truth, he cannot be convincing. At that moment, he retreats into an idealistic vision of man, and formulates an unrealistic notion of nonviolence; both are contradicted by the facts, which we know to be stubborn.

The strategy of nonviolent action

Gandhi can sometimes lose himself in idealism when he wants to justify his faith in nonviolence, but he can also show the greatest realism in the organization of nonviolent action. It is therefore necessary to adjust somehow the idealism of some of his ideas with the realism of most of his actions. For that matter, he himself was too clear-sighted not to modify his theory according to practical criteria. Hence he is aware that the Indian people who entered into the 1920 non-cooperation campaign did not do so as firm believers in the pure doctrine of spiritual nonviolence; and yet, he claims that their commitment can free India from British oppression. "Being a practical man", he writes, "I do not wait till India recognizes the practicability of the spiritual life in the political world. India considers herself to be powerless and paralysed before the machine-guns, the tanks and the aeroplanes of the English, and takes up non-cooperation because of this weakness. It must still serve the same purpose, namely, bring her delivery from the crushing weight of British injustice, if a sufficient number of people practice it." (1948: 108-109) Here, Gandhi quite naturally highlights the force of numbers as one of the key elements of the political efficiency of nonviolent resistance.

In January 1942, when Gandhi defended his policy in front of the Indian Congress, he emphasized its efficiency in order to justify the choice of nonviolence as a method of struggle for obtaining independence. "Nonviolence is my creed", he states, "the breath of my life. But it is never as a creed that I placed it before India, or for that matter anyone else, except in casual informal talks. I placed it before the Congress as a political method, to be employed for the solution of political questions. It may be a novel method, but it does not on that account lose its political character. .... As a political method, it can always be changed, modified, altered, and even given up in preference to another. If, therefore, I say to you that our policy should not be given up today, I am talking political wisdom. It is political insight. It has served us in the past, it has enabled us to cover many stages towards independence, and it is as a politician that I suggest to you that it is a grave mistake to contemplate its abandonment. If I have carried the Congress with me all these years, it is in my capacity as a politician. It is hardly fair to describe my method as religious, because it is new." (1969: 40-41)

When he tells of the struggle for India's independence, Nehru also points out the political dimension of nonviolence as suggested by Gandhi. "For years and years", he writes, "Gandhi's doctrine of nonviolence has dominated the political evolution of our country. .... It has played a capital part in our political and social life; it has also attracted considerable attention from the entire world. Naturally, it was as old as human thought. But Gandhi may have been the first to apply it massively to political and social movements. .... I believe that we can easily assert that this method of nonviolence has done us inestimable favours." (1952: 371) Elsewhere Nehru adds: "It has been said that nonviolent action was a fantasy; here it has been the only real means of political action." (1967: 204)

Yet things are not as simple as Gandhi and Nehru's assertions may imply. In reality, if Gandhi must convince his interlocutors in the Congress that the nonviolence which is he is offering India is a political—and not religious—method, it is precisely that they have reason to doubt it. He wishes to reassure them, because they are indeed worried, for many of Gandhi's words—and not only during informal conversations—have led them to question the political nature of his nonviolence. "For us and for the Congress as a whole", Nehru also writes, "nonviolence was not, could not be a religion, a faith in an infallible dogma. It could only be a policy, a tactic guaranteeing results, and it was finally to be judged by these results."

(1952: 94-95) And, on many occasions, Nehru accused Gandhi of fostering confusion between politics and religion. "I was terribly angry with him", he writes, "about the way he approached the political field through feelings and religion, as well as about his frequent references to God in the same field." (Ibid., 290)

Gandhi must therefore be taken at his word when he asserts that nonviolence is "a political method designed to solve political problems"; his non-cooperation campaigns must also be analysed by referring to political criteria. Nonviolence then appears as a technical means that makes it possible to act efficiently in the solution of political conflicts.

14

Gandhi, Architect of Nonviolence

When he chooses nonviolent resistance, Gandhi means to be realistic. "Since resort to arms was impossible and undesirable", he writes, relating the beginning of his action in India, "the only true resistance to the Government, it therefore seemed to me, was to cease to cooperate with it. Thus I arrived at the word "non-cooperation" (1964: 618) He realizes that the action of Indian people to conquer their independence is a trial of strength with the English. In March 1922, he does not hesitate to assert that dialogue between English and Indian people is as impossible as it would be between a cat and a mouse. "The average Englishman", he writes then, "is haughty; he does not understand us, he considers himself to be a superior being. He thinks that he is born to rule us. He relies upon his forts and his cannon to protect himself. He despises us. He wants to compel cooperation, that is to say, to force us to be his slaves. He too must be conquered, not by bending the knee, but by remaining aloof from him, and at the same time not hating him nor hurting him. It is cowardly to molest him. If we simply refuse to regard ourselves as his slaves and pay homage to him, we have done our duty. A mouse can only shun the cat. He cannot negotiate with her till she has filed the points of her claws and teeth." (1948: 352-353) Hence nonviolent action must put force at the disposal of justice: "It is a fact beyond dispute that a petition, without the backing of force, is useless." (1986: 21)

The end and the means

However, the necessity to "force" the adversary to acknowledge the requirements of justice does not justify the means. In the quest for truth as in that for efficiency, the quality of the means that are implemented in order to achieve the desired end, is of crucial importance. "As clear as it may be", writes Gandhi, "the definition of the goal that we wish to achieve, and our desire to do so, are not enough to lead us to it, as long as we do not know ourselves or use the necessary means. That is why I have especially endeavoured to preserve those means and to develop their use. .... I believe that we will move towards the goal insofar as our means are pure." (1960: 108) The means that are implemented must be coherent with the desired end: "The means may be likened to a seed, the end to a tree; and there is just the same inviolable connection between the means and the end as there is between the seed and the tree. .... We reap exactly as we sow." (1969: 149) In thus highlighting the organic link between the end and the means, Gandhi not only asserts a philosophical and moral principle, he also formulates a strategic principle on which he intends to base the efficiency of his political action. Violence is inefficient because, even used to serve a just cause, it holds an irreducible share of injustice. "Pure goals", Gandhi states, "can never justify impure or violent action." (1969: 83)

Nonviolent action must seek victory, but its failure—which is always a possibility—does not cause its meaning to be lost; it is a victory in itself. "The very nature of nonviolent resistance", Gandhi writes, "is such that the fruit of the movement is contained in the movement itself." (1961: 182-183) Indeed, "for a fighter, the fight itself is a victory" (Ibid., 259), on the condition that he is mistaken neither about the end nor the means.

Therefore "two kinds of forces can back petitions" (1986: 21-22): first there is the "force of arms", but Gandhi refuses to resort to it for he condemns its "evil results" (Ibid., 22). "The second kind of force can thus be stated: "If you do not concede to our demand, we shall be no longer your petitioners. You can govern us only so long as we remain the governed; we shall no longer have dealings with you." (Id.) Hence the power of rulers can be reduced to nothing if the governed refuse to submit to their authority. Constraint becomes effective when citizens' actions of non-cooperation manage to dry up the government's power sources, so that the latter is no longer obeyed. A new balance of power can thus establish itself, and allow resisters to obtain acknowledgement of their rights.

The principle of noncooperation

According to Gandhi, it is not so much the capacity for violence of English people as the capacity for resignation of Indian people which creates the power of the British Empire in India. "It is not so much British guns", he claims, "that are responsible for our subjection as our voluntary cooperation." (1969: 247) From then on, Indian people must put an end to all cooperation with the oppressive government in order to free themselves from the yoke that weighs heavily on them. "No government", Gandhi assures, "can exist for a single moment without the cooperation of the people, willing or forced. And if the people withdraw their cooperation, the government will come to a standstill. Without our support, one hundred thousand Europeans could not even hold a seventh of our villages. .... The question we have before us is consequently to oppose our will to that of the government; in other words, to withdraw our cooperation. If we stand firm in our intention, the government will be compelled to submit to our will or to disappear." (1948: 195) Gandhi's purpose here is clearly not to convert the English—even if he does not intend to give up on this aim otherwise—but indeed to constrain the British government.

The refusal to cooperate with injustice is both an ethical requirement that prevents the individual from being a party to evil himself, and a strategic principle that allows him to fight against injustice. The citizen cannot use the constraint of the law as a pretext for his cooperation with injustice. "Civil disobedience", Gandhi claims, "is the inherent right of a citizen. He dare not give it up without ceasing to be a man. .... But to put down civil disobedience is to attempt to imprison conscience." (1969: 235-236) The requirements of conscience must take precedence over the constraint of the law, for "in matters of conscience, the law of the majority has no place" (Ibid., 247). The cardinal virtue of citizens is not obedience, but responsibility: "If a government commits a grave injustice the subject must withdraw cooperation wholly or partially, sufficiently to wean the ruler from wickedness." (Ibid., 250)

Gandhi found it regrettable that an essential and often decisive part of upbringing rests on the duty of obedience to authority and that the child is thus conditioned in such a way that it becomes a subordinated citizen, not a responsible one. He castigated schools "where children are taught to think obeying the State a higher duty than obeying their conscience; where they are corrupted with false notions of patriotism and a duty to obey superiors; so that in the end they easily fall under the government's spell." (1969: 133-134) The citizen shows cowardice when he trades his personal safety and tranquility for his unconditional submission to the State. He must have the courage to disobey it each time it orders him to take part in injustice. "Civil disobedience", Gandhi wrote, "is rebellion without the element of violence in it. An out-and-out resister simply ignores the authority of the State. He becomes an outlaw claiming to disregard every immoral State law." (1969: 251)

The constraint of nonviolent action

Gandhi believes that the oppression which Indian people endure does not so much come from the personal spite of the English as from the evil-doing of the British colonial system. From then on, he intends to fight this institutional and legislative system. "Our non-cooperation", he asserts, "is neither with the English nor with the West; it is with the system that the English have established." (Ibid., 208) Nonviolent struggle thus consists in eradicating evil without eliminating the evil-doer: "I try", says Gandhi, "to track evil down wherever it may be, without ever doing harm to whoever is responsible for it." (Ibid., 142) If it is neither possible to convince nor to convert the evil-doer, he must then be prevented from committing evil, and for this he must be deprived of the support without which he becomes powerless. "Our resistance to [British oppression] does not mean harm to the British people. We seek to convert them, not to defeat them on the battle-field. Ours is an unarmed revolt against the British rule. But *whether we convert them or not*, (emphasis ours) we are determined to make their rule impossible by nonviolent non-cooperation. This method is by its very nature invincible. It is based on the knowledge that no spoliator can achieve his objectives without a certain degree of cooperation, willing or compulsory, on the part of the victim." (1969: 35)

Nonviolent resistance therefore consists in neutralizing the adversary by withdrawing all cooperation from him. "Imagine a whole people unwilling to conform to the laws of the legislature, and prepared to suffer the consequences of non-compliance. They will bring the whole legislative and executive machinery to a standstill." (1969: 240) Unity—and not only the soundness of a cause—is therefore truly strength. That is why the nonviolent resister "must mobilize public opinion against the evil which he is out to eradicate by means of a wide and intensive agitation. When public opinion is sufficiently roused against an evil the strongest will not dare to practice or openly to lend support to it. An awakened and intelligent public opinion is the most potent weapon of a nonviolent resister." (1986: 71-72) To a journalist who asks him about the pressure that he hopes to exert on British authorities by organizing the resistance movement, Gandhi replies: "I believe that, if the population suddenly withdraws its support including the slightest details, the government will find itself in a stalemate." (Ibid., 134) Non-cooperation therefore truly is a political method that seeks to neutralize the adversary before he even renounces the injustice that he is doing by himself. "We must refuse to wait", writes Gandhi, "for the wrong to be righted till the wrong-doer has been roused to a sense of his iniquity. We must not, for fear of ourselves or others having to suffer, remain participants in it. But we must combat the wrong by ceasing to assist the wrong-doer directly or indirectly." (1969: 250)

Admittedly, Gandhi knows from experience that the State is bound to resort to available means in order to fight and try to break the movement that resists its authority; but he is convinced that the people, as long as it remains united, can prevent this repression. "No police and no army", he asserts, "can crush the will of a people who is determined to resist to the last of their force." (Ibid., 240) And if the State does not succeed in breaking the will of the resistance movement, there will be no other alternative but to look for a negotiated solution to the conflict.

Nehru ultimately shows great lucidity when he writes: "Whatever may have been the role of conversion [of the oppressor] in its author's mind, nonviolence, in practice, was still a weapon, and a powerful tool of constraint, even if this constraint exerted itself in the most civilized and least reprehensible way possible." (1952: 69)

"The salt march"

The best way to demonstrate the feasibility of nonviolence as a "political method for the solution of political problems", is to analyse the campaign of non-cooperation which Gandhi organized in 1930. On 31st December 1929 at midnight, the Indian National Congress had pronounced itself in favour of Independence and had decided to organize a campaign of civil-disobedience to this end. Gandhi then decided to challenge the British government by asking Indian people to openly disobey the law which compelled them to pay a tax on salt. On March the 2nd 1930, he presented the Viceroy, Lord Irwin, with an ultimatum, in which he asserted: "If India is to live as a nation, if the slow death by starvation of her people is to stop, some remedy must be found for immediate relief. The proposed conference is certainly not the remedy. It is not a matter of carrying conviction by argument. The matter resolves itself into one of matching forces. Conviction or no conviction, Great Britain will defend her Indian commerce and interests with all the forces at her command. India must consequently evolve force enough to free herself from that embrace of death. .... The party of violence is gaining ground and making itself felt. Its aim is the same as mine. But I am convinced that it cannot bring relief to the dumb millions. And the conviction is growing deeper and deeper in me that nothing but unadulterated nonviolence can check the organized violence of the British Government. Many think that nonviolence is not an active force. My experience, limited as it may be, shows that it can be a very active force. It is my purpose to set in motion that force against the organized, violent force of British rule, as well as against the unorganised violent force of the growing party of violence. To sit still would be to give rein to both the forces above mentioned. Having unquestioning and immovable faith in the efficacy of nonviolence as I know it, it would be sinful on my part to wait any longer. This nonviolence will be expressed through civil-disobedience. .... My ambition is no less than to convert the British people through nonviolence and thus make them see the wrong they have done to India. I do not seek to harm your people. I want to serve them even as I want to serve my own. .... If the people join me as I expect they will, the sufferings they will undergo, unless the British nation soon decides to retrace its steps, will be enough to melt the stoniest hearts. The organization of civil disobedience will be to combat such evils as I have singled out. .... I respectfully invite you then to pave the way for an immediate end to those evils and thus open a way for a real conference between equals. .... But if you cannot see your way to deal with those evils and my letter makes no appeal to your heart, on the 11th day of this month I shall proceed with such co-workers of the Ashram as I can take to disregard the provisions of the Salt laws." (1969: 17-18)

Hence Gandhi reasserted his ambition to convert the English, but the action of civil disobedience that he contemplated sought to compel the British government to satisfy the Indian people's claims. He said this explicitly in a speech which he gave on 10th March, that is to say, 2 days before the start of the campaign: "Suppose", he then stated, "ten people in each of the seven hundred thousand villages in India come forward to manufacture salt and to disobey the Salt Act, what do you think the government can do? Even the worst autocrat would not dare to blow regiments of peaceful resisters out of a cannon's mouth. If only you bestir yourself just a little, I assure you we should be able to tire this government out in a very short time." (Ibid., 22)

The Viceroy was in no way convinced or moved by Gandhi's ultimatum and wrote back to express his regret that he should be "contemplating a course of action which is clearly bound to involve violation of the law of the land and danger to the public peace." (Ibid., 19) On hearing of this reply, Gandhi exclaimed: "On bended knees, I asked for bread, and received a stone instead!" (Id.) On 12th March, on the very day that the campaign began, he answered the Viceroy in these terms: "The only law the nation knows is the will of the British administrators, and the only public peace the nation knows is the peace of the public prison. India is one vast, prison house, I repudiate this law, and regard it as my sacred duty to break the mournful monotony of compulsory peace that is choking the nation's heart for want of a free vent." (Id.)

Gandhi, rebels against the British Empire

On the morning of 12th March 1920, Gandhi left the city of Ahmenabad at the head of seventy nine marchers. He proposed to head for the village of Dandi, by the Indian Ocean, about 390 kilometers away. During the march, Gandhi took the time to write articles for his journal *Young India*. On 27th March, he published an article entitled *The Duty of Disloyalty*. He notably asserted: "The present State is an institution which, if one knows it, can never evoke loyalty. It is corrupt. Many of its laws governing the conduct of persons are positively inhuman. .... This system of government is confessedly based upon a merciless exploitation of unnumbered millions of the inhabitants of India. .... It is then the duty of those who have realized the awful evil of the system of Indian Government to be disloyal to it and actively and openly to preach disloyalty. .... It is the duty of those who have realized the evil nature of the system however attractive some of its feature may appear to be, to destroy it without delay. It is their clear duty to run any risk to achieve the end." (1969: 25-26)

After twenty-five days of walking, Gandhi and his companions reached Dandi on the 5 April 1920. The following day, at 8:30 a.m., he went to the sea-shore and picked up a handful of salt that the waves had deposited on the beach. From that moment, he became a rebel against the British Empire. He then called all Indian people to civil disobedience, asking them to obtain salt illegally. On 8th April, he declared: "Today, the honour of India has been symbolized by a fistful of salt in the hand of a man of nonviolence. The fist which held the salt may be broken, but it will not yield up its salt." (Ibid., 32) Indian people enthusiastically took part in this peaceful insurrection. Nehru told of the wonder which Gandhi aroused, having had the stroke of genius to "find the gesture which struck the multitude and to bring the latter to act in an orderly and disciplined way." (1952: 193) Civil disobedience spread to other fields. "The Viceroy", told Nehru, "made things easier for us on that point, by publishing rulings forbidding us from doing such and such activity. The less these rulings were able to control the situation, the more other rulings were decreed. It was a vicious circle." (Ibid., 195)

From then on the authorities, who at first had thought it advisable not to intervene, proceeded to arrest many people. On 1st May, Gandhi wrote to the Viceroy, informing him of his intention to surround and seize Dharasana salt works. The government decided to react quickly, and arrested Gandhi on 5th May. The Dharasana raid was carried out by some two thousand volunteers on the 21 May. The latter had to endure the ferocious repression of policemen who beat them with clubs extremely brutally. Two people died, and more than three hundred were injured.

Prisons were soon to be overpopulated by some 80 000 rebels. As Louis Fischer noted in his *Life of Mahatma Gandhi*, "the situation was politically intolerable" for the British authorities (1952: 255). In an attempt to regain the initiative, Lord Irwin felt that he should make a gesture: he allowed the main leaders of the Congress—who were in prison in different places—to be taken to Gandhi's prison so that they could confer with other more moderate Indian leaders. These negotiations took place from 13th to 15th August 1930, without effect. Yet they made Winston Churchill angry: "The Indian government", he said sarcastically, "put Gandhi in prison, and came to sit behind his cell door, asking him to help overcome its difficulties." (1969: 46) The government in London, however, understood that it was not possible to control the situation without agreeing to negotiate directly with the leaders of the Congress; it suggested that the Viceroy release them. On 25th January 1931, Lord Irwin decided to release Gandhi and several of his companions. He then issued a statement: "My government will impose no conditions in exchange for these releases, for we feel that the best hope of restoration of peace lies in discussions being conducted by those concerned under the terms of unconditional liberty." (Ibid., 49)

On 17th February 1931, Gandhi arrived at the Viceroy's palace for an interview with Lord Irwin. Churchill, in his own way, was right about the event's historical significance. "It is alarming and also nauseating", he declared, "to see Mr Gandhi, an Inner Temple lawyer, now become a seditious fakir, striding half-naked up the steps of the Vice-Regal Palace, while he is still organizing and conducting a defiant campaign of civil disobedience, to parley on equal terms with the representative of the King-Emperor." (Ibid., 53)

Gandhi and Irwin signed the Delhi Pact on 5th March 1931. Many Indian people—and among them several leaders of the Congress, at the head of which stood Nehru—considered that Gandhi had shown too much conciliation towards the Viceroy. They were probably not entirely wrong, for the campaign of civil disobedience had indeed put Gandhi in a position of strength, and he could have obtained more concessions from his opponent. However, while he admitted that the pact he had concluded with the government did not ensue from a "change of heart" (Ibid., 76) on behalf of British rulers, Gandhi believed that the clauses of the resulting agreement were a good compromise. Even if independence was not established yet, he thought it possible to assert that a new door to freedom had just opened itself (Ibid., 64).

The mobilization of citizens in nonviolent resistance thus makes it possible to exert real constraint on those who have the power of decision. But there is another essential factor in all strategies of nonviolent action. As he openly defies the power of the oppressor, as he faces up to him and overcomes all fear, as he disobeys orders, as he accepts to suffer without thinking of revenge, the oppressed proves to himself that he is a dignified and free being; he restores himself in his own eyes; he reclaims power over his own life. At that moment, and whatever material power the oppressor may have, allowing him to lay down his law, the oppressed has already regained his freedom. The 1930 campaign of civil disobedience decisively allowed the

Indian people to recover its dignity. From then on, its independence—even if it was not yet written in the text of the pact signed by Gandhi and British authorities—was already etched in history. The poet Rabindranath Tagore perfectly evoked the victory which his people had then won: "Those who live in England have now got to realize that Europe has completely lost her former moral prestige in Asia. She is no longer regarded as the champion throughout the world of fair dealing and the exponent of high principle, but as the upholder of Western race supremacy and exploiter of those outside her own borders. For Europe this is, in actual fact, a great moral defeat that has happened. Even though Asia is physically weak and unable to protect herself from an aggression where her vital interests are menaced, nevertheless she can now afford to look down on Europe where before she looked up." (1952: 253)

Violence is preferable to cowardice

Gandhi was convinced that nonviolence was the most powerful weapon for obtaining justice, but he had not unlearned his belief in the efficacy of violence; he would probably not have hesitated to take up arms to fight against the British imperialism oppressing his people. "I advocate", he asserted, "training in arms for those who believe in the method of violence. I would rather have India resort to arms in order to defend her honour than that she should in a cowardly manner become or remain a helpless witness to her own dishonour." (1948: 106) He would therefore not have hesitated to "risk violence rather than the emasculation of a whole race" (1969: 179). Whoever is afraid to risk violence is incapable of risking nonviolence: "There is hope that a violent man may some day become nonviolent, but there is none that a coward will become non violent." (Ibid., 178) Hence nonviolence is a form of resistance, a confrontation, a struggle, a battle. That is why it is much further from cowardice, passivity and resignation than from violence. "Nonviolence", Gandhi claimed, "presupposes the ability to struggle. But at the same time one must consciously and deliberately restrain all desire for vengeance. Nevertheless vengeance is always superior to purely passive submission. .... But forgiveness is higher still. Vengeance is also weakness, born of the fear of harm, imaginary or real." (1971: 131)

In the face of injustice, the prevailing ideologies that assert the necessity of violence claim to impose the obligation to choose between violence and cowardice. The argument that is constantly put forward to justify violence, and which is claimed to be above all suspicion, is that it is necessary in order to fight against violence. This argument implies a corollary: to abandon just violence is to give free reign to unjust violence. From then on, the refusal of violence, with which nonviolence is generally compared, can only be the result of cowardice. As long as the debate is trapped in the "violence-cowardice" dilemma, the individual can only feel compelled to choose violence. Admittedly, man can refuse violence out of cowardice, that is to say out of a fear of the risks that it entails. But this refusal is quite contrary to the nonviolence which Gandhi advocated. "My nonviolence", he asserted, "does not admit running away from danger and leaving dear ones unprotected. Between violence and cowardly flight, I can only prefer violence to cowardice." (1969: 94) That is why it is important to find a way out of the dilemma that would have us choose between violence and cowardice.

In reality, man does not have two, but three alternatives in the face of unjust violence: cowardice, violence and nonviolence. Gandhi's thoughts on that matter are unequivocal: violence is better than cowardice, but nonviolence is better than violence. "I do believe", he wrote, "that, where there is only a choice between cowardice and violence, I would advise violence. .... But I believe that nonviolence is infinitely superior to violence." (1948: 106) When Gandhi heard that some men had fled their village in order to escape the police who were looting their houses and molesting their women, and that, in doing so, they believed that they were practicing nonviolence, he felt ashamed that his teaching may have been so badly misunderstood: "I would have expected them", he said, "to place themselves like a shield between the greater and menacing power, and those who were weaker, that their duty was to protect. Without any idea of vengeance, they could have drawn upon themselves the sufferings of combat, to the point of death, without fleeing before the storm. It was manly enough to defend property, honour or religion at the point of the sword. It would have been nobler to defend them without seeking to do evil against evil. But it was shameful, immoral and dishonourable to forsake the post of duty and, in order to save one's skin, to leave all to the mercy of the wrong-doers." (1969: 179)

Gandhi was not unaware that violence is often used as a weapon for freedom: "The page of history", he observed, "is soiled red with the blood of those who have fought for freedom." (1969: 144) He did not condemn these fighters, but it seemed to him that the time had come to end the spiral of violence which oppressors and oppressed had been sucked into. He considered the soldiers of freedom who resorted to arms of destruction to fight against oppression to have been blinded by violence. He was convinced that, in order to attain freedom, violence was in fact a detour rife with difficulties and dangers which realism orders to avoid. He wanted his people to take the shortcut of nonviolence. He was persuaded that Indian people did not need to resort to the arms of violence in order to conquer their freedom. "A nation of 350 million people does not need the dagger of the assassin, it does not need the poison bowl, it does not need the sword, the spear or the bullet. It needs simply a will of its own, an ability to say "no" and that nation is today learning to say "no"." (Ibid., 145)

Violence can seem necessary

Gandhi was aware that man's nonviolence could not be absolute: "Perfect nonviolence whilst you are not yet pure spirits is only a theory like Euclid's point or straight line." (1969: 164) If only to live, man is compelled to commit certain acts of violence. "The very fact of his eating, drinking, and moving about necessarily involves some violence, some destruction of life, be it ever so minute." (1969: 91) Man must nevertheless be content with strict necessity. As for himself, Gandhi refused to eat meat out of respect for animal life. He attached the utmost importance to the protection of the cow, as advocated by Hinduism: it "means the protection of all creatures created by God" (Ibid,.

111), "it means protection of all that lives and is helpless and weak in the world" (Id.).

The individual should not claim to be living without a compromise with all the social injustice of the established disorder that is so much structural violence. "As long as man lives in society, he can only be party to some forms of violence." (1969: 167) So if it is impossible for man to avoid all violence, "the question arises, where is one to draw the line?" (Ibid., 176) Gandhi was very careful not to give it a formal answer which would be the same for all in all situations. It is important for everyone to endeavour to draw that line as far as possible. He admitted that man can sometimes find himself in situations where he cannot do otherwise than resort to violence to prevent the worst from happening. He can even be led to killing "to protect those under his care" (1960: 118): "Suppose a man runs amuck and goes furiously about sword in hand, and killing anyone that comes in his way, and no one dares to capture him alive. Anyone who dispatches this lunatic will earn the gratitude of the community, and be regarded as a benevolent man." (1969: 93) But even this form of violence is not inevitable and Gandhi immediately added: "There is, indeed, one exception if it can be so called. The wise man who can subdue the fury of this dangerous man may not kill him. But we are not here dealing with beings who have almost reached perfection; we are considering the duty of the society, of the ordinary erring human beings." (Id.)

Some may be tempted to think that by thus acknowledging the necessity to resort to violence in order to prevent the worst from happening, Gandhi ultimately comes round to the classical theory of legitimate defence such as it is presented by all the moral doctrines based on natural law. This is in fact not at all the case. Indeed, there remains a radical difference between Gandhi's thoughts and these doctrines: the latter consider the recourse to violence as a means of defence against an aggression to be the general rule; they totally ignore the practical possibilities of nonviolence; more than that, they assert their inefficacy without even knowing them. As a result, even when they think it their duty to say—out of principle—that violence may only be used as a last resort, they offer no other concrete recourse and violence practically imposes itself as the only possibility in the face of an aggression. Gandhi, on the contrary, was convinced that nonviolence effectively offered the possibility of solving peacefully the conflicts which men must face. Hence he emphasized the fact that they should only resort to violence "when it is unavoidable, and after full and mature deliberation and having exhausted all remedies to avoid it." (1960: 119) And such a phrase is no longer simply a question of rhetoric. Finally, when he admits that violence can seem necessary, Gandhi is very careful not to fall into the legitimation processes which might justify it. The necessity of violence does not eliminate the requirement of nonviolence.

Freeing India from an Indian State

Throughout his struggle for India's independence, one of Gandhi's main concerns was not only to fight against the British Empire's state-control, but also to allow the Indian people to rule itself without resorting to the mechanisms of violent constraint that characterized the State's method of governing. According to him, the best way for Indian people to resist the British government and to deprive it of power, was to learn to rule themselves, that is to say, to become independent. This is also one of the main reasons for which he advocated nonviolence as a means of resistance. For he was convinced that those who advise violence in the fight against the English could not do otherwise—should they attain victory—than to rule India themselves by violent means: "when they succeed in driving out the English and they themselves become governors, they will want us to obey their laws." (1957: 144) To seize power by armed force is to condemn oneself to exercise it by armed force. That is why the movement of resistance which Gandhi organized did not so much aim to seize power from the English as to organize power for the Indians. The strategy of nonviolent action thus did not seek to seize power *for* the people, but to organize, as of today, the takeover of power *by* the people. "It is independence", Gandhi asserted, "when we learn to rule ourselves. It is, therefore in the palm of our hands. .... Now you will have seen that it is not necessary for us to have as our supreme goal the expulsion of the English." (Ibid., 116-117) Indians must therefore learn to "resist the tyranny of Indian princes just as much as that of the English." (Ibid., 170-171) The Indians would have gained nothing in exchanging the domination of the British State for that of an Indian State. "If, ultimately", wrote Gandhi, "the only expected change should concern the colour of the military uniform, we need not make so much fuss. In such a case, the people are not taken into account. They will be quite as exploited, if not more so, than in the current state of things." (1969: 240)

That is why, while Gandhi was organizing non-cooperation with the colonial system, he was also organizing a "constructive program" by which he endeavoured to mobilize Indians so that they might take part directly in running their own affairs. This constructive program consisted—while institutions, structures and laws that generated injustice were being fought—in suggesting other institutions, other structures and other laws which offered a constructive solution to the different problems facing the population, and to begin to carry them out so as to bring concrete proof of their feasibility. Rather than being content with demanding a just solution to the current conflict from the opposing power, one must endeavour to establish this solution in reality. According to Gandhi, there is a "inevitable connection between the constructive programme and civil disobedience" (1970: 170) and he eagerly asserted: "The whole theme of corporate nonviolence falls to pieces if there is no living faith in the constructive program." (Id.)

Gandhi considers India's schools and universities to be "under the influence of a government that has divested the nation of its honour and therefore advises the nation that it is their duty to withdraw their children from such schools and colleges." (1948: 133) But such a policy of non-cooperation only makes sense if the nation itself takes care of the education of children. "Abandonment of the present schools", wrote Gandhi, "means consciousness of our ability to organize our own educational system in spite of Himalayan difficulties." (Ibid., 134)

On several occasions, Gandhi voluntarily withdrew from the political controversies in which the struggle for independence became bogged down, and dedicated himself to concrete tasks of upward social mobility within the Indian population, starting with the poorest people. "I am not interested" he repeated, "in freeing India merely from the British yoke. I am bent upon freeing India from any form of servitude whatsoever." (1969: 241) He thus worked to organize the struggle against unemployment, untouchability, child marriage, alcoholism, lack of hygiene for the population, superstition of the masses, etc. "For Gandhi", his biographer B.R. Nanda noted, "political freedom depended on a social and economic regeneration of the country, which could only be expected from the efforts of the people itself." (1968: 108-109)

The *khadi* (indigenous textile) movement—by which Gandhi organised hand-spinning and hand-weaving in the whole of India—must be considered from this angle. The significance of the spinning wheel—which still figures on India's national flag—is indeed directly linked to the struggle for independence. It became, in the hands of Indians, a highly efficient economic and political weapon. Linked to the boycott of English textiles, the spinning wheel became the concrete symbol of the realization of economic independence; it constituted by itself a political challenge to foreign power. Thanks to hand-spinning, thousands of Indians escaped from unemployment and misery. As Nehru pointed out, it especially helped to "restore many peoples' confidence and self-respect." (1952: 368) The *khadi* movement also made it possible to bring cities and villages closer, and thus reinforced the unity of all Indians in their struggle for dignity.

Gandhi did not seek to build an Indian State using the British State—which he fought against—as a model. On the contrary, he asserted that the political philosophy of nonviolence required radical criticism of the State, in so far as violence was constitutive of the latter. "The State", he wrote, "represents violence in a concentrated and organized form. The individual has a soul, but as the State is a soulless machine, it can never be weaned from violence to which it owes its very existence." (1969: 246) He therefore wished for the cohesion of Indian society—which would result from independence—to rest not on the constraint that the State exerts on individuals, but on the responsibility and autonomy of individuals. For him, the autonomy of India « means the consciousness in the average villager that he is the maker of his own destiny" (Ibid., 239). In a real democracy, every citizen must be "the architect of his own government" (1961: 72). "Self-government", he added, "means continuous effort to be independent of government control, whether it is foreign government or whether it is national." (1969: 246)

A perfect society would be one in which no constraint would be exerted on citizens: "There is then a state of enlightened anarchy. In such a state everyone is his own ruler. He rules himself in such a manner that is never a hindrance to his neighbour." (Ibid., 238) And such anarchy by itself suggests that "There is no State" (Id.). But Gandhi was aware that this ideal was inaccessible to men. "But the ideal", he immediately noted, "is never fully realized in life. Hence the classical statement of Thoreau that government is best which governs the least." (Id.)

Democracy and nonviolence

Gandhi was convinced of the existence of an organic link between democracy and nonviolence: "I believe that true democracy can only be the outcome of nonviolence." (Id.) As soon as a democratic society cannot be conflict-free, conflicts must therefore be controlled according to the principles and methods of nonviolence. Ultimately, only the dynamics of nonviolence make it possible to combine order and justice. "True democracy or autonomy of the masses", Gandhi wrote, "can never come through untruthful and violent means, for the simple reason that the natural corollary to their use would be to remove all opposition through the suppression or extermination of antagonists. That does not make for individual freedom. Individual freedom can only have the fullest play under a regime of unadulterated nonviolence." (1961: 7) According to Gandhi, Western democracy is only formal. And he had grounds for believing that "it was not through democratic methods that Britain conquered India." (Ibid., 11) In fact, it was not through democratic means either that it ruled India. True democracy can only be realized once violence as a method of governing has been delegitimised. "If India", Gandhi wrote, "is to evolve towards democracy, there should be no compromise with violence or untruth." (1969: 348) He was convinced that a violent revolution could not achieve democracy. Referring to both the French revolution and the Russian revolution, he wrote: "It is my conviction that inasmuch as these struggles were fought with the weapon of violence, they failed to realize the democratic ideal. In the democracy which I have envisaged, a democracy established by nonviolence, there will be equal freedom for all." (1961: 20) Through the organization of actions of non-cooperation as well as the implementation of the constructive programme—which offers every individual the chance to express their power as citizens and to assume their individual responsibility—the nonviolent struggle by itself allowed Indians to learn to rule themselves. Gandhi thus hoped to prove that "Real self-rule will come not by the acquisition of authority by a few but by the shared acquisition of the capacity to resist the abuse of authority. In other words, self-rule is to be obtained by educating the masses to a sense of their capacity to regulate and control authority." (1969: 239) In order that India become truly autonomous, Gandhi thought that instead of building a powerful State, every village should be allowed to become autonomous: "Independence", he asserted, "must begin at the bottom. Thus, every village will be a republic." (1961: 73)

In 1946, on the eve on independence, Gandhi declared: "Our nonviolence has brought us to the gate of independence. Shall we renounce it after we have entered that gate? I for one am firmly convinced that nonviolence of the brave, such as I have envisaged, provides the surest and most efficacious means to face foreign aggression and internal disorder, just as it has done for winning independence." (1969: 155) But he immediately added that he knew India had not yet achieved the nonviolence of the brave. That is why he admitted that when India would be free from the British yoke, it would be necessary to maintain a police force. However, the latter would be entirely different from British police. "Police ranks will be composed of believers in nonviolence." (1961: 26) Gandhi admitted that for all that, they might have to resort to violence in some situations in order to maintain order, if they could not do otherwise.

As regards the army, Gandhi did not believe that it could be done away with overnight. Admittedly, he wanted to hope that Indians would be able to defend themselves against a foreign aggression by putting up a nonviolent resistance, and he wanted to prepare them for it. But if he could not get them to share his conviction, they would have no alternative but to prepare for defence through the means of violence. Once again, Gandhi intended to show realism and certainly did not want Indian people to renounce violence out of weakness. He described "the disarmament and consequent emasculation of a whole people as the blackest crime of the British" (1969: 158).

The main requirement, so that a society may be ruled according to the law of nonviolence, is that the greatest number of citizens should themselves have made the choice of nonviolence in adjusting their personal, social and political behaviour. Gandhi was aware that this condition was extremely difficult to achieve in practice. That is why he considered it unrealistic to believe that a government may become entirely nonviolent. "I do not today conceive of such a golden age", he wrote in 1940. "But I do believe in the possibility of a predominantly nonviolent society, And I am working for it." (1961: 10-11) But as long as the culture of a society is dominated by the ideology of violence, it can only be ruled according to the logic of violence. In order that a society may be governed according to the dynamics of nonviolence, its culture must be penetrated by the philosophy of nonviolence. The transformation that our societies therefore require is to pass from a culture of violence to a culture of nonviolence. This is precisely the challenge—and it is formidable—which we are faced with in this late twentieth century.

15

The Chances of a Culture of Nonviolence

Because it is considered irrational by a great number of our contemporaries, nonviolence is not likely to attract their attention or interest. At best, it arouses the distant sympathy of a certain number of people, without the latter losing their strong reservations towards it. Everything happens as if rational people felt—in front of others—a certain timidity which prevented them from taking nonviolence seriously.

The necessity to combat irrational violence

If nonviolence consistently appears ir-rational to the majority, it is not that the latter doubts whether it corresponds—in absolute, and therefore abstract, terms—to a rational man's moral requirements. But nonviolence considered in such a way remains a principle of pure—that is to say, purely formal—morality, that does not take into account the concrete realities of the historical world in which man must act. Every one admits that the principle of nonviolence is universal, only to add that it could only be implemented in history if all men were rational and willingly chose to renounce violence; yet, precisely, this has never happened and certainly never will.

Under these conditions, the majority considers that it is justified in believing that nonviolence—while it expresses the moral requirements of an individual who seeks to give meaning to his existence in the world—is not in a position to meet the technical needs of effective action in history. That is why the majority remains convinced that violence alone fulfils the technical imperatives of the political action which aims to build a pacified society.

The reason given by the "rational" man—he at least claims to be so and is generally seen in that light—to justify violence, is that it is necessary in order to contain, ward off, and as much as possible eliminate the violence of irrational men. And indeed, since man is naturally more likely to yield to the desires of passion than to submit to the requirements of reason, he is more "evil" than "good"; he is more inclined to do evil than good. He seeks above anything else to satisfy his needs and desires, and is naturally selfish; he sees the other as an adversary, and a rival against whom he must struggle. The image of a naturally good man who may have been perverted by society is but a myth. What really exists in the world, in concrete history, is violence, which hurts and wounds humanity; violence with its trail of destruction, injustice, suffering, unhappiness and death. And this violence which continuously weighs down on men like a deadly threat comes from both inside and outside society. So to survive and to live, men must organize and defend themselves against this double threat.

As soon as the rational man becomes aware of the objective evil which violence constitutes, he must choose to fight it in an attempt to build a world where order, law, security, justice and peace—that is to say, nonviolence—may prevail. And the only technical means that seems able to combat violence, is violence itself. Is this not one of history's constant lessons? That is why rational men have sought to build a strong State which may have all the necessary means of violence, on the one hand to force internal enemies to abide by the law, and on the other hand, to fight against external enemies that wish to lay down their own law. The State then assumes the monopoly of a legitimate use of violence, claiming that it does so in preparation for an era of nonviolence.

Violence legitimised by nonviolence

Hence violence is seen by rational men as the only way to achieve nonviolence, which is history's end. As soon as it is acknowledged that the end justifies the means, nonviolence justifies violence. From then on, the secondary violence, the counterviolence, by which rational men fight the primary violence of irrational men, itself becomes rational. More than that, violent men can rightfully boast of a superior morality to that of nonviolent men. Ultimately, violence alone is moral because it alone can achieve nonviolence in history. Violence is thus made legitimate by nonviolence, and all the criticism which nonviolent men are willing to level at violent men is suddenly reduced to nothing; indeed, the latter has grounds to use the very argument of nonviolence so as to justify his action in history. As soon as nonviolence is the indisputable argument of violence, the latter becomes totally unquestionable. And indeed, it is not disputed.

The charges are then reversed. Nonviolent men are now caught out by violent men, who accuse them of being a party to violence, of playing into its hands and of giving it free rein, of leaving history to its hold, since nonviolence by itself offers no technical means to combat the irrational acts of those who destroy the peace of the city. Nonviolent men are also accused of revelling in hypocrisy; it is pointed out that they are only entitled to *speak* of nonviolence insofar as they can benefit from personal and collective security which they owe to those who did not hesitate—by taking the greatest risks for themselves—to resort to violence. More than anyone, nonviolent men deserve the reproach which Péguy levelled at Kant's disciples: they have clean hands, but they actually have no hands. And to echo Peguy's words again, violent men recognize that they have gnarled hands, callous hands, sinful hands, but they sometimes boast of having their hands full. (Péguy, 1961: 827) In reality nonviolent men are the victims of groundless accusations when they are criticized for being a party to irrational violence by refusing to resort to allegedly rational violence. Consistent nonviolent men are aware that it is irrational violence which causes the vicious circle of violence; their refusal of violence is above all that of primary violence, which generates injustice. They are also aware that their refusal cannot be reduced to a moral condemnation; they must express it through an action in history.

Nonviolence as an obligation towards others

Admittedly, the requirement of nonviolence requests that the individual endeavour to refrain—to keep away—from the use of violence; but at the same time, and stronger still, it requests that he fight against the violence which pervades human relations within the historical community to which he belongs. The fulfilment of the first request ultimately appears to be—in the eyes of whoever has chosen nonviolence—the necessary, although not sufficient, condition, to the fulfilment of the second one. Man's individual destiny can only become meaningful in connection with the destiny of his community and, beyond it but also through it, with the whole of humanity. Someone who has chosen nonviolence is aware that they can only reach self-satisfaction in solitude. They must realize nonviolence within their own community, where others are not nonviolent, or at least are not all nonviolent. As a moral requirement, nonviolence is simultaneously and indissolubly an obligation to oneself and to others; it is therefore vain to claim to establish predominance of one over the other. In life, the obligation to oneself is only expressed through the obligation to others, and it is fulfilled through the relationship to others.

Nonviolence cannot justify a morality of pure intention that would lead the individual to lose interest in the consequences of his decisions and actions. It is precisely because he is interested in the consequences of violence that the nonviolent man refuses it. As much as anyone—and possibly even more—the nonviolent man is aware that an action is not only moral through its intentions, but also and ultimately through its consequences. The nonviolent man could therefore not withdraw from the world in order to guard against the impurity of violence. If he cuts himself off from the world, he would indeed be leaving it in the hands of those who have no qualms about acting violently; he would effectively become a party to the empire of violence. He must endeavour to live according to the requirement of nonviolence in the world as it is, that is to say, violent. What matters—in the eyes of the morality that is the basis for the requirement of nonviolence—is not the individual purity of the solitary man who refuses to jeopardise himself with reality, and renounces his responsibilities in history; what matters is the effective progress of nonviolence in the relationships between men within society.

Admittedly, if the nonviolent man renounces violence, it is to avoid being sucked into a vicious circle which would destroy his own humanity. He claims, and has no need to apologize, that the legitimacy of such a concern should be acknowledged; the latter, according to him, is indeed a constitutive element of the philosophical requirement that makes life meaningful and transcendent. But if the nonviolent man renounces violence, it is equally and inseparably in order to protect the humanity of others, so that they may at least not suffer from his own deed. The refusal of violence is not an end in itself; it does not constitute the goal which the nonviolent man seeks to achieve. The refusal of violence is but nonviolence's negative dimension. Its positive dimension lies in the fact that it generates the progress of nonviolence, that is to say of justice, in the relationships between men. It is this progress which the nonviolent man seeks to attain. And even if he is aware that he may have to accept to die in order not to renounce the convictions which make his life meaningful, he will do everything in his power to avoid such a situation. Should he consciously risk dying, it is not in order to protect his purity, but to fight against the injustices which do violence to the oppressed; to challenge the lies by which the oppressors justify these injustices.

To refuse cowardice above all

To decide how to act in the face of injustice, man is not confronted with the violence—nonviolence alternative; in fact, from the very beginning, he has another possible choice: that of refusing to act. The choice between violence and nonviolence only exists for someone who has already chosen to act against injustice. The debate on violence and nonviolence can therefore only properly be raised if it is related to a third pole: that of inaction, that is to say flight, passivity, resignation, which takes root in fear and is expressed through cowardice. Any discussion on this subject is therefore distorted as long as it is organized around two poles only (violence-nonviolence) and not around three (cowardice-violence-nonviolence).

It is important to acknowledge that someone who has chosen violence as a means to fight against injustice has already shown courage by overcoming their fear and refusing to be cowardly. If nonviolence is not above all opposed to cowardice, there will always be incomprehension when it is opposed to violence. The question of "violence-nonviolence" is only properly raised if it offers a choice between two kinds of resistance against injustice, and between two kinds of risk in the face of opposing violence. In both cases, the attitude may be courageous and intrepid, the intention may be good and pure, the willingness may be firm and determined. This must not be a matter for debate. The discussion must be concerned with two kinds of means, of technique, of method of action, which must not only be judged according to their morality, but also to their efficacy in reaching the desired end.

The nonviolent man is aware that the struggle against violence must be efficacious. He knows that it is not enough to be right against violence; it must be overcome. But there precisely is an implacable contradiction between violence's technical means and nonviolence's moral end. The man who believes himself to be "rationally" realistic intends to accept this contradiction by asserting that it is imposed on him by the technical necessity of political action. And he claims that in the end, since violence alone makes it possible to put irrational men out of harm's way, it is therefore necessary in keeping violence at bay and encouraging the progress of reason in the true history of men. But can one be so sure of this?

Violence is always unreasonable

Admittedly, the same moral judgment cannot be made on the irrational man's violence as on the rational man's counter-violence, but the latter is still a form of violence, and as such, it is not rational. It is not enough that the decision to use violence should seem rational for the violent action to be rational. Any form of violence contains an implacable part of irrationality. In the abstract, one can reasonably decide to resort to violence;

concretely, one never kills reasonably. Violence can be rational, but it is never reasonable. It may be true that every man bears the requirement of nonviolence within him, but he can only be violent if he is "beside himself".

If the rational man seeks satisfaction both in the coherence of discourse and in the coherence of life, the counter-violence to which he believes necessity forces him to resort, can only deeply displease him. The rational man evidently can not be content with allegedly rational violence. The latter breaks both the coherence of his speech and that of his life. He is aware that in order to be violent, he must give up—albeit momentarily—on having a rational attitude. He is necessarily aware that he contradicts himself when he makes the means of violence legitimate through the aim of nonviolence. He must remain aware of this contradiction which all prevailing ideologies try hard to deny. He must above all continually seek to overcome this contradiction.

Inasmuch as it may be necessary, violence is a tragic necessity. Any form of violence is a dramatic failure for the community of rational men, and no one among them could wash their hands off it and claim to be innocent. To use necessity to justify violence consequently makes violence necessary. It already serves to justify the violence to come, and to lock the future into the necessity of violence. It equals to refusing right from the start any inventiveness or creativity which might help free the future from the past. The rational man may himself—under the pressure of necessity—have to resort to violence so as to avoid a worse form of violence; this can only encourage him in the future, in a similar situation and under comparable circumstances, to try not to be the prisoner of that same necessity.

The means of violence contradicts nonviolence as an end

All things considered, the contradiction between nonviolence as an end and the means of violence is not only theoretical, it is also technical. It does not only exist in abstract principles; it is also found in the concrete results of an action, and is highly likely to jeopardize the efficacy of violence. Is not the contradiction between the means and the end ultimately the strongest?

Does not violence most often make progress? Does not the violence of the rational man give good reasons to the violence of the irrational man, who may then claim to be defending a just cause, and therefore justify his action? In fact, is there a man who does not claim his violence to be rational? Is not history filled with violence that has time and again been covered up by the argument of reason, but that has made reason regress?

Violence breaks free from the man who implements it. He who wants to seize and use it cannot hold it in his hands. It literally slips out of his hands and only obeys its own rules. It develops its own logic and becomes independent. That is why the man who has chosen violence cannot control the consequences of his actions; he completely loses control over them. Violence is a vicious circle. First of all, The irrational man's violence justifies the rational man's violence; then in return, the rational man's violence justifies the irrational man's violence. Hence is the justification of violence one of the decisive factors causing violence to become necessary. Violence is a sequence; it creates its own destiny. The rational man imitates the violence that the irrational man has implemented, while the irrational man imitates the justification of violence that the rational man has developed, so that ultimately, whether in attitude or speech, there is perfect reciprocity between the rational man and the irrational man.

Admittedly, the theory according to which the rational man's violence is necessary in order to fight against the irrational man's violence seems to be based on powerful arguments. But contrary to general belief, it seems to us that it is stronger in theory than it is in practice. Yesterday and today's history shows us that the application of this theory has generally caused a chain of violent acts which were nothing less than necessary. History thus contradicts this theory too often, and too deeply, for it to remain the basis for rational men's code of conduct. In reality, history does not function as this theory claims it does. Rather than extinguishing the irrational man's violence in the same way that water extinguishes fire, does not the rational man's violence most often keep it going in the same way that wood keeps the flame going? The question ought to be put to the rational man. More precisely, it should be asked by the rational man.

History shows that most often, the means of violence substitutes for the end of nonviolence. The means eclipses the end. To say that nonviolence is the end of history, but that the latter needs and justifies the means of violence, equals to sending nonviolence back to the end of history, but of an endless history. It places nonviolence outside history, and establishes violence in history. It deprives history of an end, which is to say, a meaning.

Violence is a blind mechanism

Rational men who choose to resort to violence rarely carry out their decision themselves. They give others the order, and it is not at all sure that those people are aware of the need to achieve nonviolence and take the necessary precautions to do so. To be honest, do they even have that possibility? The rational intention that is at the root of their action tends to disappear behind the mechanical effect of violence. In theory, their mission is to act for nonviolence; in practice, following the very logic of the technique which they have to apply, they act for violence. The agents carrying out the violence only care about being efficient, and do not have the time to trouble themselves with moral considerations. By its very brutality, the mechanism of violence is blind. It almost always leads those who act for violence to go far beyond the requirements of rationality, according to which the use of violence has been decided upon. This violence is characterized by the fact that it takes up all the space in which it acts. It therefore affects everything in that space and it is wrong to believe that it will only eliminate evil. Violence which aims to prepare for the time of nonviolence almost systematically generates pure violence in the end, that is to say, violence for violence's sake.

The contradiction between the nonviolence of the end and the violence of the means will therefore inordinately develop within the political space—which is huge—and separate the man who decides on violence from the one who carries it out. The politician claims to rationally decide to resort to violence in defence of the established order and to restore social peace, and he justifies his decision by referring to humanity's highest moral values. But first of all, to bring violence into play, it is necessary to call men to violence. This call to violence can claim to be based on reason, but in order to be heard, it appeals to passion rather than reason. In reality, it is passion—much more than reason—that arms the person who carries out violence. Violence therefore needs propaganda that appeals to passion more than it does reason. What matters in the execution of violence, is not the morality of men, but only their morale. If they cannot be rational, violent men must be convinced that they are right so that they may have others give in to their reason no matter what. And to foster the morale of those who carry out violence, they must be convinced that they are undertaking the justest and noblest possible task. The role of ideology is to prove violence innocent by removing any contradiction between its means and the end which justifies it. But violence is never *innocent*, for it has an implacable part of *nuisance* (the two words have the same root: *nocere*, to harm, to hurt). To honour violence is not only to dishonour oneself, it is above all to dishonour the victims of violence. Considered in its own right, violence is always dishonourable. To say that it is necessary does not contradict this statement; on the contrary, it reinforces it. For it is never honourable for man to be the prisoner of necessity, and especially not when the latter compels him to use violence against other men. Man's honour remains nonviolence, even when necessity forces him to resort to violence. It is crucial that at the very moment when, in the grip of circumstances, man believes he cannot do otherwise than to use violence, he should remember that the only honour lies in nonviolence. The reasons for which man resorts to violence can be honourable, but this does not necessarily make violence honourable.

Violence instrumentalizes man

So at the end of the chain of orders and obedience, henchmen carry out violence's dirty work, which is nothing less than rational and is the very negation of the values in whose name they are supposed to be acting. At this end of the chain, the executor is nothing more than an instrument for violence, a mechanical cog, a purely technical instrument. At that moment, everything leads man to the loss of his humanity. One of violence's characteristics is that it manipulates the man who exercises it. And this manipulation is equal to dehumanisation. In his book *Why freedom?*, Georges Bernanos describes the relations which "the man with a machine gun" has with his weapon: "The machine gun fires on a signal from the master of the man with a machine gun, and on a signal from this master the man with a machine gun shoots anything. .... In the man with a machine gun that I have just mentioned, the accessory is not the machine gun, but the man. The man which I am talking about serves the machine gun, but the machine gun does not serve the man; it is not "the man with a machine gun", but "the machine gun with a man". (Bernanos, 1953: 227)

So it all starts with the glorification of the nobleness of a cause, and it all ends with the acceptance of the most infamous acts of violence. The greatness of the sacrifice of those who have chosen to die for a cause is praised, but in fact these same people have received the mission to kill for it. Violence's entire "logic" precisely consists in killing in order to avoid dying. And because men have a lust for life, they also have a lust to kill. While the poet exalts the glory of those who die "in great battles .... amid all the pomp of grandiose funerals" (Péguy, 1957: 1026), while the philosopher discourses on the necessity for the rational man to resort to violence to pave the way for nonviolence, while the politician idealizes the patriotic duty of citizens to defend the honour of free men, while the general extols the courage of the soldier who braves every danger and takes the greatest risks to keep the nation safe, while the High Priest calls for the blessing of the god of armies for those who are willing to sacrifice their live in the course of duty, he which the hardness of life has forced to take up arms professionally, or that the power of propaganda has forced to enrol, the man of rank, of the lowest rank—precisely, the man with a machine gun, for in almost every war, despite the automation and sophistication of weapon systems, he has the final word—drilled for battle, trained not to be sentimental, toughened so as to forget his fear, hardened so that he may internalise the cruelty of war, this man is directly confronted with violence which instrumentalizes and dehumanizes him. No, it is not true that the man of rank, of the lowest rank, behaves like a rational man! In the exhilaration of violence, he does nothing but despise all the values which the "rational" man glorifies in order to justify war. Hence is the man of rank, of the lowest rank, raw material for the poet's lines, the philosopher's treatises, the politician's speeches, the general's announcements, the High Priest's prayers, and later, for the historian's accounts; but first of all, he is their victim.

It can be argued that the "rational" man who decided to use violence did not wish for these base deeds. This may be true, but he did wish for the process that caused them through a mechanical string of events. They are but the inevitable—practically inevitable—consequences of his decision, and he cannot refuse to take responsibility for them. It would probably be unfair to assume too much about the rational man's intentions when he decides to use violence in order to defend a just cause. His intention might be pure, but he has not paid enough attention to the consequences of his decision, which he claims not to be responsible for. In reality, violence is based on a morality of intention which in most cases excludes the possibility of a morality of responsibility. Once again, the charges are reversed. Whatever may be the intention—it may indeed be pure—of he who decides to resort to it, *violence is never a heroic deed, it is always a base deed.*

History shows that we nearly always move from the legitimation of violence which considers it to be a technical necessity, to its justification which honours it as a moral virtue. We thus develop an ideology that covers up and finally eliminates any contradiction between the end and the means of violent action. If nonviolence is indeed the end of history, the rational man is therefore challenged to invent nonviolent means to act in history.

In the past, the rational man may most often have used *violent action* to fight against the violence of oppression or aggression; this shows the necessity of *action*, but does not prove the inevitability of *violence*. Admittedly, insofar as the technical means of violence has alone been used in attempting to defeat irrational violence, it alone could show a certain efficacy. And we must admit that its beneficial effect in history has sometimes been more powerful than its maleficent effect. It was therefore better to act by this means, than not to act at all. It is true that the nonviolent man himself is also the heir to violent struggles that were carried out in the past, and that he also benefits from their experience. He keeps these struggles in mind, but this does not in the least compel him to think that violence remains a necessity *today*. On the contrary, if the end of violence has indeed justified the means of violence in the past, not only is he entitled, but it is actually his duty *today*, to ask himself whether there may be other means which would not be in contradiction with the desired end. The question that the rational man must consider *today* is whether it might be possible to invent another history, by experimenting another method of action than that of violence.

It is true that it is not simply a matter of nonviolence meeting the moral requirements which the philosopher is bound to; it must also satisfy the technical necessity which the politician has to deal with. But it also is a moral requirement for both of them to ask themselves whether the choice of nonviolence makes it possible to discover a technique that would allow people to act rationally and responsibly in history. To escape the vicious circle which philosophical reflection and political thought have been locked in for centuries, it is necessary to challenge the rightfulness of violence, and to list the technical possibilities of nonviolence.

Admittedly, every "rational" man admits that violence can only be the *ultima ratio*, the last argument, that it must only be used as a last resort, when all other means have failed; he accepts that violence should be resorted to as little as possible, and only in cases of strict necessity; and even in those cases, lesser violence ought to be chosen. The "rational" man ultimately asserts that human action must resolutely be included in the dynamics of an *economy of violence*. Someone who has chosen nonviolence could agree to subscribe to such assertions, but on the condition that the "other means", that is to say the means of nonviolent action, should also be tested. Yet, in all honesty, those who assert the necessity of violence have generally never tried nonviolence. It is one thing to say: violence should be resorted to as little as possible, and another to say: nonviolence should be resorted to as much as possible. If man is not willing to implement the means of nonviolent actions whenever possible, then violence will always be necessary. The economy of violence can only be put into practice if nonviolence is resolutely chosen. *The economy of violence is only possible within the dynamics of nonviolence.*

The need to constrain

The rational action, whose goal is to fight against violence in history, cannot be reduced to dialogues and discussions aiming to bring irrational men to reason. Violence is precisely characterized by the refusal of dialogue and discussion. Admittedly, the violent man remains a "rational" man in the sense that he might yet be reasoned with, and be able to hear reason. It might therefore be useful to try to reason with him. But violence most often makes him turn a deaf ear to the arguments of reason. In so far as rational discourse can have no hold over the violent man, it becomes impossible to persuade him to renounce violence. From then on, the only possible rational action against violence has to be a constraining action over the violent man. It would be wrong to leave nonviolence up to the goodwill of all parties involved, if it is to prevail within human relations inside the community. It is necessary to create governmental institutions that use means of constraint to ensure respect for the law—this notably involves the implementation of a "public force", of a police force and a legal system. It would be unrealistic to claim—in the name of nonviolence—to organize a society without a government which would have the right and the means to constrain citizens. Without such a government, society is given free rein for the organizing of coteries and mafias, and the latter can have no qualms about taking citizens hostage, under the constant threat of the worst means of violence. The question is then whether all forms of constraint are necessarily violent, or if nonviolent constraint may be implemented? Before this question can be answered, nonviolence must be examined.

The question which the rational man must ask himself today goes like this: can nonviolence only establish a moral attitude in the face of history, or can it establish a responsible attitude in history? Does nonviolence condemn man to refuse all forms of action, and to leave history? Should he choose to live in the desert and agree to be dead to the world? Or does it allow him to change the world? It would not be reasonable to answer immediately in the affirmative, but it would be even less so to give a definitive negative answer. There is after all a history of nonviolence that is also the history of struggles against the violence of "irrational men". It is surprising that this history may not have caught the attention of rational men who advocate and justify violence more.

It is true that a morality of pure intention that would only be based on the refusal to kill, would allow to die with dignity, but not to live. The question is therefore to know whether nonviolence can or not establish a concrete, historical morality, a morality of action, practical wisdom, allowing man not only to die for his convictions, but also to live for them. The universal requirement of nonviolence cannot simply be proclaimed in the face of history; it must be realized in history, which is violent.

It is therefore necessary to study the "feasibility" of nonviolence as a method of action. And for that, one must ask whether nonviolence can establish a practical attitude, a code of conduct, and a behaviour that may be coherent and viable, that may offer the individual, as well as the community, a real promise of long life . Admittedly, absolute nonviolence will always remain an inaccessible ideal for the individual as well as the community, but the question is to know whether nonviolence can become a practical ideal: is it possible to define an effective practice that is inspired by this ideal? In other words, is the practice of nonviolence likely enough to succeed that it may be chosen by the rational man who not only wishes to die well, but who also wants to live well? More precisely, one must ask how likely it is that the practice of nonviolence may be able to contain and reduce violence in human relations? The probabilities of failure certainly exist, and may cause the death of the individual, and even that of the community. But the same goes for violence, for this is a fact of life. To live is to risk dying at anytime. And all things considered, the chances that violence may fail are fairly considerable. But the ideology of violence, which dominates our mentalities, postulates both the failure of nonviolence and the success of violence. It is this double postulate which we feel must be questioned.

Nonviolence's great weakness lies in the fact that violence is perfectly organized and nonviolence is perfectly disorganized. The potentialities of nonviolence can only be actualized in history insofar as societies are determined to implement them at an institutional level. For that, a majority of citizens must be convinced that violence is not only desirable, but that it is also possible.

The "chances" of nonviolent action

In taking up the concept of "chance" which Max Weber defined in his essay *On some categories of interpretive sociology*, one must ask whether it is objectively likely that nonviolent action may succeed in the history of human communities. "A most understandable and important basis for the explanation of the action", Max Weber writes, "is the objective existence of those chances—that is to say, the greater or lesser probability (which can be formulated in a "judgment of objective possibility") of this expectation being justified." (1992: 321)

Each person adjusts their behaviour to that of others; each person acts in re-action to the action of others. The question here is how others may re-act to nonviolent action? A person who acts in accordance with the principles, rules and means of nonviolence nourishes the hope that others will behave in order that his action may succeed. But beyond the subjective expectations of the person who acts, the decisive factor in the success or failure of their action lies in the existing objective chances that others may behave in accordance with his expectations. Commenting on Max Weber, Julien Freund writes: "The idea of chance is therefore linked to the category of objective possibility, which means that, under given objective conditions, men are likely to act in a way which can approximately be predicted." 1966: 104)

If the person who has chosen nonviolence is to succeed in their initiative, the others must in fact consider the way in which they are expected to behave to be "valid"; in other words, it ought to make sense to them, whichever the reason for which they may do so. They may adopt this behaviour because they consider that it is equivalent to a "value" to which they may decide to adhere, but they could equally do so, while thinking that it is more in keeping with their interest. One can reasonably believe that as a culture of nonviolence progressively develops within the community, more and more individuals will adjust their behaviour according to the expectations of nonviolent action, because they recognize that it is equivalent to a "value" which gives meaning to the latter.

Since nonviolent action is only relevant in a situation of conflict, the protagonist of nonviolence expects others to adjust their behaviour by themselves accepting to enter the dynamics of a nonviolent resolution of the on-going conflict. But "the others" are not only the adversaries; they are also "all the others", that is to say all the members of the community who do not—or not yet—feel involved in the conflict. The protagonist of nonviolence expects them to become involved in the conflict resolution themselves, admitting that the behaviour that is expected of them makes sense to them. The protagonist of nonviolence ultimately hopes that it will be possible to reach that which Max Weber calls an "agreement" (1992: 341) between all the members of the community. The question is to know whether the protagonist of nonviolence can reasonably think that there are chances—that is to say, objective possibilities—that others will behave in order that his action may create the conditions for a long-lasting agreement. The prevailing ideology asserts that these chances virtually do not exist; but this is an ideological assertion, and not a sociological appreciation based on the rational evolution of objective possibilities of the success of nonviolent action. However, the same ideology asserts that the chances of success of violent action in the history of human communities are great, but then again, it is an ideological assertion much more than a sociological appreciation. In reality, it is reasonable to believe that violence's chances of success are much lesser than the prevailing ideology claims; the chances of nonviolence are also much greater than it claims. One can even reasonably consider that, in many situations, nonviolence's chances of success are much greater than that of violence. Numerous experiments have indeed shown that individuals, but also communities, can adjust their behaviour to the expectations of those who act according to the principles, rules and means of nonviolence. This means that nonviolence's chances of success really exist: it may lead individuals and communities—who were until now in a situation of disagreement and conflict—to a long-lasting agreement. In other words, there objectively is a probability according to which nonviolent action may succeed. These chances and that probability must be examined according to the concrete conditions in which the action develops, and many influencing factors must then be considered.

Max Weber points out that the validity of a social rule must be founded on "the average practical evaluation of the chances of human behaviour" (1992: 324). So in order to establish the validity of nonviolence as a normative rule of communal activity, one should reasonably consider the existence of an *average* probability according to which individuals may adjust their behaviour to the expectations of nonviolence. This hypothesis seems valid, it must nevertheless be verified. To make the political choice of nonviolence does not actually involve starting from *the ideal of nonviolence* to endeavour to put it into practice: such a task would be impossible. On the contrary, it involves starting from *the reality of violence* in an attempt to transform it, little by little, by implementing the methods of nonviolent action when it is effectively possible; and many possibilities then arise, all of which are "chances" for nonviolence.

Admittedly, for the time being, the forces of nonviolence are not in a position to effectively oppose the forces of violence that rage all across the world. When—in a circumscribed territory—all factors are present for the explosion of violence, it effectively explodes, and irreparable harm is done without anyone being able to prevent it. For it is already too late. Action must be undertaken long before the explosion occurs. There certainly is nothing inevitable about this outburst of violence against man, because it is in no way inevitable that the factors which trigger the violence should be present; but as soon as this is the case due to men's responsibility, violence inevitably bursts out. It is probable that neither the means of violence, nor those of nonviolence may be able to extinguish the frenzy of fear, passion and hate. The latter will have to burn out by themselves. The system of violence which has dominated our societies for centuries continues to inject its deadly poison into our present, but probably also into our future. As we endeavour to dismantle that system, we must understand the full extent of the irreparable harm that it continues to cause.

The greatest realism of nonviolence

We are never absolutely certain when it comes to estimating the consequences of our actions; to a large extent, the latter are unpredictable and escape us. This is equally true of violent action and nonviolent action, and it must encourage us to show great prudence in our decisions. This prudence forces us to assess the extent to which the consequences of our actions are irreparable and irreversible. Prudence thus seems to advise us to avoid violent action and to prefer nonviolent action. For, in all probability, the former holds more irreversible consequences than the latter. In comparison with the prudence that is the basis for the rational man's practical wisdom, violence appears im-prudent: it lacks fore-sight with regards to the consequences that it generates in spite of ourselves. Besides, it is important not only to judge violence's immediate consequences, but also its distant consequences, which may occur elsewhere and at other times. The efficacy of violence must not be judged in the short-term, but in the long-term. Counter-violence can have immediate effects that may lead us to believe that it has reduced the amount of violence in history. But with the passing of time, we are likely to find out that it has negative indirect consequences, perverse secondary effects, and that it has ultimately increased the amount of violence in the world. In this respect, nonviolence guarantees a better future.

 The difference between someone who has chosen nonviolence and someone who has chosen violence does not lie in greater idealism towards nonviolence, but in greater realism towards violence. For violence, when all is said and done, is a utopia. According to its etymological meaning, *u-topia* is something that does not exist *anywhere, in any place*. Yet precisely, violence may exist everywhere, but it has not in any place achieved the end which claims to justify it. Never, *anywhere*, does violence realize justice between men; never *in any place* does violence offer a human solution to the inevitable human conflicts which form the fabric of history.

Conclusion

The idea which has prevailed in our societies until now, is that it is only possible to fight against violence effectively by opposing a counter-violence. If so many philosophers, having asserted the ethical requirement of nonviolence, have ultimately not been able to do otherwise than acknowledge the necessity and legitimacy of counter-violence, it is because they have not been in a position to conceive a nonviolent action against violence. Everything in our culture leads us to consider our relation to violence through the *violence / counterviolence* combination, and not through the *violence / nonviolence* combination. The conviction that explains the choice of nonviolence, is that counter-violence does not effectively fight against the system of violence, because it is in fact part of it, and it only contributes to its maintenance and its perpetuation.

The principle of nonviolence requires the search for a nonviolent way to act effectively against violence. Many struggles have shown the efficacy of the strategy of nonviolent action in allowing men and peoples to recover their dignity and their freedom. Admittedly, this efficacy is always relative and failure is always a possibility, but nonviolent action makes it possible for man to have a coherent and responsible attitude in the face of other men's violence. However, *the efficacy of nonviolent action does not justify the principle of nonviolence*. If we only sought to justify the pertinence of the principle of nonviolence with the efficacy of nonviolent action, sooner or later we would be confronted with the limits of that action, and we would then have to question the relevance of that principle.

The principle of nonviolence has led us to bring about a Copernican revolution in the way that we consider the efficacy of the struggle against violence. For centuries, we have been used to considering efficacy as being essentially the effect of violence. More or less consciously, we have reached a point where we identify efficacy with violence. But we only wish to feel *the efficacy of violence*, and refuse to see *the violence of efficacy*: we therefore let ourselves become blind to *the violence of violence*.

With the *violence / counter-violence* combination, the struggle against violence is led through a head-on opposition to its mechanical effects. This shock opposes two physical forces of the same nature. It is then necessary to carry out greater violence in order to defeat violence. Admittedly, in the short-term, counter-violence can successfully put an end to the drive of opposing violence, and have us believe that we have gained a victory. But in reality, this victory is highly likely to be illusory, for we have ultimately reinforced violence's hold over history; we have contributed to confining history to the logic of violence; we have made violence a necessity. To resort to counter-violence in the struggle against violence increases the risk of stretching the string of violent acts indefinitely. The violence / nonviolence combination aims to break that string. Of course, nonviolent action also seeks to interrupt the effects of violence, but it starts by attempting to fight against its causes. Rather than seeking to hold back the torrent, one should seek to dry up its spring.

Henri-Bernard Vergote rightfully pointed out that "violence cannot be considered a mere kind of force": "In the light of spirituality which sees it at its opposite, it appears to be an attitude as well as a way of being." (1987: 368) Similarly, he adds, spirituality is not a force, but an attitude. In this light, he denounces "the misconception of spirituality, considered from the sole point of view of its possible efficacy: the fact that it resembles a force is thus justified, as long as it seems symmetrically opposed to physical force, producing the same effects but by other means." (Ibid., 364) Indeed, more than an action, *violence is an attitude*; it is an attitude towards other men which generates an attitude towards death and killing. (Let us point out that cowardice is also an attitude.) In the same way, *nonviolence is above all and essentially an attitude, an attitude other than (cowardice and) violence*, another attitude towards other men which generates another attitude towards death and killing. It is the ethical and spiritual attitude of the "standing man" who recognizes violence as the negation of humanity, and refuses to submit to its domination. Such an attitude is based on the existential conviction that nonviolence is a more powerful resistance to violence than counter-violence. Nonviolent action ultimately seeks to create the conditions that allow the adversary who has chosen violence to change his attitude. This aim is a gamble which contains a risk of death. And this risk, precisely, holds the hope for life.

If nonviolence were but a method of action that sought to achieve that which violence aims for through other means, it ought then to be judged on its results, which alone could justify it. And it would be best to change that method soon as it is considered ineffective. But if nonviolence is an attitude—the attitude of the rational man who seeks to give his life meaning and transcendence—it then serves to justify itself. And the rational man has no reason to change his attitude.

But even if nonviolence is an attitude that results from a personal choice, it fosters a civilization project which is set to take its place in history. The stakes are high in the building of such a nonviolent civilization today, for the future of humanity as well as for that of each of our societies. It requires the best of the energy of all men of goodwill. Each man, in his own way, can act in order to make a dent in the system of violence that dominates our societies; these dents all open onto a future in which man will see other men as his fellow men. It would not be reasonable to assert that this civilization of nonviolence will triumph—it is sadly not true that "truth always triumphs"—it is nevertheless reasonable to act so that it may little by little prevail over the archaisms of which we are still prisoners. We are deeply convinced that at the beginning of the 21th century, this is where the hope of men lies.

References

Alain, pseud.; Chartier, Émile Auguste (1939). *Convulsions de la force*. Paris: Gallimard.
Andrews, C. F. (1934). *M.-K Gandhi à l'oeuvre. Suite de sa vie écrite par lui-même*. Paris: Les éditions Rieder.
Aquinas, Thomas (n.d.). *Summa Theologica*.
Arendt, Hannah (1972). *Du mensonge à la violence* (On Violence). Paris: Calmann-Lévy.
Arendt, Hannah (1985). *Essai sur la révolution* (On Revolution). Paris: Gallimard.
Arendt, Hannah (1988). *Condition de l'homme moderne* (The Human Condition). Paris: Calmann-Lévy.
Arendt, Hannah (1992). *La crise de la culture* (The Crisis in Culture). Paris: Gallimard.
Bakunin, Mikhail (1965). *La liberté* (Liberty). Paris: J. J. Pauvert.
Bayada, Bernadette (1993). "Préjugés et stéréotypes, sources de violence", in *L'éducation à la paix*. Paris: Centre national de documentation pédagogique.
Berdyaev, Nikolai (1963). *De l'esclavage et de la liberté* (Slavery and Freedom). Paris: Aubier.
Bernanos, George (1948). *Le chemin de la Croix-des-âmes* (The Way of the Cross-of-Souls). Paris: Gallimard.
Bernanos, George (1949). *Les enfants humiliés* (The Humiliated Children). Paris: Gallimard.
Bernanos, Georges (1953). *La liberté pour quoi faire?* (Why Freedom?). Paris: Gallimard.
Bisot, Anne-Catherine and Lhopiteau, François (1993). "La résolution non-violente des conflits", in Best, Francine and Julien, Claude, Eds., *L'éducation à la paix*. Paris: Centre national de documentation pédagogique.
Bondurant, Joan V. (1969). *Conquest of Violence*. Berkley and Los Angeles: University of California Press.
Buddha (1991). *Paroles du Bouddha*. Paris: Le Seuil.
Bukovsky, Vladimir (1978). *Et le vent reprend ses tours* (To Build a Castle). Paris: Robert Laffont.
Camus, Albert (1951). *L'homme révolté* (The Rebel). Paris: Gallimard.
Canetti, Elias (1966). *Masse et puissance* (Crowds and Power). Paris: Gallimard.
Canivez, Patrice (1990). "La révolution, l'État, la discussion", in *Discours, violence et langage : un socratisme d'Èric Weil, Actes du colloque de Paris, 18-19 novembre 1988, Le Cahier, n° 9-10*. Paris: Éditions Osiris.
Clausewitz, Carl von (1955). *De la guerre* (On War). Paris: Les Éditions de Minuit.
De la Boétie, Étienne (1978). *Le discours de la servitude volontaire* (Discourse on Voluntary Servitude). Paris: Payot.

Dostoyevsky (1948). *Les frères Karamazov* (The Brothers Karamazov). Paris: Gallimard.

Duval, Étienne (1993). "L'espace intermédiaire", in *La médiation, dossier de Non-violence actualité*. Montargis: Non-violence actualité, pp. 32-34.

Duvignaud, Jean (1980). "Violence et société", in *Raison présente*, 54.

Einstein, Albert (1979). *Comment je vois le monde* (The World as I See It). Paris: Flammarion.

Fischer, Louis (1952). *La vie du Mahatma Gandhi* (The Life of Mahatma Gandhi). Paris: Calmann-Lévy.

Fornari, Franco (1969). *Psychanalyse de la situation atomique* (Psychoanalysis of the Atomic War). Paris: Gallimard.

Freud, Sigmund (1981). *Essais de psychanalyse*. Paris: Petite Bibliothèque Payot.

Freud, Sigmund (1993). *L'inquiétante étrangeté et autres essais* (The Uncanny). Paris: Gallimard.

Freud, Sigmund (1993). *Le mot d'esprit et sa relation à l'insconscient* (Wit and its Relation to the Unconscious). Paris: Gallimard.

Freund, Julien (1966). *Sociologie de Max Weber* (The Sociology of Max Weber). Paris: PUF.

Fromm, Erich (1983). *De la désobéissance* (On Disobedience). Paris: Robert Laffont.

Gandhi, Mahatma (1948). *La jeune Inde* (Young India). Paris: Stock.

Gandhi, Mahatma (1957). *Leur civilisation et notre délivrance*. Paris: Denoël.

Gandhi, Mahatma (1958). *Satyagraha*. Ahmenabad: Navajivan Publishing House.

Gandhi, Mahatma (1959). *What Jesus means to me*. Ahmenabad: Navajivan Publishing House.

Gandhi, Mahatma (1960). *Lettres à l'ashram*. Paris: Albin Michel.

Gandhi, Mahatma (1961). *Democracy: real and deceptive*. Ahmenabad: Navajivan Publishing House.

Gandhi, Mahatma (1961). *Satyagraha in South Africa*. Ahmenabad: Navajivan Publishing House.

Gandhi, Mahatma (1964). *Autobiographie ou mes expériences de vérité* (An Autobiography: The Story of my Experiments With Truth). Paris: Presses Universitaires de France.

Gandhi, Mahatma (1969). *Tous les hommes sont frères* (All Men Are Brothers). Paris: Gallimard.

Gandhi, Mahatma (1971). *All Men are Brothers, Life and Thoughts of Mahatma Gandhi*. Ahmenabad: Navajivan Publishing House.

Gandhi, Mahatma (1986). *Résistance non-violente* (Nonviolent Resistance). Paris: Buchet/Chastel.

Girard, René (1978). *Des choses cachées depuis la fondation du monde* (Things Hidden since the Foundation of the World). Paris: Grasset.

Guéhenno, Jean (1968). *La mort des autres*. Paris: Grasset.

Gusdorf, Georges (1960). *La vertu de force* (The Virtue of Fortitude). Paris: PUF.

Havel, Vaclav (1989). *Essais politiques* (The Power of the Powerless). Paris: Calmann-Lévy.

Havel, Vaclav (1989). *Interrogatoire à distance* (Disturbing the Peace). Paris: Éditions de l'Aube.

Hegel, Georg (1988). *La raison dans l'histoire* (Reason in History). Paris: Union générale d'éditions.
Hegel, Georg (1989). *Principes de la philosophie du droit* (Elements of the Philosophy of Right). Paris: Librairie philosophique J. Vrin.
Hegel, Georg (1992). *Phénoménologie de l'esprit* (The Phenomenology of Spirit). Paris: Aubier.
Herbert, Jean (1969). *Ce que Gandhi a vraiment dit*. Paris: Stock.
Jankélévitch, Vladimir (1967). *Le pardon* (Forgiveness). Paris: Aubier.
Jaurès, Jean (1969). *Histoire socialiste de la Révolution française* (Socialist History of the French Revolution). Paris: Éditions sociales.
Jonas, Hans (1993). *Le principe de responsabilité, Une éthique pour la civilisation technologique* (The Imperative of responsibility). Paris: Le Cerf.
Jouvenel, Bertrand de (1977). *Du pouvoir* (On Power). Paris: Hachette.
Kant, Immanuel (1952). *Fondements de la métaphysique des moeurs* (Groundwork of the Metaphysics of Morals). Paris: Librairie Delagrave.
Krischer, Gilbert (1992). *Figures de la violence et de la modernité*. Lille: Presses Universitaires de Lille.
Lacroix, Jean (1968). "Raison et histoire selon Eric Weil", in *Panorama de la philosophie contemporaine*. Paris: PUF.
Lassier, Suzanne (1970). *Gandhi et la non-violence*. Paris: Le Seuil.
Levinas, Emmanuel (1990). *Autrement qu'être ou au-delà de l'essence* (Otherwise than Being: Or Beyond Essence). Paris: Le Livre de Poche.
Levinas, Emmanuel (1990). *Difficile liberté* (Difficult Freedom). Paris: Le Livre de Poche.
Levinas, Emmanuel (1991). *Entre nous, Essais sur le penser-à-l'autre*. Paris: Grasset.
Levinas, Emmanuel (1992). *Éthique et Infini* (Ethics and Infinity). Paris: Le Livre de Poche.
Levinas, Emmanuel (1992). *Totalité et Infini, Essai sur l'extériorité* (Totality and Infinity: an Essay on Exteriority). Paris: Le Livre de Poche.
Levinas, Emmanuel (1993). *Cahier de l'Herne*. Paris: Le Livre de Poche.
Levinas, Emmanuel (1994). *Humanisme de l'autre homme* (Humanism of the Other). Paris: LGF, Le Livre de Poche.
Livre des morts des anciens Égyptiens (The Egyptian Book of the Dead) (1985). Paris: Stock Plus.
Luutu, Vincent Tsongo (1993). *Penser le socio-politique avec Emmanuel Levinas*. Lyon: Profac.
Machiavelli, Niccolo (1962). *Le Prince* (The Prince). Paris: Le Livre de Poche.
Malraux, André (1967). *Antimémoires* (Anti-memoirs). Paris: Gallimard.
Maritain, Jacques (1927). *Primauté du spirituel* (The Things That Are Not Caesar's). Paris: Plon.
Maritain, Jacques (1933). *Du régime temporel et de la liberté* (Freedom in the Modern World). Paris: Desclée de Brouwer.
Maritain, Jacques (1965). *L'homme et l'État* (Man and the State). Paris: PUF.
Mellon, Christian (1980). "Violence des bombes et violence des structures et Une inflation à maîtriser", in *Alternatives non-violentes*, 37: 37-48.
Milgram, Stanley (1974). *Soumission à l'autorité* (Obedience to Authority). Paris: Calmann-Lévy.

Morin, Edgar and Kern, Anne Brigitte (1993). *Terre-patrie* (Homeland Earth). Paris: Le Seuil.
Mounier, Emmanuel (1961). *Oeuvres*. Paris: Le Seuil.
Mounier, Emmanuel (1961). *Révolutions personnaliste et communautaire, Oeuvres*. Paris: Le Seuil.
Nanda, B. R. (1968). *Gandhi, Sa vie, ses idées, son action politique en Afrique du Sud et en Inde*. Verviers: Marabout Université.
Nehru, Jawaharlal (1952). *Ma vie et mes prisons* (Toward Freedom). Paris: Denoël.
Nietzsche, Friedrich (1963). *Ainsi parlait Zarathoustra* (Thus spoke Zarathustra). Paris: Gallimard.
Ostrogorski, Moisei (1979 [1903]). *La démocratie et les partis politiques* (Democracy and the Organization of Political Parties). Paris: Le Seuil.
Pascal, Blaise (1963). *Oeuvres complètes* (Complete Works). Paris: Le Seuil.
Patanjali (1991). *Yoga-Sutras*. Paris: Albin Michel.
Péguy, Charles (1957). *Eve, Oeuvres poétiques en prose*. Paris: Gallimard.
Péguy, Charles (1961). *L'Argent suite, Oeuvres en prose, 1909-1914* (On Money, continued, 1909-1914). Paris: La Pléiade.
Péguy, Charles (1961). *Victor Marie, Comte Hugo, Oeuvres en prose (1909-1914)*. Paris: Gallimard.
Plato (1965). *Apologie de Socrate* (The Apology). Paris: Garnier-Flammarion.
Plato (1965). *Criton* (Crito). Paris: Garnier-Flammarion.
Plato (1967). *Gorgias*. Paris: Garnier-Flammarion.
Poirié, François (1992). *Emmanuel Levinas*. Besançon: Éditions La Manufacture.
Poirié, François (1996). *Emmanuel Levinas: Essai et entretiens*. Paris: Actes Sud.
Popper, Karl (1993). *La leçon de ce siècle* (The Lesson of This Century). Paris: Anatolia.
Popper, Karl and Condry, John (1994). *La télévision : un danger pour la démocratie* (Television: a Danger to Democracy). Paris: Anatolia.
Prabhu, R. K. and Rao, U. R. (ed.) (1969). *The Mind of Mahatma Gandhi*. Ahmenabad: Navajivan Publishing House.
Prairat, Eric (1988). "Pour une éducation non-violente", in Bayada, Bernadette et al., Eds., *La médiation, dossier de Non-violence actualité*. Montargis: Non-violence actualité, pp. 45-46.
Refalo, Alain (1989). "Place et rôle des associations dans une stratégie de dissuasion civile", in *Alternatives non-violentes*, 72: 27-35.
Rehnicer, Raymond (1993). *L'adieu à Sarajevo*. Paris: Desclée de Brouwer.
Rey, Alan, dir. (1993). *Dictionnaire historique de la langue française*. Paris: Le Robert.
Ricoeur, Paul (1955). *Histoire et vérité* (History and Truth). Paris: Le Seuil.
Ricoeur, Paul (1990). *Soi-même comme un autre* (Oneself as Another). Paris: Le Seuil.
Riobe, Guy (1988). *Le Père Riobé, un homme libre*. Paris: Desclée de Brouwer.
Rojzman, Charles (1992). *La peur, la haine et la démocratie* (Fear, Hatred and Democracy). Paris: Desclée de Brouwer.
Rousseau, Jean-Jacques (1762). *Du contrat social* (Of the Social Contract). Amsterdam: Marc-Michel Rey.
Scheler, Max (1953). *L'idée de paix et le pacifisme* (The Idea of Peace and Pacifism). Paris: Éditions Aubier Montaige.

Schopenhauer, Arthur (1991). *Le fondement de la morale* (On the Basis of Morality). Paris: Le Livre de Poche.
Serres, Michel (1992). *Eclaircissements* (Clarifications). Paris: François Bourin.
Serres, Michel (1992). *Le contrat naturel* (The Natural Contract). Paris: Flammarion.
Sharp, Gene (1980). "A la recherche d'une solution au problème de la guerre", in *Alternatives Non-Violentes*, 34: 3-16.
Six, Jean-François (n.d.). *Brèche*, 40-42.
Solzhenitsyn, Aleksandr (1974). *Lettre aux dirigeants soviétiques* (A Letter to the Soviet Leaders). Paris: Le Seuil.
Sorel, Georges (1972). *Réflexions sur la violence* (Reflections on Violence). Paris: Éditions Marcel Rivière et Cie.
Sublon, Roland (1979). "Narcisse au service du pouvoir", in *Cahiers de la réconciliation*, February: 14-17.
Tendulkar, Dinanath Gopal (1969). *Mahatma: Life of Mohandas Karamcha Gandhi*. New Dehli: Ministry of Information and Broadcasting.
Thoreau, Henry-David (1967). *La désobéissance civile* (Civil Disobedience). Paris: J.J. Pauvert.
Tolstoy, Leo (1891). *Que faire* (What is to be done?). Paris: Éditeur Albert Savine.
Tolstoy, Leo (1901). *Rayons de l'aube*. Paris: Stock.
Tolstoy, Leo (1906). *Une seule chose est nécessaire* (The Only Need). Paris: Librairie Universelle.
Tolstoy, Leo (1923). *La vraie vie*. Paris: Bibliothèque Charpentier.
Vergote, Henri-Bernard (1987). "Esprit, violence et raison", in *Études*, 366(3), March: 363-377.
Weber, Max (1979). *Le savant et le politique* (Politics as a Vocation). Paris: Plon.
Weber, Max (1992). *Essais sur la théorie de la science* (Methodology of Social Sciences). Paris: Plon.
Weil, Eric (1974). *Logique de la philosophie* (The Logic of Philosophy). Paris: Vrin.
Weil, Eric (1982). *Philosophie et réalité, Derniers essais et conférences* (Philosophy and Reality). Paris: Vrin.
Weil, Eric (1984). *Philosophie politique* (Political Philosophy). Paris: Vrin.
Weil, Eric (1990). *Problèmes kantiens* (Kantian Problems). Paris: Vrin.
Weil, Eric (1991). *Essais et conférences* (Essays and Conferences). Paris: Vrin.
Weil, Eric (1992). *Philosophie morale* (Moral Philosophy). Paris: Vrin.
Weil, Simone (1951). *Cahiers I* (Notebooks I). Paris: Plon.
Weil, Simone (1953). *Cahiers II* (Notebooks II). Paris: Plon.
Weil, Simone (1953). *La source grecque* (The Greek Source). Paris: Gallimard.
Weil, Simone (1955). *Oppression et liberté* (Oppression and Liberty). Paris: Gallimard.
Weil, Simone (1956). *Cahiers III* (Notebooks III). Paris: Plon.
Weil, Simone (1957). *Ecrits de Londres et dernières lettres*. Paris: Gallimard.
Weil, Simone (1960). *Écrits historiques et politiques* (Historical and Political Writings). Paris: Gallimard.
Weil, Simone (1962). *L'enracinement* (The Need for Roots). Paris: Gallimard.
Weil, Simone (1963). *Attente de Dieu* (Waiting for God). Paris: Chrétien.
Weil, Simone (1985). *Intuitions préchrétiennes* (Pre-Christian Intuitions). Paris: Fayard.
Weil, Simone (1988). *Écrits historiques et philosophiques* (Historical and Political Writings). Paris: Gallimard.

Index

A

Alain, 28, 41, 116, 190, 285, 289
Alexander the Great, 114, 165
Aquinas, Thomas, 77
Arendt, Hannah, 51, 84, 140, 141, 142, 143, 158
Aristotle, 40, 69, 83, 139, 140

B

Bakunin, 124, 285
Barret-Kriegel, Blandine, 176
Bayada, Bernadette, 178
Berdyaeff, Nicolas, 126
Bernanos, George, 63, 98, 125, 271, 285
Bethsaida, John of, 26
Bondurant, Joan, 225
Buddha, 58, 168, 285
Bukovsky, Vladimir, 98

C

Caesar, 114, 288
Camus, Albert, 92, 119
Canetti, Elias, 42
Canivez, Patrice, 214, 215
Churchill, Winston, 248
Clausewitz, Carl von, 181, 182, 183, 184, 185, 186, 187, 286
Confucius, 66

D

de Gaulle, Charles, 154
de la Boétie, Étienne, 93, 94

Dostoyevsky, 73, 286
Duvignaud, Jean, 143

E

Einstein, Albert, 219

F

Fischer, Louis, 248
Fornari, Franco, 43, 44
Freud, 44, 45, 51, 103, 104, 152, 286
Freund, Julien, 276
Fromm, Erich, 53

G

Galtung, Johan, 11, 36
Gandhi, 5, 10, 219, 220, 221, 222, 223, 224, 225, 226, 227, 228, 229, 230, 231, 232, 233, 234, 235, 236, 237, 238, 239, 240, 241, 242, 243, 244, 245, 246, 247, 248, 249, 250, 251, 252, 253, 254, 255, 256, 257, 258, 259, 285, 286, 287, 288, 289, 290
Girard, René, 20, 21, 33, 79, 166
Guehenno, Jean, 125
Gursdof, Georges, 177

H

Havel, Vaclav, 92, 101, 102, 103, 157
Hegel, 41, 111, 112, 113, 114, 115, 116, 117, 220, 287

I

Irwin, Lord, 244, 248

J

Jankelevitch, Vladimir, 84
Jaurès, Jean, 95
Jonas, Hans, 64, 162, 163
Jouvenel, 125, 135, 287

K

Kant, 35, 36, 193, 263, 287
Kern, Anne Brigitte, 166
Krischer, Gilbert, 208

L

Laozi, 44, 45, 62, 168
Lenin, 221
Levinas, Emmanuel, 5, 15, 35, 43, 69, 70, 71, 72, 73, 74, 85, 181, 217, 218, 219, 287, 288, 289
Luutu, Tsongo, 219

M

Machiavelli, Niccolo, 107, 108, 109, 110, 220, 288
Maritain, Jacques, 77, 124, 220
Mauss, Marcel, 14
Milgram, Stanley, 50, 52, 288
Mirabeau, 95
Morin, Edgar, 166
Mounier, Emmanuel, 135, 221

N

Nanda, B.R., 255
Napoleon, 114
Nazareth, Jesus of, 26, 66, 67, 79, 119, 153, 166
Nehru, Pandit, 224, 237, 238, 244, 247, 248, 256, 288

Nietzsche, 40, 124, 288

O

Ostrogorski, Moisei, 127, 128, 154, 155, 157, 289

P

Pareto, Vilfredo, 49
Pascal, 29, 91, 104, 105, 106, 289
Pasqua, Charles, 135
Patanjali, 59, 289
Péguy, Charles, 26, 263, 271, 289
Plato, 40, 58, 69, 78, 168, 289
Popper, Karl, 148, 149, 160, 175, 176
Prairat, Eric, 177, 178

R

Rehnicer, Raymond, 49
Ricoeur, Paul, 34, 64, 74, 221, 289
Rojzman, Charles, 151
Rousseau, Jean-Jacques, 124, 290

S

Scheler, Max, 28
Schopenhauer, Arthur, 63
Serres, Michel, 28, 67, 163
Sharp, Gene, 10, 190
Six, Jean-François, 173
Socrates, 40, 58, 68, 78, 168
Solzhenitsyn, Aleksandr, 100, 290
Sorel, Georges, 96
Sublon, Roland, 126

T

Tagore, Rabindranath, 249
Taine, 125
Tao Te Ching, 44, 62, 168
Tarsus, Saint Paul of, 62

Thoreau, Henry-David, 94, 95, 257, 290
Tolstoy, Leo, 10, 66, 160, 167, 290

V

Vergote, Henri-Bernard, 61, 282

W

Weber, Max, 117, 118, 119, 120, 121, 123, 141, 276, 277, 278, 286

Weil, Eric, 5, 9, 193, 194, 195, 196, 197, 198, 199, 200, 201, 202, 203, 204, 205, 207, 208, 209, 210, 211, 212, 213, 214, 215, 216, 217, 219, 220, 222, 287
Weil, Simone, 5, 22, 27, 33, 34, 36, 41, 49, 56, 58, 61, 78, 90, 130, 131, 135, 153, 155, 156, 157
Wojtyla, Karol, 65, 66, 131

www.ingramcontent.com/pod-product-compliance
Lightning Source LLC
Chambersburg PA
CBHW021146160426
43194CB00007B/703